IN SEARCH OF
A SOLAR HERO

IN SEARCH
OF
A SOLAR HERO

THE KING TRILOGY

Adam King

The Magician

I

ALEXANDER FRANCIS
HORN

A Nadder Book

ELEMENT BOOKS LTD

© Alexander Francis Horn

First published in Great Britain 1987 by
Element Books Ltd, Longmead, Shaftesbury, Dorset

All Rights Reserved
Printed in Great Britain by
Billings, Hylton Road, Worcester
Cover design by Leslie Watkins
Supervised by David Robey and Janice Crosby

"Stopping by Woods on a Snowy Evening" from *The Poetry
of Robert Frost* edited by Edward Connery Lathem.
Copyright 1923. © 1969 by Holt, Rinehart and Winston.
Copyright 1951 by Robert Frost. Reprinted by permission of
Holt, Rhinehart and Winston, Publishers.

Reprinted by permission of Joan Davies: I Have A Dream: ©
1963 by Martin Luther King, Jr.; I've Been To The
Mountain-top © 1968 by the Estate of Martin Luther King,
Jr.; Sermon: Washington Cathedral: © 1968 by Martin
Luther King, Jr.; Drum Major Instinct: © 1968 by Martin
Luther King, Jr. Estate.

British Library Cataloguing in Publication Data
Horn, Alexander Francis
In search of a solar hero: the King
trilogy.— (A Nadder book).
I. Title II. Horn, Alexander Francis. Adam
King III. Horn, Alexander Francis.
Magician IV. Horn, Alexander Francis. I
812'.54   PS3558.068/

ISBN 1-85230-001-9

Contents

Author's Preface

The theatre — a reflector of reality, a celebration of life, the conscience of the nation, the conscience of the world . . . The murders of John Kennedy, Robert Kennedy, Martin Luther King . . . The sixties, Vietnam, the peace marches, the Kent State shootings . . . These plays begin here.

But their real history began the day I met the woman who was to become my wife. It may be a pardonable offense against the spirit of our times for a man to love his wife: to also sing her praises as teacher, actress, director, producer is surely unforgivable.

Yet the truth must be stated. If ever a playwright had a teacher, she has been mine: if ever a work has been a collaboration, these plays have. For me, writing has been the most difficult of tasks, and I am grateful to have such a comrade by my side.

Socrates had his Diotima, Dante his Beatrice, Shakespeare his Dark Lady of the Sonnets, and I, my Sharon. I cannot compare myself to these giants in greatness, they outdistance me as the stars the earth; yet I hold myself their equal in grace and fortune, for I have been blessed with a love that completes my life and my work.

It's time to send these children of ours out into the world. May they be robust and strong and have long life. May they help you attain that happiness I wish for you with all my heart.

Alexander Francis Horn

ALEXANDER FRANCIS HORN

Theatre and the Esoteric Tradition

In *The Idea of the Theatre,* Francis Ferguson states that there have been three great theatres in the Western tradition: the Greek, Aeschylus and Sophocles; the Elizabethan, Shakespeare; and the medieval, Dante (taken as theatre). All three were cosmic theatres. All theatres since Shakespeare have been partial perspectives. In Racine there is a split between reason and passion, in which reason triumphs over passion. In Wagner passion is triumphant over reason.

The modern theatre founded by Ibsen, great as he is, is also a partial perspective, which culminates in Chekhov, the pathetic modality, and which is inferior to heroic man seen in the round, as part of the universe, and part of divinity. Modern theatre lacks cosmic dimension. Hebbel, Ibsen, Chekhov, Brecht, Miller, Williams, Strindberg, Shaw, Cocteau, Anouilh, O'Neill, Ionesco all remarkable, each a partial perspective.

For theatre to become truly great again, it must be restored to its cosmic dimension, lost to it since the theatre of Shakespeare.

The mirror has cracked, that great mirror of Man which in Hamlet is held up to the world to reveal all the multiple facets on various levels of Man, the microcosmos that reflects his entire society and the great world, the macrocosmos. This mirror of man is now in fragments, in as many fragments as there are different varieties of theatre. Therefore, for the restoration of cosmic theatre there must be a restoration of man. Man, fallen into multiplicity, must be restored to his original unity. The great work of the cosmic theatres in the past: the *Orestia,* the Oedipus trilogy of Sophocles, *Hamlet, King Lear, The Tempest, The Divine Comedy* contain the psychology of man's development, from multiplicity to unity, and are in fact the restoration of the divinity of man. This is his evolution. The Eleusinian mystery, the transformation of man symbolized as an ear of corn that can die to be reborn, the sacred drama of cosmic dimensions performed in the Egyptian temples to select initiates, is made public in the Christ drama, the passion play, the death and resurrection of man's spirit. This single universal theme is implicit in all the great works.

These plays are an effort to create a cosmic theatre for our time.

x

They embody many esoteric traditions: Western theosophy (the Pythagorean Platonic tradition and the great sage philosophers, Thales, Heraclitus, Parmenides, Empedocles), the Cabala, Egyptian Hermetic teaching, Zen Buddhism, Sufism, and of course the teaching of G.I. Gurdjieff, Peter Ouspensky, Dr. Maurice Nicoll, and Rodney Collin, known to us in the twentieth century as representatives of a system called The Work. This work was in earlier periods called The Work of Law, the Work of Love, and in our time, as Rodney Collin has said, should be called the Work of Harmony, because never before in our recorded history, in our war-torn, fragmented, computer-driven society, never has HARMONY been such an IMPERATIVE.

With the culmination of the nineteenth century, Nietzsche proclaimed God dead; by the middle of the twentieth century Sartre had proclaimed man dead, a useless passion. Surely the old God is dead, as surely as man as we have known him is dead, and has been since the 1600's when divinity was banished from the world, from man's consciousness. God, once the greatest pride of man, gave way to a mechanistic universe — Kepler, Galileo, Newton — where a magical living universe, God-informed, was replaced by a mechanistic and functional universe, informed by the Void. Man fell into dualism, the universe was ruptured, man's psyche became divorced from Reality, his consciousness diminished to the idols of the cave. From this time the science of faith was replaced by the science of doubt. The Cartesian world view triumphed. Man became the servant of the scientific method which cut off the heads of Kings, replaced the Pope with the Mob, and gave birth to the Frankenstein of the French Revolution. The new tyrant, reason, seceded from the heart, and all the children of that revolution arose: Darwin, Marx, Freud, Einstein, and the humanistic tradition, in which man danced gaily away from his creator to the edge of the precipice, following the siren song of the carpetbaggers of the twentieth century — the logical positivists, the deconstructionists, and all the other professors of meaninglessness. The adulteration of all sacred traditions, the confusion of tongues, the cafeteria of the spiritual supermarket where the great teachings are consumed like a Bloomingdale's potpourri, have so unsettled what little is left of man's sanity that only a thorough housecleaning of all the sophistries that beset us can now redeem us. We are all the lost children of Israel, suffering the Egyptian plagues.

There are two lines in all sacred traditions — not only the Old

Testament and the New Testament, but the Mahabarata, the Homeric, the Chaldean, and Babylonian, as well as the Chinese, Indian and Persian traditions — that is the line of kings and the line of priests, the Brahmins and Shatiras. Whether it be the Arthurian cycle of the wizard Merlin and King Arthur, or the Old Testament of Samuel and Saul which unites in the great priest-king David (giving birth to the splendor and wisdom of Solomon when Israel reaches its apex of glory), always the contemplative priest is seen side by side with the king, the leader of sacred action, Bhakti, Raja and Jana yoga — that is the yogas of devotion, consciousness and knowledge side by side with Karma yoga — the yoga of action.

In the ancient theocracies, such as the Hebraic and Egyptian the two functions are united: the sacred priest king, Moses, Hermes Trismegistus, the sage kings of ancient China, the divine priest kings of Babylonia and Chaldea, and South America.

Sometimes we see these two functions running side by side in two separate beings, or together in one being; sometimes the lines diverge, or clash — as in the long conflict between the popes and kings of Western Europe. These dual functions are exemplified in the sacred books of the *Tarot* (the Magician and the Emperor), the *I Ching,* the *Po Vuvul* of South America.

Ponderings of a Citizen of the Milky Way is the line of contemplatives; its companion volume, *In Search of a Solar Hero* the line of kings. Yet this sharp division can only exist in discursive thinking; in reality they are never apart. In *I,* the last play of *The King Trilogy,* which comprises *In Search of a Solar Hero,* the two lines unite in the Magician and Daniel.

Referring to these distinct lines, Plato makes clear that when a man leaves the cave and achieves true contemplation, i.e. the vision of God, he must return to the cave and aid his fellow men. When these two lines are sundered, false esotericism arises; when they are united they produce true esotericism. This is the main point upon which all esotericism inevitably founders and degenerates in the course of time, giving rise to the need for the esoteric impulse to be constantly revivified and redefined.

When the line of priests, or contemplatives, loses its true vision of God, or retaining it loses its connection with the line of kings, or conversely when the line of kings loses its true validity, which can only stem from the vision of God imparted to it by the true priests, then esotericism becomes false and the civilization which is based upon it inevitably degenerates. For example, the transcendental Indian civilization became sterile and life-denying when the yogis became so divorced from the line of kings that they ended up on mountaintops and lost their union with action.

This problem, which can be called the central problem of esotericism, and therefore of all civilizations, is apparent in our time. When contemplatives and men of action find each other mutually despicable, this rupture produces the barbarism of today. The line of kings has so degenerated that the men who rule the world are simply shopkeepers in a universal assembly line turning out objects of consumption for a debased humanity. With the rarest of exceptions, the contemplatives have degenerated into sterile pseudo-intellectuals teaching courses in universities that have no relation to active life. Consequently we have no civilization, no contemplatives pondering the meaning of existence (philosophy having ended with Nietzsche), and no true men of action. Thus the vision of God actualized in a living community has been lost. And Yeats could only cry "The centre cannot hold;/ Mere anarchy is loosed upon the world,/ The blood-dimmed tide is loosed, and everywhere/ The ceremony of innocence is drowned;/ The best lack all conviction, while the worst/ Are full of passionate intensity." Rilke lamented in the *Duino Elegies,* "Earth! invisible! What is your urgent command, if not transformation?" While Elliot despaired throughout *The Wasteland* of modern life. The last time in our tradition there was a struggle for a unified world view was the Renaissance — all efforts since being quickly aborted.

Plato has stated that until philosophers are kings or kings are philosophers there will never be an end to the miseries of the world. Nothing ever said could be truer. All civilizations of the past prove this axiom. Wisdom and love must be united with courage and strength for there to be real doing. When these are separated the end is idle states of mind: pseudo-mystical states, or power-mad dictators. Consequently, to understand the central dilemma of Western civilization, which is usually stated as the split between idealism and realism, spirit and matter, as stemming from the sundering of the lines of philosophers and kings, is to understand not only the main problem of human life, but the solution to it.

The King Trilogy is an example of the two lines united: Adam King, Luke King and Matthew King in the line of kings, and the line of priests exemplified by Joseph Man. In *The Magician* Luke exemplifies the line of kings and the Magician the line of priests. In *I* these two lines unite in the Magician and Daniel to overcome the problem of

Evil, i.e. Tyrant, and transform evil to restore the Golden Age. *In Search of a Solar Hero* is *the* search for Man who unites these two separate functions, the line of contemplatives and the line of action, long sundered, into one, and thereby restores Man to his primordial unity and the world to its primeval simplicity, the Garden of Eden, when Man was one with Nature and God. Psychologically, in the work of Gurdjieff, these lines are called the line of knowledge and the line of Being. Their union produces divine understanding which leads to great Doing.

The King Trilogy traces this evolution psychologically and cosmologically.

Journey to Jerusalem, empowered by many traditions, such as the Sufi, is a cabalistic, hermetic, alchemical work. Adam and Eve (Eros) and the Serpent of Wisdom (the Logos) journey through all space and time to the kingdom of consciousness, Jerusalem, where the two halves of Man, the female and the male, divided since the fall, are reunited in the mystic marriage of Christ (Eros united with Wisdom). In an ever recurring spiral, exemplifying paradise lost and paradise regained, man and women together struggle to unite themselves and all worlds to their source, that first principle of their existence, God. The history of the world in time and eternity.

The Legend of Sharon Shashanovah expresses the idea found in the sacred tradition that, as he is, man is a puppet waxing and waning under the power of the moon, but who can, under the right conditions and with proper help, transform himself into a human being. The theatre, a sacred discipline, is the transforming force that shocks and awakens man from his sleep of death in the puppet theatre, and which can enable man to enter the cosmic theatre whereby he becomes a spectator of all time and all existence.

The Fantastic Arising of Padraic Clancy Muldoon is a demonstration that the gods, willfully banished from the modern drawing room, have in fact always been with us, and that only man asleep has failed to see them. When he awakens to his blindness, his illusions, his self-deceit, his paralyzed state of impotence, and takes the decisive step of dying to himself, he can be reborn as a conscious being in their company — to the heavenly kingdom that lies within him, and which has always awaited him, and inherit the Earth at last.

The Argument has been going on since the beginning of time. Man, under the authority of his own self will, versus Man, under the authority of the one true God. Two religions: the religion of power and money versus the religion of true power, derived from God.

All of these plays are mystery plays deriving from the great tradition: Aeschylus, Sophocles, Dante, Shakespeare, and, to a lesser degree, Goethe. They are a complete break with the psychology and the aesthetic of modern drama, and are a return to the ancient psychology, metaphysics, ethics, and natural philosophy. They are an attempt to move toward a cosmic theatre and away from our present theatre, which, with the rarest of exceptions, is disgraced with an exclusive attention to the trivial, the mundane, the incomprehensible, the absurd, the nihilistic.

The objective science of Aeschylus, Sophocles, Shakespeare, and Dante depicts the true relationship of the part to the whole: of the individual to humanity, humanity to Nature, and Nature to God, in one unified world vision. These philosopher-kings unite science with art, philosophy and religion. This fusion accounts for the primordial force of their works and is a demonstration of the unity of priest and king, of contemplative and active, of visionary and empiricist.

The barbarism of our time once again is exemplified in the fragmentation of art, religion, science and philosophy. Once united in one body of wisdom-knowledge, it has become fragmented in separate domains, again a sign of the barbarism of our times. When these sacred disciplines lose their primordial unity with one another, we have knowledge instead of wisdom and all the accumulation of data without meaning of modern science, so that science now degenerates into pseudo-science, pseudo-art, pseudo-religion, pseudo-philosophy, technicians running around like squirrels gathering nuts. The return to true science, art, religion, and philosophy can only come about through the union of man's heart and mind, which have been at war with one another since Descartes.

The prophetic insight of Tolstoy, who cried out against a pseudo-science and a pseudo-art that could only lead to man's destruction (first speaker in *The Argument*), passionately pleaded for the wisdom of a true science and a true art that would contribute to true greatness — man's transformation under God.

Tyrant, the fallen angel, who is both a cosmic principle without man and within man, is that Luciferian rebellion against God which leads to the fall of man. This rebellion is occurring in the cosmic levels outside man and the psychological levels within man, since man as a citizen of the galaxy embraces higher worlds as well as the lower. The rebellion of fallen man, Tyrant, against God and His universe, which we retrace throughout all the ancient scriptures culminates in the nihilism of today. Man, led by the spirit of Tyrant within him, seeks to destroy his Creator and His universe, and authorize himself as the god of the Void.

It is clear to all men and women of good will that man is at the end of the line; that the medieval natural order of man in nature installed under the spiritual order of God, which was broken by a Renaissance maimed irreparably by a tyrannical inquisition, and which refused to recognize the perfect equality of men and women, and therefore turned Eros into a Cinderella living in terror of her life, of her two step-sisters, obscenity and heartless rationality, was a wrong turning in the life of mankind. For four hundred years we have been descending into deeper and deeper hells. Since the reformation (Luther), and the counter-reformation, which produced the religious wars that destroyed the civilization of Europe and plunged man into the Thirty Years War of the seventeenth century, the enlightenment of the eighteenth century, which could better be called the endarkenment, the gross materialism of the nineteenth century which produced the atheism of industrialism and the collectivism of communism, socialism, Americanism, Utopianism and every other ism, and the twentieth century technology of two world wars, the horrors of Buchenwald and Hiroshima, three quarters of the population of the earth going to sleep hungry, the murder of man's spirit, the mass starvation of the body and the soul, a growing universal illiteracy, the beginning of the Third World War the day the Second World War ended, that Third World War we have been in forty years during which time we have witnessed the mass deaths of Korea, Vietnam, Cambodia, Indonesia, Nicaragua, Guatemala, Brazil, the enslavement of an entire continent of Africa, and the wholesale murder of an entire people, the rape of our youth, deaths, maiming and tortures of five million in the First World War, fifty million in the Second World War, and untold millions in the Third World War in our terrible and terrifying century of madness; the incalculable psychic damage of all the diverse cultures of the world being uprooted and thrown into the blender of America which has churned them up and produced a new species of man: unthinking, unfeeling — clones — the perfect victims of the Anti-Christ, we have reached the lowest hell of Dante's *Inferno* yet. Man, who has followed the spirit of that fallen angel, Tyrant, spirit of darkness and denial, of daemonic defiance of our creator and His created order, in our rebellion against Heaven whereby we have made a tyranny of life on this earth, both for our neighbors and ourselves, has cast this earth, which is designed to be a heaven, into a cauldron of Hell. It is clear that unless we make the turning now, and recognize, with Dante's pilgrim, that midway in our life we are lost in a dark forest and that we seek to find the true way back, that we will have irretrievably damned ourselves and that *our* humanity, at least, will perish from off the face of this earth. The return to our original selves is imperative, because beings, no longer men, but masquerading as such, have so fallen under the tyrannical impulse of their own false nature, that not content with having raped and exploited God's earth and humanity, seek now to put hotels on Mars and divide the planets of our Solar System into profitable parcels of real estate toward the greater glory of their own comfort and freakhood. It is now either lights-out, or a return to Love united with Wisdom. These plays are written out of the desperate need of our time: ponderings of a citizen of the Milky Way in search of a solar hero.

AFH
January 1, 1987

ADAM KING

A Play in Two Acts

1973

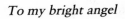

To my bright angel

He who can protest and does not
is an accomplice to the crime.

The Talmud

CHARACTERS

Storyteller

Tyrant

King Family
Topman, financier and former Ambassador
Destiny, his wife
Adam, the President
Matthew, Attorney General } their sons
Luke, a Senator
Vanity, Adam's wife
Prudence, Matthew's wife
Fashion, Luke's wife
Daniel, son to Adam and Vanity
Peter, son to Luke and Fashion

The Big Ten, bankers
 and industrialists
Wolf
Fox
Snake
Weasel
Leech
Jackal
Shark
Pig
Crocodile
Vulture

Joseph Man, a Christian minister
Martyr, his wife
Samuel Y, a Muslim leader

General
Fingerman, head of the Secret
 Police
The Greek, an industrialist
Pearl, a hired assassin
Chief Justice Whorein
Peacock, Vice President
Knocksin, a presidential
 candidate
Araby Araby
Washout }
Fall Guy } patsies
Fall Guy's Wife

Cardinal Common Tribute,
 friend to Topman
Senator Staunch } friends to Matthew
Blackman }
Fortress, a District Attorney
Goodman, chief witness
Farmer, a minority labor leader
Miss Quincy, secretary to
 President King

Reporters, Sheriffs, Doctors,
Nurse, Judge, Witnesses,
 Greysuits
Chorus

ACT I

PROLOGUE

STORYTELLER: Gather close around me, for I've a story that must be told; a story for each man and woman, a story for every child. It determined the future of humanity, it described the past of human-kind. The event began at noon one day . . . and never ended. The murder of these three men was one event, not three, but one.

It was a comfortable hour, on a comfortable day, in a comfortable time, in a comfortable land, when a highly uncomfortable young man leaped up the Capitol stairs, coatless, hatless, and vaulted into power. It was a time when everything was possible; it was a time when nothing was possible. And he matched us.

(*Adam enters, assumes pose with arm outstretched in handshake; he remains in freeze throughout the first scene.*)

With seven-league boots he strode the world. He reached for the moon. His hands stretched across the oceans in peace. He called to the nation. The elders shook their heads, but the people heard, and our country began to waken from her long slumber. He spoke for freedom, and he meant it.*

SCENE 1: A STREET IN WASHINGTON

TYRANT: I am Tyrant,
    Foul, hideous, misbegotten;
    Born from the whim in each man's heart.
    The true child of democracy,
    The impotence and rage of the world.
    I am all that creeps in petty spite
        upon the earth.
    I am panic, chaos, rout,
    The disorder and anarchy of the world,

*Music p. 89

License, madness, flight from freedom,
Disbelief, all that's inert, vulgar, coarse.
I am life's revenge on life;
Loved by those who cannot love themselves.
I am blame, deceit, suspicion, slavery.
I am the limit and guardian of life.
Topman!

TOPMAN: Who's calling?

TYRANT: Have you forgotten so soon!

TOPMAN: I don't know you.

TYRANT: You know me.

TOPMAN: Get out of my way!

TYRANT: But I am your way.

TOPMAN: Who are you?

TYRANT: Don't you remember? A man came to a far country.
He was poor. He hungered and thirsted for Mammon.[1]
He bowed down and worshipped before . . .

TOPMAN: Tyrant!

TYRANT: Yes! Ha! Ha! Don't run away, Topman. I want to talk to
you.

TOPMAN: What do you want?

TYRANT: I've come for my payment.

TOPMAN: Get away from me, you devil!

TYRANT: Is this the way for old friends to meet? Come, it's a simple
thing. I'll take your son, and be gone.

TOPMAN: You won't have my son! Oh God, not Adam!

TYRANT: God can't hear you. And if He could, He wouldn't interfere.
Here's the contract: made, signed and sealed. The fate that's once
decreed can never be undone. Unless . . .

TOPMAN: Unless . . .

TYRANT: Unless it can . . . Ha! Ha! Unless . . . it can! Where are you
going, Topman? There's nowhere to run to. Besides, we haven't
concluded our business yet. Ha! Ha!
(*Blackout.*)

SCENE 2: THE WHITE HOUSE, AN OUTER OFFICE

TYRANT: (*Calling from afar.*) Behold the dreamer! Let us slay him,
and cast him into the pit. And we will say, some evil beast has
devoured him; and we shall see what becomes of his dreams.[2]

(*Adam breaks freeze and comes to life. Enter entourage, followed by two Reporters tap dancing. Tyrant puts on half-mask and watches from afar.*)

REPORTER 1: A great day, Mr. President! You must be dancing on air. How do you feel?

ADAM: I must've been out of my mind to take this job. My father always said politics beat working. I was misinformed. I'm deeply disillusioned. What's the world coming to when a man can't trust his own father?

TOPMAN: Ha . . . Ha . . . Now, now, Adam.

REPORTER 1: How do you feel about the President's remark? Any comment, Mr. King?

TOPMAN: Ask me how it feels to raise a rocket to the sun.

REPORTER 2: How was Moscow?

ADAM: Beautiful.

REPORTER 1: What about Goodman Peasant? Was he tough?

ADAM: A natural catastrophe, until we started drinking. The Premier's too intelligent to make peace with a man who doesn't drink.

REPORTER 2: The Russians love their vodka.

ADAM: No more than we Irish like our whiskey.

MISS QUINCY: Welcome home, Mr. President. A wonderful day!

ADAM: It was all Vanity's doing. How the monarchs of the world trembled at her feet.

MISS QUINCY: She's the First Lady of the land.

ADAM: Of the world. On a day like this, the least we can do is wire the Pope and tell him the Catholics have finally conquered America.

MISS QUINCY: But it's not quite true, sir.

ADAM: If the Attorney General has been given the opportunity to gain a little experience before entering private practice, I don't see what harm it can do to give the Pope a little encouragement; do you, Miss Quincy?

MISS QUINCY: Does he really expect me to send that message?

MATTHEW: You know my brother.

(*Miss Quincy shrugs, then exits.*)

REPORTER 2: About that shot to the moon, sir?

ADAM: It's all my brother's fault. He bet I couldn't leap over the moon and take all men with me.

REPORTER 1: Is what the President says true, Senator?

LUKE: In a manner of speaking. Have you ever known a president to lie?

ADAM: Don't answer that question, gentlemen.

REPORTER 2: (*Laughing.*) But many people are asking what we shall do when we conquer the moon.

ADAM: Why, see if we shall find God, or nothingness.

REPORTERS: Thank you, sir.

(*Exit Reporters tap dancing.*)

GENERAL: A great victory, Mr. President.

ADAM: The glory of our times demands a head of state who's resolute, warlike, prudent, conscientious, and most grave. God forbid, gentlemen, I am none of these, but what poor simple nature can do, I shall undertake.

FINGERMAN: More than undertake. My congratulations, sir; a stunning achievement!

WOLF: A happy day, Topman. Peace at last.

TOPMAN: Though Saul hath conquered his thousands, and David his tens of thousands, Adam King has outdone them all. He has conquered his hundreds of thousands.

ADAM: I hope I have purchased a lasting peace.

TOPMAN: Long life to all my sons.

WOLF, GENERAL and FINGERMAN: Long life!

TOPMAN: Ah, what can be sweeter than the day a man reaps the harvest of his work and lives again in his sons' achievements?

WOLF: Well said. And now, for the President, a long deserved rest.

ADAM: Rest? In this drowsy age when men still pay homage to the idols of the cave? We are but shadows of our former selves. I've come to office in a dark time, and whether by accident or fate, I must be helmsman of the world's purgatorial ascent. This country hasn't been born yet. Let's pick it up by the scruff of the neck and give it a shaking it will never forget!

WOLF: What more can you do than you've already done?

ADAM: I've only just begun.

FINGERMAN: Hypocrisy's the fashion of the times. There's a limit to what one man can do.

ADAM: One man? Seven Adams rage within my breast. The first Adam: co-ruler with God in heaven. The second: he who fell from grace. The third: redeemer of the race. The fourth, fifth, sixth: prophet-warrior, lover, sage. The seventh: he who shall be nameless, I, myself, a poor nothing who shall be king over all the rest. With all this panoply of greatness, who would fear to wage war against tyranny? I dreamed the other night, the bomb, like the sword of Damocles,[3] fell upon my head. Oh, for a lasting peace.

GENERAL: You have it.

ADAM: In theory, yes. But an abyss lies between the conception and the action. We have yet to disarm.

FINGERMAN: All in due time and in accordance with custom.

ADAM: Time's a robber, and custom's a rogue that steals our life away. It takes no King Solomon to tell us this. Only a fool would place his faith in time and custom.

FINGERMAN: You have no choice. Congress must ratify the peace.

ADAM: Congress be damned! Do you think I'm going to allow an assembly of blockheads to throw humanity's life away?

FINGERMAN: Sir, protocol demands . . .

ADAM: I say protocol be damned! Disarm! Then let Congress ratify.

FINGERMAN: If you will not heed the voice of experience . . .

ADAM: Listen to men of experience; that's to say, study with a toad.

GENERAL: Mr. President, there are certain interests you must pacify. You're moving too fast.

ADAM: Since I was a boy I never stood in line, but jumped every fence I found. Whether it be a flaw in nature, or a too hasty appetite for life, I know not; but I never could be second to any man, save One above.

GENERAL: That's all very well; but the people require a more measured pace or you'll lose them.

ADAM: The power and glory of our time make a refuge for fools. See how they hide in every nook and cranny of the age. Don't they know God's sufferance keeps them on the earth? Why, this is hell: to wait until my countrymen discover there's a sky above.

GENERAL: Mr. President . . .

ADAM: I find, gentlemen, that I'm suddenly very tired. More of this tomorrow.

FINGERMAN: As you wish, sir.

TOPMAN: Remember, Wolf, and you too, gentlemen, I expect you this evening for a little celebration. It's not every day a man brings home the peace of the world in the palm of his hand.

GENERAL: Our pleasure. Mr. President . . .

FINGERMAN: 'Til this evening.

WOLF: Topman.

(*Exit Wolf, Fingerman and General.*)

ADAM: Sun and moon in strife contend.

> Jackals cry; hyenas laugh.
> Always the wolf devouring the earth.

TOPMAN: You've learned to rule with a strong hand, my boy. Ha! Ha! I could hardly keep a straight face. Insolent bastards. Did you see the way they looked when Adam tore into them?

LUKE: We'll show them what a Catholic, an Irishman, and a King can do.

TOPMAN: Goddam right, my boy! Rotten WASPs! For over forty years they've been stinging us to death.

MATTHEW: But they haven't succeeded, Dad. We're too tough.

TOPMAN: Yes, too tough. But it hasn't been for want of trying. Now let them get a little of their own back. Oh, what a day! Ha . . . Ha . . . what a day! Like I always said, boys, don't get angry; get even!

ADAM: On top of the world, Ambassador?

TOPMAN: Revenge is sweet, Adam. It's sweet!

ADAM: They threw the mold away when they made you.

TOPMAN: Naturally.

ADAM: Dad, you're the biggest scoundrel I know.

TOPMAN: Well! What of it?

ADAM: And I'm happy for you.

TOPMAN: Ha! I know you are, my boy. I know you are! Am I to take your brothers with me?

ADAM: No, I have need of them. We'll meet again tonight.

TOPMAN: Then I'd best get out of here. I have things to do. 'Til tonight then, boys.

MATTHEW: 'Til tonight.

(*Exit Topman.*)

SCENE 3: THE KING FAMILY HOME

(*Tyrant, masked, watches from afar throughout scene.*)

TOPMAN: (*Packing.*) I must get away from here.

DESTINY: Topman, what is it? Our guests are below.

TOPMAN: Guests be damned! He's come for me.

DESTINY: I've never seen you like this.

TOPMAN: He's come again.

DESTINY: He . . . ?

TOPMAN: That man. The one who came for Mark. He's come again. He wants Adam.

DESTINY: Dear, you're upset.

TOPMAN: He took Mark. Now he'll take Adam.

DESTINY: Topman . . .

TOPMAN: You don't believe me, do you?

DESTINY: I believe you're overwrought again, dear.

TOPMAN: Don't you understand? I've danced with the devil. Now, I must pay . . . with my sons. Can't your God above hear me? One prayer . . . isn't there one prayer in your heart for me . . . that can reach Him?!

DESTINY: Topman . . .

TOPMAN: Ugh! Get away from me. You and your church, and your puking little prayers and your Hail Marys. Oh my soul is sick . . . It's sick unto death.

(*Enter Cardinal Common Tribute.*)

CARDINAL COMMON TRIBUTE: Well, Destiny, the guests have arrived; the champagne is flowing and we await a toast from our host. Is this the way to . . . What is it, Topman? . . . You're the shadow of yourself.

TOPMAN: Shadow . . . shadow did you say? Oh, Father, is there no power in heaven or hell that can change our fate?

CARDINAL COMMON TRIBUTE: There's God.

TOPMAN: My shadow blocks the way. He's stolen my life . . . Mark . . . and now Adam.

CARDINAL COMMON TRIBUTE: Your shadow?

DESTINY: He thinks he's met the devil, Father.

CARDINAL COMMON TRIBUTE: Well, if the devil exists, he's the man to meet him.

TOPMAN: I'll give the church all I have. I'll not keep back a penny. But save my sons . . . save them! I must warn Adam!

CARDINAL COMMON TRIBUTE: Get a grip on yourself, man!

TOPMAN: Oh, is there no magic in your church can fight this devil? Fifteen years ago he came for Mark. I thought my life was over. I locked myself in my room and waited for him. I wanted to die. But he never came — clever swine . . . slowly my life returned to me. I thought I was done with him. And then all my early plans and ambitions returned . . . I would have Mark again in Adam. And now . . . see how he tortures me . . . he's returned for Adam! He'll damn my remaining sons forever!

CARDINAL COMMON TRIBUTE: My God! Topman . . .

TOPMAN: Oh help . . . someone help me . . .

CARDINAL COMMON TRIBUTE: Send for the doctor.

TOPMAN: I don't need a doctor, you goddamn fools. I need . . . Where's Adam? I must warn him.

DESTINY: He's downstairs, dear, with all our guests.

TOPMAN: Guests! What guests?!

DESTINY: For the victory celebration.

TOPMAN: Victory . . . yes. I mustn't disturb him now. Later . . . I'll talk to him.

CARDINAL COMMON TRIBUTE: That would be a good idea.

DESTINY: Lie down now. You're tired.

TOPMAN: Can't . . . must go down to our guests. They'll be missing me.

DESTINY: Just for a little . . . rest.

TOPMAN: Rest . . . yes. Oh, will I ever rest again!

DESTINY: Shh . . .

(*Blackout.*)

(*A short time later. Tyrant, masked, has entered the room.*)

DESTINY: Shh . . . you don't want the boys to hear you.

TOPMAN: I said I'm talking.

DESTINY: Lower your voice, dear.

TOPMAN: I'll speak as loud as I goddamn please!

DESTINY: Alright, Topman.

TOPMAN: Where do you think that kind of money and power comes from? But you never dared to ask, did you? You turned away and went sniveling to the church.

DESTINY: I knew where it came from, and I tried to stop you, but you wouldn't listen; you were possessed.

TOPMAN: You went along with me.

DESTINY: No! As God is my witness.

TOPMAN: Don't give me any of that God stuff.

DESTINY: All my life I've had to guard my sons from you.

TOPMAN: Guard your sons from me! Why, you fool, I made my boys what they are.

DESTINY: No, Topman, while you were out womanizing and lusting for power, I stayed at home and made sure of their souls.

TOPMAN: You made them sniveling weaklings to be exploited by the first strong man to come along.

DESTINY: With all your strength, Topman, you're a weak man.

TOPMAN: Is that what you told my sons while I was gone?

DESTINY: You know better than that. I've taught them there's a Greater Power and it is that they must obey. And not you, the world, or the devil can ever take that from me.

SCENE 4: ANOTHER ROOM IN
THE KING FAMILY HOME

(*Later that evening.*)

VANITY: Why Dallas?

ADAM: Peacock wants me to go.

VANITY: What for?

ADAM: To heal the party differences.

VANITY: It's too dangerous, Adam.

ADAM: A president who can't walk among his own people is no president at all.

VANITY: You've received too many threats. Your own ambassador to the United Nations was attacked down there. They spit all over the man and almost killed him. He told me, under no circumstances, to let you go. Those Texans are mad.

ADAM: I won't play the coward.

VANITY: You're an anachronism, Adam. A religious president in these absurd times! You're like the little boy who stuck his finger in the dike and lost his life. Must you court death?

ADAM: He and I are good friends. We met one dark night in the Pacific, and now we're on the best of terms.

VANITY: Yes. I know all about it: Lieutenant, Harvard, war hero, the cult of manhood. Why do you always have to prove yourself? I do believe you're half in love with death.

ADAM: Death's a good advisor.

VANITY: Count me out. I want to live.

ADAM: You promised, Vanity.

VANITY: I have my own life to lead.

ADAM: I've noticed . . . and your own friends.

VANITY: Oh, now it comes out. You're jealous.

ADAM: You're the mother of my children. That man's no friend to me, Vanity.

VANITY: Afraid of what the world will think?

ADAM: You're to stay away from him!

VANITY: There's no need for you to be jealous, darling . . . I'll see whom I please and when I please. You don't own me.

ADAM: They're gossiping all over Washington.

VANITY: Washington is always gossiping. Let them!

ADAM: Over my dead body.

VANITY: Then it will be over your dead body! Who do you think you are? You don't care for me. All you care for is the great Adam King whose father bought him the world as a plaything. You can't keep pushing people around and telling them what to do. The world got on very well before you came into it, and will get on very nicely when you leave it. And so will I. Do you hear me? I can't bear living with you another moment.

ADAM: Then why have you stayed?

VANITY: Ask your father!

ADAM: What!

VANITY: You heard me.

ADAM: Vanity, what are you talking about?

VANITY: Didn't you know, dear! I thought everyone knew!

ADAM: What has my father got . . . to do . . . with this?

VANITY: Never mind.

ADAM: Explain yourself.

VANITY: Why, your father's a great man, Adam. You go to him to solve all your problems. And so do I.

ADAM: What kind of promises did my father make you, Vanity?

VANITY: That's my business.

ADAM: Oh, God! You too?

VANITY: Well, that's politics, Adam.

ADAM: What have I done?

VANITY: I wouldn't feel too bad about it, Adam. You got what you wanted.

ADAM: Have I, Vanity? Have I? . . .

(*Blackout.*)

SCENE 5: THE WHITE HOUSE
THE PRESIDENTIAL OFFICE

(*Tyrant, masked, watches from afar.*)

MATTHEW: Mr. President . . . Adam . . . Wolf has raised the price of steel!

ADAM: No! Am I dreaming, or is this a nightmare? It can't be real.

MATTHEW: I'm afraid so. It just came through the wire.

ADAM: The greedy hog grunts in bondage to the moon. How long will Wolf and Fox rule the earth? They and Weasel and all their sleazy crew?

MATTHEW: There's more, Adam. Fox has broken the ceiling on oil. Shark, Leech, and the rest of the Big Ten are following suit.

ADAM: A munition maker's dream — the international cartels are at it again. Those treacherous bastards.

MATTHEW: After they'd given their word to you.

ADAM: Men without honor! What can their word be worth? What low connivance, deceit and cunning, mendacity, and all its brood can teach, I've learned. The Wolf was my brother, the Fox my friend; Weasel warmed me; Snake comforted me, 'til I awakened to my human nature and cast them off. Now I'll turn the tables on these money lenders. Shall greatness be forever slain by the Shark and the Leech? Shall they take usury on the human race, and have their pound of flesh forever? Oh, why have I hesitated so long to declare eternal war on the enemies of man?

MATTHEW: My God, Adam, you've done the best you can!

ADAM: No! I've been the whipping boy of corruption and sat idly by while abuse and privilege railed at justice. I've lent my high office to the corruption of the times; I've been a whore. I've wanted heaven and this world too. Seeing I couldn't take this world with me, I've balked . . . stood between two worlds, and in my fear of losing both, enacted scripture in reverse — turned my eyes from the usage of the times, lent a servile knee to hypocrisy — taken bribery with the left hand, while with the right discounted all knowledge of the doing.

MATTHEW: To hear you talk, you're the most corrupt man that ever entered office.

ADAM: I'll never be hung for a saint, that's for sure. But it's not that, Matthew. It's the lies I've told myself. My God, how long can a man want to be the sweetheart of America?

MATTHEW: If you want to be critical, fine — but don't peck yourself to death.

ADAM: Am I an imposter? Can I be other than myself? How long shall I eat the flattery of the world and apologize for my life? In this preposterous time when men *seem* to be, but never are, when will I dare to be myself? I feel like the man in the iron mask. I've got to break out and live this moment and every moment of my life.

MATTHEW: Well, if you're bound for the truth, go!

ADAM: You think so?

MATTHEW: There's no other train worth taking.

ADAM: Thanks, Matt. That's all I needed to hear.

(*Enter Reporters tap dancing.*)

REPORTER 1: Statement!

ADAM: My father always told me that all businessmen were sons of bitches. I'll be damned if he wasn't right; but I never believed him 'til now.[4] I cannot believe that the people of our country will permit a small band of ruthless businessmen to trample on the rights of others, just so they may make a profit at the expense of the common good.[5]

REPORTERS: Thank you, Mr. President. Wow!!

(*Exit Reporters tap dancing.*)

ADAM: Matthew, slap anti-trust proceedings against Wolf and Fox. And while you're at it, the whole pack of them. We'll have this out once and for all.

MATTHEW: All of them?

ADAM: All of them.

MATTHEW: Oh boy!

ADAM: The whole country is on the take — corruption from top to bottom. The military sleeps with the munition makers, who are necessary to protect our economic interests throughout the world. And every bureaucrat from top to bottom must have his cut. A monstrous war machine, a gigantic bureaucracy, an insatiable munitions-chemical-oil complex that must be fed . . . and the little men, the citizens of the republic, must go to feed it with their lives.

MATTHEW: What's to be done?

ADAM: Scrap it. The premise is wrong.

MATTHEW: Scrap it?

ADAM: We must. Unless we want another Rome, gorged with the blood of its victims and glutted with mediocrity. These monstrous multinationals have a stranglehold on every country in the world. We've got a terrible fight on our hands.

(*Tyrant, disguised as staff member, enters office carrying papers to be signed.*)*

TYRANT: Your papers, Mr. President.

(*Adam signs papers, hands them back to Tyrant. They exchange a look, Tyrant exits.*)

ADAM: Matthew . . .

MATTHEW: Yes, Adam . . .

ADAM: If anything were to happen to me, what would you do?

*Music p. 89

MATTHEW: What is it, Adam?

ADAM: Nothing . . . But if anything were to happen to me . . .

MATTHEW: I'd carry on.

ADAM: That's what I thought.

MATTHEW: Is there anything you wanted to tell me?

ADAM: No . . . That's all I wanted to know.

(*Enter Luke.*)

MATTHEW: Here's Wonder Boy, the esteemed Senator in all his glory.

LUKE: Adam, come away with me.

ADAM: "The woods are lovely, dark, and deep,
But I have promises to keep,
And miles to go before I sleep.

ADAM/MATTHEW: And miles to go before I sleep." [6]

LUKE: Come play with me, Adam. Let's lazy out to sea and float downstream forever.

ADAM: Upstream for me, Luke.

LUKE: The world's a dream.

ADAM: Oh, to rouse it from its slumber.

LUKE: Would you give your life for that, Adam?

ADAM: Yes, Luke, I would

LUKE: Die for the world? Not I. The world's not worth the trouble.

MATTHEW: Cut it out, Squirt, we're busy.

ADAM: What would you give your life for, Buddy Boy?

LUKE: A clear day, a fair wind for sailing, and a pair of eyes to see the world as it is.

ADAM: For me, the center of action. The presidential office.

LUKE: Drop the world, Adam. The world's too hot to handle. Round and round she goes, and where she stops, nobody knows. Let's get off before we're spun for a loss.

ADAM: Where would we go?

LUKE: Where would we go?! Where would we go? Why, where would we go? Let's see . . . for starters, there's Waikiki. We'll launch out to sea and ride the foamy wave, the briny deep. Then we'll surfboard from sea to shore. And the ladies, Adam, the ladies! They're all asking for you.

ADAM: I'd be recognized.

LUKE: Not if you were man enough to swim in the clothes you were born in.

ADAM: Stranded in the raw?

MATTHEW: I can see the headlines now: "President appears as God made him. Demands we get down to bare facts."

LUKE: Off with the old, on with the new.

ADAM: The whole truth.

LUKE: Exactly.

MATTHEW: You could hold a baby in your arms and win the homage of the nation.

LUKE: "What a human guy," they'd say.

ADAM: The oil interests would accuse me of polluting the ocean.

MATTHEW: "Congress impeaches President. Oil interests accuse President of pissing in the raw."

ADAM: It won't work.

LUKE: You see, I was right. You've no life at all. Why Adam, you're caught in the mask of office. You think you drive the world, but the world drives you . . . (*Buzzer sounds and Matthew picks up telephone.*) Why it's a good night's work to mount your own wife! Mount the world and you mount Vanity, and the world runs away with you while you cry out to your mother, Destiny, "Look, Ma, I'm dancing." Be careful, Adam, your Vanity will undo you. (*Exit Luke.*)

MATTHEW: Mr. President, Joseph Man is waiting.

ADAM: Oh God! Matthew, this Joseph Man, is he honest?

MATTHEW: I'd swear he is.

ADAM: And a great lover of woman, they say.

MATTHEW: He's a match for Dionysus.[7]

ADAM: He's a true Christian, then. A priest of love. No wonder women rush to him for Holy Sacrament. Fingerman must be in seventh heaven. I bet he's contrived a dossier of filth and slander a foot deep.

MATTHEW: He means to bury him in three feet of dirt.

ADAM: And . . . ?

MATTHEW: He doesn't care what they say about him.

ADAM: What courage! A man who dares to be himself, despite the hypocrisy of the age. Christ, he outfaces the world. This is either greatness or madness!

MATTHEW: Perhaps both. Greatness has always borrowed something of madness.

ADAM: I never admired a man more than this black priest. Sodom and Gomorrah, see how he marches through all the Cities of the Plain . . . a newborn prophet, striding in giant steps through Montgomery, Birmingham, Selma, Atlanta. How can it be that I, born to wealth and circumstance, can be thrown in the shadow by this

Pied Piper of virtue who steals the people's hearts away — the grandson of a slave who marches by foot to greatness. God, I could throw away the world, and walk side by side with him, but that vanity, like a canker in my soul, cannot give up the ceremony of office. Office, what's that? An outhouse where all vices congregate!

MATTHEW: What will you do when he marches up the Capitol steps?

ADAM: Unbolt the windows, unlock the doors. A country that keeps out its prophets and artists will not long deserve to live. If we banish our seers and sages, our lovers and poets, who shall teach us the meaning of our lives?*

(*Enter Chorus tap dancing in locomotive rhythm which they use throughout play. Chorus speaks as individuals except where indicated. Tyrant disguised as member of Chorus.*)

CHORUS: Mr. President, don't touch this issue.

Don't commit yourself.

This man is political suicide.

ADAM: He's the only man in the country who's got the guts to stand up for what's right. What a country! I am the President and I can do nothing.

CHORUS: (*All chanting.*) Get in line! Get in line! Get in line!

ADAM: Remarkable! Every clerk, mechanic, or messenger boy can speak out on this issue, but not the President.

CHORUS: (*All.*) You must follow public opinion.

ADAM: And who is to be responsible for the state of the country?

CHORUS: (*All.*) Get in line! Get in line! Get in line!

(*Exit Chorus tap dancing.*)

(*Enter Miss Quincy.*)

MISS QUINCY: Joseph Man, Mr. President.

ADAM: Show him in.

(*Exit Miss Quincy; Matthew remains.*)

(*Enter Joseph Man.*)

JOSEPH MAN: Mr. President.

ADAM: Mr. Man.

(*They shake hands.*)

JOSEPH MAN: I wish to express my gratitude for the help you have given me. Will you now extend your friendship to my people? They are in great need of it.

ADAM: They have that already.

*Music p. 90

JOSEPH MAN: No, Mr. President, we have your sympathy, not your friendship.

ADAM: I have instructed the Attorney General to help your people to the full extent that his office will allow.

JOSEPH MAN: That he has done. But as President you have not yet committed yourself.

ADAM: As the President, I could hardly do that.

JOSEPH MAN: As the President, you could hardly do otherwise.

ADAM: I believe, Mr. Man, that I can best serve the cause of your people by remaining above the struggle.

JOSEPH MAN: While men, women, and children are beaten to death in the streets . . . ?

ADAM: The conscience of this country — of the world — has been touched.

JOSEPH MAN: And your conscience, Mr. President, has that also been touched?

ADAM: Yes. My people are . . .

JOSEPH MAN: My people are also your people, Mr. President.

ADAM: I appreciate that.

JOSEPH MAN: We are one people, indissolubly bound together. It is your duty before God and man to bear witness to the truth.

ADAM: I am doing everything . . . I am seeking every possible means to correct the present situation.

JOSEPH MAN: Are you, Mr. President? All save one. You are not taking a moral stance.

ADAM: I do not think that advisable in the present atmosphere.

JOSEPH MAN: Each of us has a destiny for good or evil. You can't run away from yourself, Mr. President. If you're the man I think you are, you won't succeed. Sooner or later a man must stand up and be counted.

ADAM: At the proper time, Mr. Man.

JOSEPH MAN: The time is now. There is no other. My people ride the tide of history. They cannot wait. The forward march of events cannot be stopped; history demands your decision. And history cannot wait.

ADAM: As an historian, I am almost tempted to agree with you. However, a premature reading of history can be a grave mistake.

JOSEPH MAN: The responsibility rests far more heavily on the shoulders of those who, through timidity and delay, cause catastrophe.

ADAM: You have a point. Until philosophers are kings . . .

JOSEPH MAN: Or kings, philosophers, there shall be no end to the sorrows of the world. Now is the time to rouse yourself to greatness, and set a moral example that will inspire the world. You cannot allow the few to hold back the forward march of the world. Humanity stands at a great crossroads. You have stated the issue: freedom or slavery. And you have said, "Let us begin." And you have done so. As the leader of the free world, only your voice can sound the clarion call of conscience, indisputably and irrevocably, that can be heard by all the world. You cannot deny that responsibility.

ADAM: Nor will I. But as minister to your people, you enjoy a confidence I can scarcely hope for. If God gives you your sanction, men give me mine.

JOSEPH MAN: You are the highest officer in the land.

ADAM: By the will of the people. I can't do much if I lose their confidence.

JOSEPH MAN: You can't do anything if you lose God's.

ADAM: And what if the people are not ready to follow my moral example?

JOSEPH MAN: I'm afraid they must. Or you will have to follow theirs. I once heard it said that a leader is a man who goes forward without looking back to see if anyone is following him.

ADAM: The man who said that was never an elected official. Well, Mr. Man, what do you want?

JOSEPH MAN: Your sanction.

ADAM: I'm listening.

JOSEPH MAN: To march on the Capitol and redeem the promise of our forefathers.

ADAM: You're asking for the impossible.

JOSEPH MAN: Are we on this planet to ask for anything else?

ADAM: You're asking for the stars.

JOSEPH MAN: For us it's the whip or the stars. For four centuries my people have been under the whip of degradation and brutality. And yet the black man is the future of our country.

ADAM: I know it.

JOSEPH MAN: My people are caged by the great beast of prejudice and fear. You have the key to unlock the cage and release them. Will you use it?

(*Enter Chorus from both sides; they cross over and exit, in locomotive tap dance routine, chanting.*)

CHORUS: Get in line! Get in line! Get in line! Get in line! Get in line! Get in line! Get in line!

ADAM: I will. Though I fear I sign my death warrant.

JOSEPH MAN: Will you purchase your re-election with the blood of my people?

ADAM: You know the answer to that question.

JOSEPH MAN: I had hoped to tell my people I have met a man. I was not mistaken.

ADAM: You understand, Mr. Man, if I do this I will be putting my entire office on the line.

JOSEPH MAN: Yes.

ADAM: Can you guarantee me that if your people march . . . there will be no violence?

JOSEPH MAN: Yes.

ADAM: What assurance can you give me?

JOSEPH MAN: You have my word. What can I tell my people, Mr. President?

ADAM: Tell them, Mr. Man, it is not the whip, but the stars.

(*They shake hands.*)

JOSEPH MAN: 'Til we meet again.

ADAM: 'Til we meet again.

(*Blackout.*)

SCENE 6: THE WHITE HOUSE
THE PRESIDENTIAL OFFICE

(*Tyrant, masked, watches from afar.*)

WOLF: You're asking us to change our entire way of life.

ADAM: Or perish like the dinosaur.

WOLF: It would cost incalculable billions to retool our industry.

ADAM: Spend it! A country that can't empty its own garbage isn't fit to live. We're infecting the entire world with our pollution.

WOLF: But the problem is insoluble.

ADAM: We are committing sacrilege, exploiting and murdering the earth — and you dare tell me the problem is insoluble, when the life of every man, woman, and child is at stake — now, and for all future time to come!

FINGERMAN: How can we speak of the future? It is Nature that will determine our course.

ADAM: You presume a great deal upon Nature. Is she to huff and puff while we parasites loot and rape her?

FINGERMAN: What we do here on earth is of very little account in the scheme of things.

ADAM: What man, holding your philosophy, would not desire to hang himself at once?

FINGERMAN: I think I see as clearly as any man.

ADAM: Then it's a wonder you have not seen this: that we men are a part of this majestical creature the earth, and that the spirit of man shall lift earth, planets, sun, and all living things, 'til they touch every star in heaven; the whole shimmering on the ever-turning wheel of the vast unchanging universe.

FINGERMAN: This is poetry.

ADAM: Fact. We are here not to sow discord, but harmony.

FINGERMAN: I take man as I find him.

ADAM: You mean as the treachery of the world has made him.

FINGERMAN: Call it what you will. He's a rebellious, intractable creature.

ADAM: Made so by the injustice of the state.

FINGERMAN: Men must have order.

ADAM: Order without freedom leads to the bee and the ant.

FINGERMAN: I do not understand your freedom.

ADAM: It is precisely because it is beyond your comprehension that it will lead us to the stars.

FINGERMAN: And is this how you propose to deal with the Third World?

ADAM: Do you know of a greater force than reason?

GENERAL: There's war.

ADAM: War's a wastrel. Why should humanity be led out to slaughter, forever and a day? Let us be men, and declare war on war, on poverty, on injustice, on the whole exploitative machinery of the past. Pollution, slavery, war, they are all one issue. Either they must go, or man must go from the face of the earth.

GENERAL: You're asking for a moral revolution.

ADAM: Yes, a moral revolution. I welcome it!

FINGERMAN: But you can't turn the world upside down.

ADAM: Why not? It's been wrong side up long enough. The world was made for man, not man for the world.

GENERAL: Mr. President, I hardly know if you're joking or if . . .

ADAM: Perhaps the Attorney General can help you. Matthew?

MATTHEW: Will this clarify your thinking, General?

GENERAL: "A de-escalation order for all troops in Southeast Asia." But that's impossible.

ADAM: It may be impossible. But that's the way we're going. We're pulling out of Vietnam.

GENERAL: But why?

ADAM: Too many boys would die, General. Too many boys would die.

MATTHEW: And this . . .

GENERAL: "Closing down our nuclear bases overseas."

ADAM: That's correct.

GENERAL: You won't get away with this!

ADAM: That will be all, General.

GENERAL: Why . . . !

WOLF: General!

ADAM: I have a word or two further to say to you, Mr. Fingerman. You're fired!

FINGERMAN: Why you high-handed . . . !

ADAM: Rather high-handed than low-handed. There are not two governments in this country. There is only one. And I am running it. Now, I think you understand that.

FINGERMAN: The Secret Police is my organization. I built it. How far do you think you can get without it?

ADAM: Very far indeed. You've set up your last dictatorship throughout the world. I'm going to break the C.I.A., scatter it in a thousand pieces, and throw it to the wind.[8] We are not friends to those assassins throughout the world who wait in dark alleys to murder justice. As long as I am President of these United States . . .

FINGERMAN: How long do you think that will be?

ADAM: Why you insolent son-of-a-bitch. I ought to break every bone in your body! Get out of here!

FINGERMAN: Very well, Mr. President. But there are forces in this country that will not tolerate what you are doing. I don't think you know what you are up against.

ADAM: Get out of here before I have you thrown out!

STORYTELLER: . . . At last we had a winner.

SCENE 7: A CORPORATE BOARD ROOM

(*Enter Big Ten and General driving limousine, stomping feet, smoking cigars. Each member of the Big Ten wears a large bronzed mask revealing the essence of his animal. They stop, unfold limousine into conference table, sit down in unison. Enter Topman, who sits at middle of table. Tyrant, wearing half-face mask, watches from afar.*)

WOLF: What's the matter with your boy, Topman? I thought he was working for us.

CROCODILE: We can't shit without him being there to tell us how to do it.

SNAKE: After all we've done for him, you think the least he would do . . .

TOPMAN: Is let you rob the country.

SNAKE: That's not funny.

TOPMAN: I didn't mean it as funny.

SNAKE: I'll overlook that remark, Topman. As I was saying, you'd think the least he would do is show us the milk of human kindness.

FOX: True, Snake, true. After all, we made him what he is today. Who the hell does he think bought him the presidency? You can't trust anyone nowadays. Things aren't what they used to be.

TOPMAN: Now wait a minute.

WOLF: No offense meant, Topman. We know those sons of yours are the apple of your eye. But you can't blame the boys for getting a little upset. They've taken all the abuse they're about to take from your son . . . I might say both your sons. Isn't that right, boys?

BIG TEN and GENERAL: That's right.

WOLF: Now don't misunderstand me, Topman. I like Adam. I think he's a fine man. Isn't that right, Fox?

FOX: We have nothing but the highest respect for him.

WOLF: I've always said that boy would make a hell of a president. (*Nudging Topman.*) A branch off the old tree, eh. Like father, like son. And damned if I wasn't right. Can't recall such a well-loved man in office. Can you, Shark?

SHARK: Can't recall it.

WOLF: The people's choice. Wouldn't you say so, Crocodile?

CROCODILE: The people's choice.

WOLF: Like I was saying, I like your boy just fine, Topman. I'd like him to be our boy, too. Our motto well could be: any son of Topman's is a son of ours. Now, we know he's got a lot of fancy ideas. Peace, he wants peace. Well, that's alright. We're for peace, aren't we boys?

BIG TEN and GENERAL: Sure.

WOLF: He wants to clean up the cities. What's wrong with cleaning up the cities? Am I right, boys?

BIG TEN and GENERAL: Right.

WOLF: He wants to help the poor, the down and outers — that's alright too; we were all poor once. I'm not against giving a break to the down and outers. He wants to feed the hungry multitude. That's christian . . . that's christian! But when he wants to take the money out of our pocket to do it, that's where we draw the line. Isn't that so, boys?

(*All stare intensely at Topman.*)

So you see how it is, old friend? I'd have a talk with him.

FOX: Live and let live, I always say.

JACKAL: One man's meat is another man's poison.

CROCODILE: We've all got to live with one another.

WEASEL: Get our share.

SNAKE: Sleep in the same bed.

JACKAL: After all, what's good for us is good for the country.

WOLF: Exactly. It would be a lamentable thing if we had a falling out.

FOX: The way I see it, we go along with him, he goes along with us. We all go along together. Everybody's happy. Everybody knows that.

VULTURE: Sure, everybody knows that.

WOLF: Otherwise . . . See what I mean?

TOPMAN: I'll talk to him.

(*Exit Big Ten; they rise, fold table back up into limousine, exit, stomping feet.*)

SCENE 8: THE WHITE HOUSE
THE PRESIDENTIAL OFFICE

(*Tyrant continues to watch from afar.*)

TOPMAN: Politics is a game that only fools take seriously.

ADAM: Then I'm a fool.

TOPMAN: I didn't raise my sons to be fools. I raised them to win.

ADAM: That's what I intend to do.

TOPMAN: Then take in your sails. Give a little.

ADAM: And be a paper president.

TOPMAN: Now, Adam . . .

ADAM: That's the issue, isn't it?

TOPMAN: You're putting an unkindly light upon it. I've always taught you not to sail against the wind. When the wind's against you, bend a little.

ADAM: I've bent so far backward, if I bend any further, my back will break.

TOPMAN: Try to see it from their position.

ADAM: I've done nothing else since I've come to office. Whose side are you on, anyway, Father?

TOPMAN: You've got to cooperate with these boys, Adam. How far would you have gotten without them?

ADAM: But they want too much. They want everything.

TOPMAN: Give it to them.

ADAM: What!

TOPMAN: Ha! There isn't a businessman in the world that doesn't want everything. The question is, can he get it?

ADAM: Not as long as I'm President.

TOPMAN: Well, then, promises never hurt anyone.

ADAM: Promises . . . We don't owe them anything. We never made that kind of promise.

TOPMAN: Then where's the harm? They don't expect you to keep them. No politician ever keeps his promise.

ADAM: Well, then, what's the point?

TOPMAN: Let's just call it a token of your affection. They'd like to know you appreciate them, that you're not against them.

ADAM: They've been humored enough.

TOPMAN: What else can you do? They're the backbone of the country.

ADAM: I intend to modify the backbone of the country.

TOPMAN: Not without their consent, son.

ADAM: With or without their consent.

TOPMAN: You're joking.

ADAM: I'm not joking.

TOPMAN: You're talking crazy, my boy.

ADAM: Am I?

TOPMAN: Why, they'd have your scalp in a minute. They're the power of this country — of the world. Money talks. Don't you know what you'd be bucking?

ADAM: Did they send you here, Father?

TOPMAN: No, of course not.

ADAM: You're an awful good liar, Dad, but you could never lie to your sons.

TOPMAN: No, I never could lie to you or your brothers. Damn it to hell.

(*Adam laughs.*)

Sometimes, I think you boys will be the death of me.

(*Adam still laughing.*)

No, I mean it. You're too high-spirited — all of you — and stubborn. You want your own way and you won't give an inch.

ADAM: Whose fault is that, Ambassador?

TOPMAN: Mine, I suppose. The only trouble is there's not much room for high-spirited men in this world. They're crowding you, Adam.

ADAM: I can take care of myself.

TOPMAN: I know.

ADAM: What is it, Dad?

TOPMAN: Aw, it's nothing.

ADAM: Come on, Old Man.

TOPMAN: I'm worried, Adam.

ADAM: There's nothing to worry about.

TOPMAN: These men are scum. They wouldn't be beyond . . .

ADAM: They wouldn't dare.

TOPMAN: Can you be sure of that, Adam?

ADAM: Can we be sure of anything?

TOPMAN: You know what I'm saying.

ADAM: No, I can't be sure.

(*Enter Vanity and Destiny carrying hatbox.*)

VANITY: Oh, we didn't mean to disturb you, Grandpa Topman. I'm sure you two men are talking about something of grave importance.

ADAM: No, not really.

TOPMAN: Besides, there's always room for you, my dears.

VANITY: Oh, Grandpa Topman.

TOPMAN: I was just trying to talk some sense into your husband, but he won't listen.

DESTINY: Adam is president now, dear. Adam, I just got this most wonderful hat. It's such a pretty color. Do you like it?

ADAM: It's wonderful, Mother.

DESTINY: Shall I try it on?

(*Adam looks at his watch.*)

I understand, dear. Of course, you're busy. I just came to collect your father.

ADAM: Remember me in your prayers, Mother.

DESTINY: I always do, Adam.

VANITY: You ought to pay more attention to your father, Adam. He knows best.

TOPMAN: I hope so.

(*Exit Destiny and Topman.*)

(*Silence.*)

VANITY: What is it, Adam? What's the matter? You need rest. You must sleep.

(*Vanity starts to rub his neck and shoulders during the following speech. Adam becomes increasingly drowsy, and by the end of the scene he is fast asleep slumped over his desk.*)

ADAM: The last time I slept, I dreamed I had a rendezvous with Death. He came with a bright trumpet sounding my name. We maim ourselves, forever hacking off one another's limbs, walking the earth like disembodied ghosts — so much misery in the world. Had I the power, I'd lift the earth off its axis and hurl it to the stars. The world's falling in a thousand pieces. I seem to be elected to hold it together and I don't know how. Patch it one place; it falls apart in another. Every time I go to fight these men, they hide like shadows. I feel the world creeping like a snail, sitting, sitting, forever sitting — as if creation made some mistake and made us worms instead of men. We're in a race against catastrophe. The world is drifting to a bad place in this long twilight. I'm a watchman on the tower of freedom. Unless God gives the victory, the city cannot hold.

VANITY: Oh, Adam, you want men to be brave and strong, but people aren't that way, and one day, I'm afraid they'll break your heart.

SCENE 9: THE WASHINGTON PEACE MARCH

(*Enter Joseph Man, coming down through audience.*)

JOSEPH MAN: So I say to you, my friends, that even though we must face the difficulties of today and tomorrow, I still have a dream. It is a dream deeply rooted in the great dream that one day this nation will rise up and live out the true meaning of its creed: "We

hold these truths to be self-evident, that all men are created equal."
I have a dream that one day, on the red hills of Georgia, sons of former slaves and the sons of former slave owners will be able to sit down together at the table of brotherhood.

I have a dream that one day even the state of Mississippi, a state sweltering with the heat of injustice, sweltering with the heat of oppression, will be transformed into an oasis of freedom and justice.

(*Enter Adam.*)

I have a dream that my four little children will one day live in a nation where they will not be judged by the color of their skin, but by the content of their character. I have a dream today!

I have a dream that one day, down in Alabama — with its vicious racists, with its governor having his lips dripping with the words of interposition and nullification — one day, right there in Alabama, little black boys and black girls will be able to join hands with little white boys and white girls as sisters and brothers. I have a dream today!

I have a dream that one day "Every valley shall be exalted and every hill and mountain shall be made low. The rough places shall be made plain and the crooked places shall be made straight, and the glory of the Lord will be revealed, and all flesh shall see it together."

This is our hope. This is the faith that I go back to the South with. With this faith we will be able to work together, to pray together, to struggle together, to go to jail together, to stand up for freedom together, knowing that we will be free one day. This will be the day when all of God's children will be able to sing with new meaning: "My country 'tis of thee, sweet land of liberty; of thee I sing; land where my fathers died, land of the Pilgrims' pride; from every mountainside, let freedom ring." And if America is to be a great nation, this must become true.

And when we allow freedom to ring, when we let it ring from every village and every hamlet, from every state and every city, we will be able to speed up that day when all of God's children — black men and white men — Jews and Gentiles — Catholics and Protestants — will be able to join hands and to sing in the words of the old Negro spiritual: "Free at last, free at last; thank God Almighty, we are free at last." [9]

ADAM: I have a dream.
  (*They embrace.*)
  (*Exit Joseph Man.*)

SCENE 10: ADAM ALONE WITH HIS SON

(*Enter Daniel.*)

ADAM: Have you never heard the Earth crying out for help? Sometimes alone, or by the sea shore, or on a windswept walk, or my head on a pillow in the middle of the night, I hear her calling: "Adam King, help me; as you are a man, help me." Not loudly, but quietly and gently: in a leaf, a meadow, the rain falling upon my face and then the leaf, the meadow, the rain, become that voice, calling from a long way away; not a strange voice, but one within me that I've always known . . . almost a voice I've known before I was born and then, whatever I am doing, whether in affairs of state, or the heat of battle, I must stop and listen.

Sometimes, when I look at the history of the Earth and all the men who ever struggled, bled and died for her, it seems to me, sometimes, that they are all one man — the struggles of one man — and you and I and all of us are just a small part of it.

They want to destroy everything wild, fiery, tender and magnificent in life . . . the wind singing in the trees. But we won't let them. For the Earth is calling: "Remember me. Don't let me die."

(*Exit Daniel.*)

SCENE 11: THE WHITE HOUSE
THE PRESIDENTIAL OFFICE

(*Enter Topman.*)

ADAM: Don't you see what these men are doing?
TOPMAN: Of course I see.
ADAM: If they have their way, they'll wreck the country.
TOPMAN: If you stand in their way, they'll have your head.
ADAM: Someone has to do it.
TOPMAN: Why you?
ADAM: I'm the President.

TOPMAN: They'll kill you.

ADAM: Then they'll kill me.

TOPMAN: You're talking like a goddamn school boy, wet behind the ears. Leave well enough alone.

ADAM: You're sounding like one of them!

TOPMAN: I am one of them!

ADAM: Are you, Father?

TOPMAN: My hands aren't clean, Adam.

ADAM: Who's talking about dirty hands? We're talking about the cold-blooded murder of the human race.

(*Enter Tyrant, masked, watching from afar.*)

TOPMAN: Let me talk to them. I've done business with them all my life.

ADAM: You can't do business with them. If they have their way, there won't be a blade of grass left to lay your head on, a clear sky to see the day. Is that what you want for your grandchildren, Ambassador?

TOPMAN: There are those who eat the earth — and those that watch them do it. No one's ever found a way to change it.

ADAM: Then the world must change.

TOPMAN: Who can change it?

ADAM: I can. I will. I must. You taught me to win, not to lose.

TOPMAN: They're too strong.

ADAM: I'm stronger.

TOPMAN: They're too many.

ADAM: There are millions of people crying for help.

TOPMAN: The truth has blinded you.

ADAM: The people see the truth.

TOPMAN: The mob sees the truth when it's convenient, but they won't fight for it. If you ever get in trouble, they'll desert you like the Plague.

ADAM: But I work for the people; I'm accountable to them.

TOPMAN: You're accountable to keep your wits about you, or you'll lose them. Public office is a mask you have to change from time to time.

ADAM: You didn't.

TOPMAN: That was different.

ADAM: It's always the same issue: the raw bruising truth or the expedient lie.

TOPMAN: All right, it was the same. And look what happened.

Ruined for public office. And it did no good. I wasn't listened to. Is that what you want . . . your highest hope cut off; hated, despised, by the very thing you love?

ADAM: If I could hope to be the man you are, the man you have been; if I could take my stand as you have stood . . .

TOPMAN: Oh, Adam, give them the earth and all that's in it.

ADAM: No! I'd rather die.

TOPMAN: Oh, blast them all. I want my son. After Mark . . . I couldn't bear it if I lost you, Adam.

ADAM: You won't lose me, Ambassador. These men are impotent. You've said so yourself. Why, you and I and Matthew could take on an army of them.

TOPMAN: There's nothing more dangerous than impotence when you unmask it. It will strike like a snake in the night.

(*Exit Adam.*)

SCENE 12: A CORPORATE BOARD ROOM

(*Enter Big Ten wearing their masks, and General, in limousine. Tyrant, masked, watching from afar.*)

GENERAL: "War's outmoded."

JACKAL: "It's out of date."

FOX: Our profits! Our profits!

LEECH: Did you hear him? Did you hear him?

PIG: Did I hear him? Why the man is mad; he's mad.

WOLF: Didn't I tell you?

GENERAL: Ha, ha, "War's outdated," he said.

PIG: "It's obsolete."

LEECH: "Outmoded!"

FOX: And how are we to make a profit? How, I ask you, gentlemen, are we to make a profit?

WOLF: He must go. That man must definitely go . . .

JACKAL: "Pollution must end," he said.

WEASEL: Impossible!

LEECH: Preposterous!

PIG: Out of the question!

SHARK: "The destruction of the environment must end," he said.

VULTURE: And how are we to live? How are we to live?

WEASEL: Impossible!

LEECH: Preposterous!

PIG: Out of the question!

VULTURE: "Protect the independent businessman," he said.

WEASEL: Impossible!

LEECH: Preposterous!

PIG: Out of the question!

FOX: He wants to kill us all.

WOLF: Yes, Fox, and to think we trusted him to represent our interests.

FOX: We were misled.

SNAKE: Naive.

WEASEL: Too trusting.

WOLF: Yes, Weasel, he betrayed our trust. It's time to admit we made a mistake. It pains me to say this, gentlemen, but for the good of the country he must be . . .

TOPMAN: No!!

FOX: It's sad but true. He brought it on himself.

TOPMAN: I said no!!

WOLF: You know the rules, Topman.

TOPMAN: Let him go. I'll talk to him. I'll . . . his term is nearly up. He won't run again. I won't let him. Please.

(*Big Ten laugh.*)

Take everything I've got, but not my boy.

WOLF: There's too much at stake.

TOPMAN: You won't murder my son!

(*Begins to strangle Wolf, sees Tyrant approach, has stroke, and collapses.*)

LEECH: He's finished.

FOX: Nothing to stop us now.

(*Big Ten stand, unmask in triumph and display their masks in various places.*)

TYRANT: At your service, gentlemen.

WOLF: (*In terror.*) Who are you?

TYRANT: I am Tyrant.

WOLF: How did you get here?

TYRANT: Your thoughts summoned me.

FOX: We don't know you.

TYRANT: Thoughts have wings that fly beyond your wildest dreams.

LEECH: What is this talk?

TYRANT: Come, come, gentlemen. I would have got here sooner, but our friends throughout the world would not let me go.

WEASEL: Our business . . .

TYRANT: Is murder.

WEASEL: Murder! No one spoke of murder.

TYRANT: But you thought it, felt it, sensed it. Gentlemen, let us be frank. The smell of murder's in the room. And since murder is the business of the day, proceed.

WEASEL: Murder the President!

SHARK: He's a man just like you.

WEASEL: It's not the man, but the office.

PIG: Murder the President and we murder the land. An act not lightly forgiven in this world or the next.

TYRANT: Why, murder is a holy act when it rids us of this menace. The man's a pestilence, a fever in the blood of humanity.

WOLF: I'm for murder: calculated, pure, and simple.

FOX: Why murder? Let's say eliminate. It's more discreet.

SHARK: Yes . . . eliminate, eliminate.

TYRANT: And there's more. A dynasty is in the making. After Adam come his wretched brothers, Matthew and Luke, and then Joseph Man. They breed like rabbits. Why be timid? Eliminate the four.

SNAKE: Why then, gentlemen, there's nothing for it but to eliminate them all.

SHARK: Now for the vote.

WOLF: Gentlemen, I know nothing of what occurred here today.

FOX: I wash my hands.

SNAKE: I turn the other cheek.

TYRANT: This is by its very nature a corporate decision. There is no question of individual responsibility. This is the twentieth century, gentlemen. Not the dark ages.

WOLF: I have no objection in principle. But the actualization might prove awkward.

FOX: Difficult.

JACKAL: Embarrassing . . .

TYRANT: Nothing simpler, gentlemen. For a small fee, anything can be done.

FOX: And the payment . . .

TYRANT: Let's not think of payment at a moment like this. I offer you the moon, the earth, the stars.

FOX: But there's a price for everything. What is it?

TYRANT: Your friendship. Your good will is all I ask for.

WOLF: What will you do with it?

TYRANT: Take it, and use it as I will. I'm a member of the Universal
Church of Matter, in good standing, as are you all, gentlemen.
Our business: to promulgate insatiable desire.
"Matter, measure, weight," that's our motto.
What's above's beyond us; what's below is ours. Can you touch it,
taste it, see it, smell it? The five senses, that's our god.

SNAKE: But can we trust you? Are you reliable?

TYRANT: In our universe there's room for crime. It's one of the
processes that makes the world go 'round; therefore I am as
constant as the night.

SHARK: How do we know you won't change your mind in the middle?

TYRANT: As you can see, I've always played my role in history. I will
be with you 'til the end of time.

(*During Tyrant's speech, Big Ten in heartbeat rhythm gasp in
increasing frenzy. Music begins and slowly mounts.*)

Since Adam fell from heaven*
Mediocrity's in fashion.
Come, come, gentlemen,
Do not despair
There'll be no one to stand against you;
You've done your work too well.
The public mind's corroded with fear
By the ground you've paved with corruption.
Get these four, and I promise you
Not a man will stand against you.
We'll teach the lie,
Our text shall be this:
The beauty of equivocation.
We'll hew truth into a thousand fragments,
Each in enmity against the other
'Til truth, in consternation,
Forswears itself
And turns into a lie.
Flattery and terror shall do such a work
That men will walk humpbacked
Across the earth,
Their tongues lapping up the dirt,
Until they swear to those not yet born

* Music p. 92

They never heard of truth.
Before we're done we'll set
Man against man in rancorous hatred.
Civil discord, anarchy, and madness
Shall be the watchword of the day.
Now, gentlemen, what have you to fear?
To your work: Destroy! Destroy! Destroy!
Men must be taught a lesson this day.
Let the whole world see what happens
To the man who dares to stand against us.
I want the brain, the brain, the brain!
Let the bone, the tissue, the blood
Of his shattered brain spill
Out, out, out, and
Drip, drop by drop, in the gutters of
    the world.
(*The music reaches its peak. The Big Ten freeze in a grotesque of
The Last Supper with Tyrant behind them. Blackout. Silence.
Three gunshots.*)

SCENE 13: DALLAS

VOICE: The President is dead.
    (*Lights up, enter Chrous chanting in locomotive tap dance
    routine; Tyrant is disguised as Chorus member.*)
CHORUS: Not in the cover of the night,
    But in the great light of day,
    The assassins came
    And blotted out the life of reason.
    His mind, oh, his mind
    Was shattered.
    The earth cried out;
    Men gaped in amazement.
    The nation swayed, fell,
    Broke into a thousand pieces.
    Men shivered on the edge of chaos.
    The abyss had opened
    And from its depths
    The Great Beast held on God's great leash
    Had broken loose; in his train

Came panic, chaos, rout.

Something had gone out of
The heart of life forever.
Not a man died that day,
But you and I, my brothers.
Therefore in the name of the people we will . . .
(*All in syncopated rhythm.*)
Find the killer! Find the killer!
Find the killer! Find the killer!
Find the killer! Find the killer!
Find the killer!
(*Enter Fall Guy; enter Jackal, Pig, Shark, Crocodile, who stand apart; enter Grey Suits. Grey Suit 2 remains, at all times, silent, sinister, menacing.*)

CHORUS: (*All point to Fall Guy.*) The Fall Guy!
(*Enter Sheriff 1.*)

SHERIFF 1: This is the gun that did it!

CHORUS: (*All.*) This is the gun that did it!
(*Enter Sheriff 2.*)

SHERIFF 2: No, *this* is the gun that did it!

CHORUS: (*All.*) Oh, *this* is the gun that did it!
(*Enter Sheriff 3.*)

SHERIFF 3: No, *this* is the gun that did it!

REPORTERS: (*Breaking away from Chorus.*) Statement.

FALL GUY: I am innocent. I want to see a lawyer.

SHERIFFS: No lawyer.

REPORTERS: Witnesses?

JACKAL, PIG, SHARK AND CROCODILE: (*Pointing to Fall Guy.*) He did it!

FALL GUY: Innocent . . . Innocent . . . INNOCENT!
(*Enter Pearl; Tyrant hands him revolver.*)

PEARL: Justice must be done. (*Shoots Fall Guy.*)

REPORTERS: Statement.
(*During Pearl's speech, he is surrounded by Jackal, Pig, Shark, and Crocodile, who keep stuffing money in his hands and pockets; one Sheriff holds a prompter's board, from which Pearl reads his speech. At one point, Pearl breaks down crying, and wipes his nose with a handful of bills.*)

PEARL: I have a very soft heart. I was carried away with emotion and my very soft heart broke when I learned of our wonderful

President's death at the hands of this villain, leaving our beloved country orphaned and alone. I know that every right thinking citizen will applaud me for ridding society of the menace that committed this unspeakable crime. Although I am of Jewish faith, I am sure that every Christian countryman will understand that I am a very nice man and was swept away by the tender feelings in my heart.

(*Sheriffs gag Pearl and tape his mouth shut; they hustle him off stage.*)

(*Enter Peacock and Judge.*)

PEACOCK: I understand the President is dead. It's a shame that some folks ruin all the fun for the rest of us. One rotten apple ruins the whole barrel. In my term of office, I pledge to throw all the rotten apples away, leaving one great prosperous barrel — yes sir, a great society. Now, I don't have to tell you folks that what happened here today was a tragedy. Not just an ordinary everyday tragedy, but a real tragedy. Our head of state is dead. But you all know that. It behoves me as your new leader to ask you to bow your heads in prayer with me as we ask the Lord to give us the strength to bear this terrible calamity that has befallen our beloved country. And while we are at it, I am going to make a little personal prayer asking the Lord to give me the wisdom and the strength to fulfill the pledge made by my predecessor, our late beloved President, to the poor, the hungry, the unfortunate, and to give me the courage to bear the burden of office and lead this great nation rightly.

JUDGE: Do you swear under the power vested in you to uphold the Constitution and laws of this land?

PEACOCK: I swear.

JUDGE: To fulfill justice, mercy and righteousness?

PEACOCK: I swear.

JUDGE: To defend the widow, the orphan, the needy?

PEACOCK: I do.

FALL GUY'S WIFE: (*Breaking from Chorus.*) There has been a miscarriage of justice. My husband was innocent! I wish to testify.

CHORUS: (*All.*) She wishes to testify.

REPORTERS: You wish to testify

FALL GUY'S WIFE: I wish to testify.

GREY SUIT 1: Your husband was . . .

FALL GUY'S WIFE: Innocent.

GREY SUIT 1: An enemy.

FALL GUY'S WIFE: Innocent!

GREY SUIT 1: An agent. You realize that anyone aiding and abetting the enemy is subject to deportation? On the other hand you may decide not to testify, and cooperate with the government of this country. In that case we will help you in any way we can . . . You have a child.

FALL GUY'S WIFE: A little girl.

GREY SUIT 1: What is your decision?

FALL GUY'S WIFE: I am confused.

GREY SUIT 1: You realize your former husband was a counter-intelligence agent for the enemy?

FALL GUY'S WIFE: I . . .

GREY SUIT 1: A spy. Engaged in espionage against the republic.

FALL GUY'S WIFE: I . . .

GREY SUIT 1: Do you wish to be implicated in his crimes?

FALL GUY'S WIFE: I . . .

GREY SUIT 1: Or do you wish the protection of this mighty country?

FALL GUY'S WIFE: I wish for protection.

GREY SUIT 1: A plea for protective custody!

REPORTER 1: Testimony.

FALL GUY'S WIFE: I do not wish to testify.

CHORUS: She doesn't wish to testify.

(*Exit Sheriffs, carrying off Fall Guy's Wife.*)

GREY SUIT 1: She doesn't wish to testify.

(*Exit Grey Suits.*)

WITNESS 1: (*From Chorus.*) I saw the whole thing. I'll testify.

JACKAL: She doesn't understand. (*Strangles witness, carries her away.*)

WITNESS 2: (*From Chorus.*) I saw it, I'll testify.

PIG: He doesn't understand. (*Stabs witness, carries him away.*)

WITNESS 3: (*From Chorus.*) I saw it. I'll testify. It was a group of . . .

SHARK: He doesn't understand. (*Shoots witness, carries him away.*)

WITNESS 4: (*From Chorus.*) I was a witness. I'll testify. These men, they . . .

CROCODILE: He doesn't understand. (*Beats witness to death, carries him away.*)

REPORTER 2: Witnesses?

(*Re-enter Jackal, Pig, Shark, Crocodile with Tyrant.*)
(*Silence.*)

REPORTER 1: No more witnesses.

JACKAL, PIG, SHARK and CROCODILE: Now they understand.

(*Exit Jackal, Pig, Shark and Crocodile.*)

JUDGE: Do you swear not to bear false witness but before God and man to be a witness to the truth?

PEACOCK: I do.

JUDGE: Then by the power vested in me by God and the Republic, you have taken the sworn oath of office and are now President and Commander In Chief of the land.

CHORUS: (*All.*)
Everything will be all right now . . .
Everything will be all right now . . .
Everything will be all right now . . .

REPORTERS: It's official. The Fall Guy did it.

CHORUS: (*All.*)
Everything will be all right now . . .
Everything will be all right now . . .
Everything will be all right now . . .

(*Enter Vanity, Nurse.*)

VANITY: We murdered him.

CHORUS: What did she say?

CHORUS: She said we murdered him.

CHORUS: No.

CHORUS: Yes, she said we murdered him.

VANITY: I want Matthew. Where's Matthew? Oh, won't someone please help me?!

NURSE: He's in the Capitol, Mrs. King.

PEACOCK: Mrs. King . . .

VANITY: Don't touch me. I'm afraid.

NURSE: Afraid?

VANITY: Of what they might do. Of what might happen.

PEACOCK: Everything is under control, Mrs. King.

VANITY: They killed him . . . We all did . . . They want to murder us all. But they won't murder my babies — not my little ones.

NURSE: Shh . . . Shh . . . It's all right, Mrs. King, everything is all right now. I think you want to lie down now and get a little rest. We'll just slip you out of these clothes.

VANITY: I want to wear it; I want them to see what they've done.

NURSE: Now, now, Mrs. King.

VANITY: His head was gone . . . The bullet shattered his brain. Oh

my God! Oh my God! They tore out his brain! MURDERERS . . .
MURDERERS!

(*Exit Vanity, Nurse, Peacock.*)

(*Enter Doctors, with Tyrant disguised as doctor, followed by
Reporters.*)

DOCTOR 1: No question . . . the bullet entering from the front tore off
his head.

REPORTERS: Are you certain, Doctor?

DOCTOR 2: Positively. Our autopsy shows three bullets. One from
behind . . .

DOCTOR 3: One from in front . . .

DOCTOR 1: And one from the side.

REPORTERS: Then the Fall Guy could not have acted alone.

DOCTOR 3: Not unless he was capable of being in three different places
at the same time.

REPORTERS: There is no doubt of your findings?

DOCTOR 2: None whatsoever.

REPORTERS: May we quote you?

DOCTOR 2: Absolutely, the people must know the truth.

(*Exit Reporters.*)

(*Enter Grey Suits.*)

GREY SUIT 1: Permit me to disagree with you, Doctor. The people
must not know the truth.

DOCTOR 1: Who are you?

(*Grey Suits flash their badges.*)

I see.

DOCTOR 3: But justice must be done.

GREY SUIT 1: We are from the Justice Department. Can there be any
question that we could act in any way contrary to the interests of
justice?

DOCTOR 3: But . . .

GREY SUIT 1: You see, Doctors, we have every reason to believe that
this unfortunate murder of our late beloved President was a plot to
overthrow the government.

DOCTOR 3: A plot to overthrow . . .

GREY SUIT 1: A plot to overthrow the government.

DOCTOR 1: But who would want to . . .

GREY SUIT 1: Engineered by the enemy.

DOCTOR 1: Dreadful.

GREY SUIT 1: And that is why we must ask you, Doctors, to cooperate with the government at this time.

DOCTOR 1: Of course. What do you want us to do?

GREY SUIT 1: Change your story.

DOCTOR 2: But if what you say is true, then it is to the good of the country that the people know of it.

GREY SUIT 1: Permit me to disagree with you, Doctor. You know our people: generous to a fault, touchy, temperamental, emotional, with a sense of fair play unknown in the annals of history; quick to arise and to settle any affront to the national pride by wiping out the enemy ruthlessly. What would be their response to this? It would mean nuclear war . . . perhaps the destruction of the human race. So now you understand, Doctors, why we must do everything in our power to avoid such a catastrophe.

DOCTOR 3: Of course!

DOCTOR 1: Certainly.

GREY SUIT 1: I knew we could count on you, Doctors, men of your intelligence and stature, to understand the situation.

DOCTOR 1: Certainly you can count on us!

GREY SUIT 1: Just the mention of one bullet entering from behind will be sufficient.

DOCTOR 3: In . . . our . . . autopsy report?

GREY SUIT 1: In your report.

DOCTOR 2: But that would be lying. A false medical report is grounds for . . . our licenses could be revoked.

GREY SUIT 1: Revoked . . . It's more like grounds for the Congressional Medal of Honor!

TYRANT: Well, Doctors, if it's for the good of the country . . .

DOCTOR 2: But how can we take the responsibility to . . .

GREY SUIT 1: Oh, if that's all that's troubling you, Doctor, ease your mind at once. It's not your responsibility. The government takes full responsibility.

(*Tyrant removes disguise, exits.*)

DOCTOR 2: For the consequences as well?

GREY SUIT 1: For the consequences as well.

DOCTOR 2: I see. All right then, I'll go along with you.

GREY SUIT 1: That's fine, Doctor.

DOCTOR 2: But won't there be a hearing, an inquiry of some kind?

GREY SUIT 1: Oh, there will be a public hearing, all right, but this won't be part of it. I assure you this will be strictly a confidential matter.

(*Exit all.*)

SCENE 14: JOSEPH MAN'S HOME

(*Telephone rings; Martyr answers, replaces phone.*)

MARTYR: Adam King is dead!

JOSEPH MAN: I tell you, this nation is sick! (*To audience.*) Does any one hear me? I say again, does any man hear me out there?

(*Enter Samuel Y, stepping out of audience.*)

SAMUEL Y: I hear you!

JOSEPH MAN: Is that you, Samuel Y?

SAMUEL Y: Yes, it is me, brother.

JOSEPH MAN: These people are crazy. They kill their own president. Oh, what is the use? It's hopeless!

SAMUEL Y: Want to lay down and die?

JOSEPH MAN: Sometimes, Samuel Y; yes, sometimes I do.

SAMUEL Y: Mustn't do that. You must go on, brother.

JOSEPH MAN: Why'd they want to go and kill him? He was for them!

SAMUEL Y: That's why, brother, that's why. White devils! I told you not to count on him. They'll never let a white man help a black.

JOSEPH MAN: He was our friend.

SAMUEL Y: Was. He's a dead president; and a dead friend is no friend. Got Pork Chop in office now. The days of milk and honey are over. They're laughing over his dead ass. The whites are scared. A white man would have to turn black to help us now.

JOSEPH MAN: Christ was white.

SAMUEL Y: You got a little white blood yourself, ain't you, brother?

JOSEPH MAN: Don't talk that way!

SAMUEL Y: That's what folks are saying.

JOSEPH MAN: What are they saying?

SAMUEL Y: That you're part white, brother, otherwise you wouldn't go around kissing whitey's ass! Of course that's what your enemies say. Your friends say that ain't true. Your friends say you just a little smug.

JOSEPH MAN: We got to get along with these people.

SAMUEL Y: Ain't a white man worth his ass . . .

JOSEPH MAN: We got to bend a little.

SAMUEL Y: You are smug.

JOSEPH MAN: We got to live and let live.

SAMUEL Y: I am a man, brother.

JOSEPH MAN: I know that, Samuel Y.

SAMUEL Y: And no man gives me the right to live. Black man been trying to live for four hundred years and white man still ain't gonna allow it. They gonna kill me. You know that, don't you brother?

JOSEPH MAN: I know that. They gonna kill me too.

SAMUEL Y: We gonna be two dead men in the land of plenty. Brother, I just thought of something to tickle your bones. You fixin' to go to heaven? I know you got your heart set on it. Wouldn't it be funny if I landed up in heaven and you ended in hell? You'd be mighty disappointed, after being so good and all. That's the trouble with you, brother, acting like an angel in the land of the apes. Yeah, they gonna kill me; then you be all alone. What you gonna do without me?

JOSEPH MAN: I don't rightly know.

SAMUEL Y: You be real nice — and maybe, just maybe, they gonna let you live.

JOSEPH MAN: And you're gonna spit harder and harder in their face.

SAMUEL Y: That's right, brother. One black man in the whole world gotta stand up and be unafraid.

JOSEPH MAN: Samuel Y, don't spit too hard yet.

SAMUEL Y: Why not, brother?

JOSEPH MAN: I need you . . . I need you from time to time, to tell me how smug I am.

SAMUEL Y: You can count on me, brother. 'Til we meet again.

JOSEPH MAN: 'Til we meet again.

SCENE 15: THE KING FAMILY HOME

(*Destiny, Luke, Fashion, Blackman, and Tyrant, disguised as family friend, are in downstairs living-room. Topman, in wheelchair, is wheeled by Nurse into upstairs bedroom. The stroke has paralyzed Topman, except for use of one arm. He has lost the ability to speak.*)

DESTINY: How can I tell your father?

LUKE: I've kept all news from him.

FASHION: But he's restless. He keeps asking.

DESTINY: He knows.

LUKE: He can't.

DESTINY: He knows.

FASHION: But how? It's impossible. He's got no word. No newspaper, nothing.

DESTINY: I can tell by his eyes.

LUKE: Where's Matthew?

PRUDENCE: Vanity's plane is late. They'll be along presently.

LUKE: We can't wait any longer. We must tell him now. Mother . . .
   (*All, except Blackman and Tyrant, go to bedroom.*)

LUKE: Adam's dead . . . Dad.

DESTINY: Yes . . . Topman. He was . . . killed.
   (*Topman begins moaning in effort to communicate; he struggles to rise from wheelchair.*)

NURSE: Mr. King, please, please.
   (*Enter Matthew, and Vanity, who go to bedroom; Fashion, Luke and Prudence return downstairs to living room.*)

VANITY: I'm going to tell you everything, Grandpa Topman, exactly as it happened. It was a clear bright day . . . the sun was shining . . . the crowd was waving . . . the band was playing as we drove . . .

LUKE: I'll kill them all! The dirty, filthy murderers!

FASHION: Luke!

PRUDENCE: What can we do?

LUKE: The rotten filthy killers! They won't get away with it!

FASHION: Not this way, Luke! Not this way!

LUKE: Let me go!
   (*Destiny returns to living room.*)

PRUDENCE: Blackman, stop him! He's crazy!

BLACKMAN: Hold on, man! Hold on!

LUKE: I have a fire in my brain that could ignite the world.

PRUDENCE: Luke, come to your senses. Mother and Father are upstairs.

DESTINY: No, Prudence, I'm here.

LUKE: The jackals! I'll blow the whistle on them all!

DESTINY: What is it, Luke?

LUKE: Nothing! Nothing! Nothing!

BLACKMAN: Luke, come outside; I want to talk to you. (*To Luke aside.*) Keep your mother out of this, man. Do you hear?

FASHION: No, no, stay here.

LUKE: I can't.

DESTINY: Talk to me, Luke.

LUKE: Not a word. Not a word.

DESTINY: What is it?

LUKE: I must not speak . . .must not. I'll kill them all!

PRUDENCE: He's gone mad!

DESTINY: (*She slaps him.*) Silence! I brought you into this world, Luke. You will do as I say. You must think of the family.

LUKE: You know who killed him. Our own friends murdered him.

DESTINY: Luke!

LUKE: A demon did this to mock us. The world is laughing. I can see the mockery in men's eyes. I've a sickness in my heart no medicine can ever cure.

DESTINY: You must bear it. We all must.

LUKE: Bear it? Not a thousand days. They didn't even give him a thousand days. How could it have happened? Does God breed monsters for men, or is this the work of some demon? Damn, damn, damnation take them all! What offence had my brother committed that he must die for it? He only wished to help mankind. And for this, and this alone, he was struck down. For as the world reckons, there is no greater crime than to help your brother.

(*Matthew leaves bedroom.*)

MATTHEW: Frail humanity.
We worship the fist that beats us,
And slay the tender heart
That feeds us.
I want to cry out, but I can't.
What shall I say: "Stop the earth"?
A crime so monstrous, so hideous,
It breaks the bounds of reason,
Terrifies the mind,
Paralyzes the will.

Oh pain, pain, pain!
All the pain in the world.
Not heaven or hell
Can ever wipe this pain way.
I have a grief that could unlock
The gates of hell.
I'll keep it private,
Buried in my heart.

DESTINY: It's too horrible to think of. Promise me you'll never speak of it again.

LUKE: I swear it. I'll never speak of it again.

DESTINY: All of you promise me.

PRUDENCE: We do, Mother.

(*Exit all, except Topman.*)

(*Big Ten members, one by one, enter tap dancing. Each speaks to Topman, then exits. As they do so, Topman swings cane wildly at them in a fit of grief and rage.*)

WOLF: Sorry about your son, Topman.

FOX: Yes, it was a shame.

LEECH: A terrible tragedy . . . terrible.

JACKAL: Awful.

WEASEL: Wish there was something we could do.

SHARK: Are you all right, Topman? Is there anything we can do for you?

VULTURE: You can count on us. You know that, Topman.

CROCODILE: Sure.

PIG: Anytime.

FOX: We're your friends. Hah, hah!

WOLF: We'll be seeing you. And, uh . . . Topman, give our best to the Mrs. Tell her we're sorry about your boy. It must be terrible for you both.

(*Enter Storyteller.*)

STORYTELLER: Our young president was dead. He had given his life for the land he loved. He had done in his death what he failed to do in his life. He had brought us all together that shameful day the six white horses brought his body to the grave.

Something dark and ugly clawed at the edges of our minds; betrayal . . . and something worse — the thought that we had killed him. Harsh and terrifying knowledge, too unbearable to face.

SCENE 16: WASHINGTON: THE FUNERAL

(*Enter Matthew, Vanity, Daniel. Drumrolls.*)

DANIEL: And could no one save my daddy?

VANITY: No, my son.

DANIEL: Not even the army and the navy?

VANITY: Not even the army and the navy.

DANIEL: Will he come back?

VANITY: No, my little boy.

DANIEL: Don't they want him to be president?

MATTHEW: Out of the mouths of babes . . .

VANITY: Oh Daniel . . .

DANIEL: If he comes back and isn't president, then can he live?

VANITY: Hush, my son.

DANIEL: Daddy can be with us then, and everything will be all right.

VANITY: (*Aside.*) Nothing will ever be right again.

ACT II

SCENE 1: AN APARTMENT IN WASHINGTON

VANITY: You've come.

THE GREEK: You said you needed me.

VANITY: You must help me. You mustn't refuse me.

THE GREEK: Anything in my power.

(*Silence.*)

Yes?

VANITY: Find out who killed my husband.

(*Shakes his head "no."*)

Please.

THE GREEK: What about Matthew?

VANITY: Matthew is shattered. And Luke is a boy.

THE GREEK: And the father . . .

VANITY: . . . is crippled. I have no one else to turn to but you.

THE GREEK: You are asking me to do this for you?

VANITY: Yes.

THE GREEK: You will not change your mind?

VANITY: No.

THE GREEK: All right. You shall know the truth.

VANITY: Oh, thank you.

THE GREEK: You shall know the truth, but you will regret it. And later, when you know, I am wondering, will you still thank me then?

(*Blackout.*)

(*Lights come up; some time later.*)

VANITY: I don't believe it.

THE GREEK: I told you, you would regret it.

VANITY: I can't believe it.

THE GREEK: These are the men.

VANITY: You could be mistaken.

THE GREEK: My sources are unimpeachable. There's no question.

VANITY: I won't believe it.

THE GREEK: Betrayal is as old as the world.

VANITY: What am I to do?

THE GREEK: Nothing.

VANITY: Nothing?!

THE GREEK: Leave it alone. You have what you wanted.

VANITY: These men must be brought to justice.

THE GREEK: Justice! Foolish girl. Still you do not understand.

VANITY: What are you talking about?

THE GREEK: The men who killed him, they are the government. Can a government be brought to justice?

VANITY: But I will know. I will always know. I must tell Matthew.

THE GREEK: That is a mistake. You will kill him.

VANITY: What?

THE GREEK: You will see.

SCENE 2: A PUBLIC SQUARE

(*Enter Matthew. Chorus, carrying newspapers, chanting in locomotive tap, Tyrant disguised among them. Newspapers are raised and lowered in staccato rhythm as they alternately speak and hide.*)

MATTHEW: These are the men who did it.

CHORUS: (*All.*) Are you certain?

MATTHEW: These are the names. Wolf, Fox, Crocodile, Leech.

CHORUS: (*All.*) We don't believe it. It can't be true. It can't be true.

MATTHEW: Yesterday, when Vanity tried to give the evidence to Peacock, the lives of her children were threatened.

CHORUS: (*All.*) This can't be happening here.

MATTHEW: Will you help me?

(*Silence.*)

The spirit of my martyred brother will haunt this land forever. His death will give men no rest 'til they turn and see what he lived and died for. And until you become worthy of that spirit, you will have no rest.

CHORUS: (*All.*) And you, Matthew, do you see it?

MATTHEW: I am always in my brother's presence. Always.

CHORUS: (*All.*) If we do what you are asking, we will bring the country down in ruins.

TYRANT: (*Stepping out of Chorus.*) Do you honestly believe Adam would have wanted that?

MATTHEW: I don't know . . . Who are you?

TYRANT: A friend of your brother; a friend to the republic—and all right-thinking men. Adam King lies a martyr to the nation. Let him so lie. You wish us to speak the truth. Think what it would mean: a country disillusioned, its faith in the powers that rule it, broken. Have we that right? No. This is egotism. Let those who are your friends guide you. There are truths too dangerous for anyone to know, truths that do not lead to the welfare of the people. To speak such a truth would be a lie. Fate has decreed that the exalted memory of your brother shall give comfort to generations yet unborn. It would be the greatest cruelty, the greatest lie, to upset the people. Therefore, for the good of the country, we must bury the truth, bury the truth, bury the truth forever.

MATTHEW: Can you live with yourselves, breathe the air, sleep in your beds, walk, talk, chatter . . . Can you do all this? And not one man, I say, not one, cry out for my dead brother?
(*Silence.*)
Not one voice in all the land cry out? No, I will not believe this. Can't you speak? Have you lost your tongues? Are you men or dogs! Are you stone! Have you forgotten? Is there no one who remembers my brother ADAM KING?

CHORUS: (*All in syncopated rhythm.*) Keep cool! Keep cool! Keep cool! Don't rock the boat! Don't rock the boat!

(*Matthew crosses stage, goes up steps to his home.*)

MATTHEW: They've beaten me. They've beaten me.

PRUDENCE: No, no, my boy.

MATTHEW: I've failed.

PRUDENCE: Hush.

MATTHEW: Prudence.

PRUDENCE: I'm here, Matthew.

MATTHEW: They don't want the truth. They don't want it.

PRUDENCE: I know.

MATTHEW: No one wants it.

PRUDENCE: Yes.

MATTHEW: What am I to do? Oh, what am I to do?

PRUDENCE: Hush, hush.

MATTHEW: Help me. Help me.

PRUDENCE: Shh . . . Shh . . .

MATTHEW: I don't want to live.

CHORUS: (*All in syncopated rhythm.*) Keep cool! Keep cool! Keep cool!

(*Knocking.*)

PRUDENCE: Who's there? Who is it?

SENATOR STAUNCH: (*From offstage.*) Matthew, open the door. It's me, Staunch.

PRUDENCE: It's Senator Staunch.

(*Enter Senator Staunch.*)

(*Exit Prudence.*)

SENATOR STAUNCH: Matthew, I think I know a way to help you. The district attorney of my state is beholden to me. He's a good man. Through his office we can introduce the evidence and get the truth to the people. It's a long shot — but it's worth a try.

MATTHEW: Yes.

SENATOR STAUNCH: If we could discredit or even cast reasonable doubt on the official version . . .

MATTHEW: It would be a beginning. Meanwhile, I must play a waiting game.

(*Exit Senator Staunch.*)

(*Chorus members scatter. They become citizens involved in various occupations — waiter, carpenter, gambler, secretary, janitor, etc. Tyrant is disguised as newsvendor. They pursue these occupations during the following scene. From time to time they all stop their activities and, in unison, either watch the investigation intently, or conspicuously hide behind newspapers.*)

SCENE 3: THE INVESTIGATION

(*Enter Big Ten and Chief Justice Whorein in limousine. Throughout Chief Justice Whorein's discussion of money, Big Ten fill two large satchels with gold bricks.*)

FOX: I assure you, Chief Justice, there's a great deal of money behind this.

CHIEF JUSTICE WHOREIN: Money! The root of all evil. I knew it. I knew it! Money is filth. I never touch it. What is it, after all . . . paper, just plain paper. How foolish for men to corrupt their souls for that . . . paper. In my thirty years on the bench, has anyone ever seen this hand touched by money?

BIG TEN: NEVER!

CHIEF JUSTICE WHOREIN: NEVER! In thirty years on the bench, has anyone every been able to prove my mind has been swayed by the large economic interests in the land?

BIG TEN: THEY'VE NEVER BEEN ABLE TO PROVE IT.

CHIEF JUSTICE WHOREIN: NEVER . . . BEEN ABLE TO PROVE IT! Am I not, Chief Justice of the land, above suspicion?

BIG TEN: ABOVE SUSPICION.

CHIEF JUSTICE WHOREIN: ABOVE SUSPICION. Gentlemen, let me speak with candor. In a lifetime devoted to dignity and virtue — a life dedicated to the law — I have watched the ebb and flow of money. When I have seen my fellow men drowning in despair in this ocean of paper money, I knew there could be only one honorable course open to me. I have seen others, deceived by the fretful shadows of life, have a lower standard, yet mine has been and always shall be, the GOLD STANDARD. Does happiness desert you? Gold will not. Does friendship, love, family, fly from you? Gold will not. Does appetite, health, betray you? Gold will not. For she is reliable, solid, trustworthy, and true — the one certitude in an uncertain world. Ah, fair empress to whom all must come . . . But I fear I grow prolix. (*Sits on the two satchels of gold.*)

The Whorein Commission is now in session. Let the whoring . . . I mean hearing . . . begin.

(*Enter Senator Staunch. All freeze except Staunch and Matthew.*)

SENATOR STAUNCH: We've done everything in our power to get Washington to release those photographs.

MATTHEW: And . . .

SENATOR STAUNCH: The government won't budge.

MATTHEW: I see . . .

SENATOR STAUNCH: I'm sorry.

MATTHEW: Thank you for your efforts. And your daughter . . . ?

SENATOR STAUNCH: Still missing. (*Matthew shakes his head.*) What will you do now, Matthew?

MATTHEW: Follow the investigation, and . . . wait and see.

(*Exit Senator Staunch.*)

REPORTERS: Statement!

MATTHEW: I see no reason to believe my brother was killed by anyone other than the Fall Guy acting as a lone assassin.

(*Enter Fortress.*)

FORTRESS: A request for the photographs of the President's autopsy.

CHIEF JUSTICE WHOREIN: (*Consulting Big Ten each time before speaking.*) Denied.

FORTRESS: For what reason?

CHIEF JUSTICE WHOREIN: DENIED FOR THE GOOD OF THE COUNTRY!

FORTRESS: These photographs and documents are the final link that proves beyond doubt the true killers of President King.

CHIEF JUSTICE WHOREIN: DENIED FOR THE GOOD OF THE COUNTRY!

FORTRESS: The people have a right to the truth.

CHIEF JUSTICE WHOREIN: DENIED FOR THE GOOD OF THE COUNTRY! The Whorein Commission is now adjourned . . .

FORTRESS: Wait. I have witnesses!

CHIEF JUSTICE WHOREIN: You have witnesses?

CHORUS: (*All.*) He has witnesses!

FORTRESS: I wish to call Senator Staunch, who first brought the conspiracy to my attention, to the stand.

CHIEF JUSTICE WHOREIN: Call Senator Staunch to the stand.

(*Machine gun fire offstage.*)

FOX: Senator Staunch is dead.

FORTRESS: Dead!

FOX: Yes . . . poisoned . . . by a box of candy . . .

SNAKE: A well-wisher sent him . . .

LEECH: While in mourning for his . . .

VULTURE: Kidnapped daughter.

FORTRESS: I wish to present the testimony of Ferrari Ferret. He flew the hired assassins to South America.

(*Machine gun fire offstage.*)

CROCODILE: Ferrari Ferret is dead.

PIG: He met with an unfortunate automobile accident three years after the assassination.

CHIEF JUSTICE WHOREIN: His testimony is therefore inadmissible.

FORTRESS: But . . .

CHIEF JUSTICE WHOREIN: Certainly the District Attorney knows dead men cannot talk. Ha, ha . . .

(*Big Ten laugh.*)

FORTRESS: But I can prove . . .

CHIEF JUSTICE WHOREIN: Overruled! I am beginning to enjoy this. Proceed with the hearing.

FORTRESS: I wish to enter as evidence certain proven facts relating to Ferret's co-conspirators.

CHIEF JUSTICE WHOREIN: Produce the evidence.

FORTRESS: May I proceed?

CHIEF JUSTICE WHOREIN: You may. Mr. District Attorney, this is an impartial inquiry. Let me assure you that you have our good will. This commission is interested in nothing but the truth.

FORTRESS: Thank you, Chief Justice. I have a sworn witness willing to testify to the fact that he saw and heard Ferret's associates . . . Call Mr. Goodman to the stand.

(*Enter Goodman with Sheriff 1.*)

SHERIFF 1: Do you solemnly swear . . . (*Muttering incoherently in gibberish.*) . . . So help you God.

GOODMAN: I do.

FORTRESS: Mr. Goodman, were you present at a gathering of five men, besides yourself, last fall?

GOODMAN: I was.

FORTRESS: What did you hear these men saying? Please tell the commission.

GOODMAN: I heard them say that they were going to kill the President.

FORTRESS: Would you please tell the commission the names of these men?

GOODMEN: They were Hatchet, Mottel, Wreck, Slew, and another man whose name I can't recall.

(*Tyrant smiles.*)

(*Machine gun fire offstage.*)

LEECH: Unfortunately, Hatchet . . .

SHARK: Mottel . . .

SNAKE: Wreck . . .

JACKAL: And Slew . . .

FOX: Are dead.

CROCODILE: They met with various forms of death.

LEECH: In each case by accident.

CHIEF JUSTICE WHOREIN: Highly regrettable!

LEECH: Highly!

CHIEF JUSTICE WHOREIN: Therefore the evidence is inadmissable. The witness's testimony shall be STRUCK FROM THE RECORD!

BIG TEN: (*Strike table.*) STRUCK FROM THE RECORD!

FORTRESS: But Mr. Goodman is a sworn witness under oath.

CHIEF JUSTICE WHOREIN: The testimony concerns dead men, who obviously, Mr. District Attorney, cannot be here at this hearing to refute the charges against their good name. Let it never be said that there is prejudice toward the dead in my court. This inquiry is impartial toward the living and the dead. The evidence is therefore hearsay and must be STRUCK FROM THE RECORD!

BIG TEN: (*Strike table.*) STRUCK FROM THE RECORD!

FORTRESS: But this is outrageous!

CHIEF JUSTICE WHOREIN: Overruled. The witness is excused. The commission wishes to thank, and I personally wish to congratulate, Mr. Goodman for his rectitude and high-mindedness in coming here today. Often in the solitude of my chambers, I have prayed to God to send me witnesses to the truth. You are such a man, Mr. Goodman, if I see rightly, and I think I do. All I can say is if there were more men like you, this country would be a far better place to live in.

(*Goodman is politely escorted out of courtroom by two Sheriffs. Gunshots heard from offstage. Sheriffs re-enter.*)

As for you, Mr. District Attorney, President Peacock warned me about you. We have ways of dealing with men like you.

(*Two Sheriffs handcuff Fortress and drag him out of courtroom.*)

The Whorein Commission is now adjourned.

(*Exit Big Ten in limousine. Chief Justice Whorein exits, weighed down by carrying two satchels of gold.*)

MATTHEW: But it's a lie!

CHORUS: (*All.*) What can you do? What can anyone do?

(*Exit all, except Matthew. Tyrant watches.*)

MATTHEW: Why don't I speak,
  Rise up and cry out?
  To see the nation topple,
  The people in disorder,
  Chaos throughout the land?
  And all for what . . .
  To avenge a dead brother?
  Am I my brother's benefactor
  That I may revenge him
  On the land he loved,
  Lived for, died for?
  Truth they say,
  For truth's sake,
  Is the greatest havoc
  That can be wreaked.
  Have I that right . . . ?
  But then my brother lies unjustified
  And that's the greatest lie of all.

Then speak I will.
I'll shout "Villainy!" from every housetop,
Broadcast this foul murder
And those that did it.
I'll tear down the world,
And think it no great matter,
So that justice will be heard
For but an hour.
An hour . . . no,
Give me but a minute
To break the men
Who broke my brother,
Less than a minute
To pull down the carrion
Who slew my brother,
Usurped his place
And whose feet are planted on his grave.
In seconds they murdered a president,
Stole a country,
And gave mortal anguish to the world.
Second for second then . . .
I'll expose them to the judgment of history.
In full power of my office,
I will prosecute them
Before the conscience of the world.
Tear off their rags of seeming virtue,
That hide the ulcered leprosy
Of vice beneath,
And prove . . . prove . . .
But I have no proof.
What if I'm not believed?
Then from an instrument of justice,
I'm turned into the laughingstock
Of the world.
I must be silent,
For it was ever so
That virtue must be slow to learn of vice.
But when I'm called
Before that great and final judgment,
Where my every deed must be accounted

And weighed in that sure
And certain balance,
What am I to say . . . ?
I had a brother,
As virtuous as he was kind,
So balanced in his disposition,
So impartial in his mind,
That beauty, shining through him,
Lit up his every motion,
'Til envy in a rage rose up and slew him.
Athlete, hero, scholar, statesman,
He was the bright hope of the world.

SCENE 4: AN APARTMENT IN WASHINGTON

THE GREEK: The strong take everything.

VANITY: Everything?

THE GREEK: Everything! Now you see the truth.

VANITY: The truth. What is the truth?

THE GREEK: The world as it is.

VANITY: That's not much.

THE GREEK: Is there anything else?

VANITY: There is . . .

THE GREEK: There is nothing. That's all there is.

VANITY: I won't go with you.

THE GREEK: Have you any choice?

VANITY: I have my children, my country.

THE GREEK: The country that killed your husband?

VANITY: Adam despised you. You're everything he detested in a man.

THE GREEK: Fortunately his wife did not share his opinion. She had better taste.

VANITY: Don't talk that way.

THE GREEK: How would you like me to talk?

VANITY: Adam was right about you. You're vile and gross.

THE GREEK: You like it.

VANITY: Like it! You're not one hundredth the man my husband was.

THE GREEK: Yes, you like it. You missed this in your husband, no?

VANITY: You are vile! The comparison is obscene. My husband . . .

THE GREEK: Your husband understood nothing of the world, or the men who run it. What he had he did not make with his own hands. So it was taken from him. He was a fool.

VANITY: You steal it.

THE GREEK: Ideas again . . . that your husband teach you. A husband that did not even understand you, the woman he loved.

VANITY: And you understand me?

THE GREEK: Yes, I understand you. He make you stupid in head, but I will teach you what you are.

VANITY: With a whip, no doubt.

THE GREEK: When that makes you happy, yes, a whip.

VANITY: Do you expect me to stand here and listen to this? A woman in my position?

THE GREEK: You do not understand your position.

VANITY: I have the respect of the world.

THE GREEK: You are the plaything of the world. Woman alone is . . . tipota . . . nothing. But I will give you and your children my protection and my strength.

VANITY: Your protection?

THE GREEK: Yes . . . here you have no world to stand on. But I will give you the world . . . my world. A world in which to rest.

VANITY: You make it sound almost tempting.

THE GREEK: My islands are the most beautiful at this time of year. Once you wished you might never leave them. Do you remember?

VANITY: Oh, if wishes could come true.

THE GREEK: I will make them come true.

VANITY: These past five years . . .

THE GREEK: Have been a dream. This is reality. You and I.

VANITY: But I must consider the opinion of the world.

THE GREEK: The world is a whore that must be taken by force and held by force. A wild animal that must be tamed. I do what I do. Nobody to stop me. And if you are with me, nobody to touch you.

VANITY: But to the people, I am Mrs. Adam King.

THE GREEK: Adam King was a crowd pleaser. The crowd killed him. He was murdered by his own publicity, as they are murdering you, bit by bit. Is that what you want, foolish girl?

VANITY: No.

THE GREEK: Well . . .

VANITY: What do you want me to do?

THE GREEK: Forget him.

VANITY: You shameless beast!

THE GREEK: Is the nature of man to be shameless for woman he love.

VANITY: You don't love me, you desire me.

THE GREEK: Is there a difference? I give you my name. I give you everything. In return . . .

VANITY: In return?

THE GREEK: I take everything. Do you understand?

VANITY: Yes.

THE GREEK: We will be married in a month.

SCENE 5: THE WEDDING FEAST OF HELL

MATTHEW: Who can I be, if not myself?
 What shall I be,
 If not what I was born to be?
 I'll join the general masquerade.
 I've fallen to the bottom of myself
 And found the Great Beast[10]
 That I've loved and hated, within.
 I, myself, am the entrance
 To heaven and hell.

 TYRANT!!! Where are you? TYRANT!!!

TYRANT: (*From afar.*) Right here, Matthew, inside your mind. I've been expecting you. (*Unmasking.*) What can I do for you?

MATTHEW: Come out.

TYRANT: As you wish.

MATTHEW: You're . . .

TYRANT: Yes, I am. You're trembling.

MATTHEW: I've seen you in a thousand faces.

TYRANT: But never recognized me. It's alright Matthew. You needn't be alarmed.

MATTHEW: I didn't believe you existed.

TYRANT: Very few do. But the moment you wished to find me, you did. That is because I am everywhere.

MATTHEW: You're always in disguise.

TYRANT: I come to people in the likeness of themselves. I'd never be recognized if it weren't for the few, the elect, who can bear to see me as I am.

MATTHEW: The elect?

TYRANT: Yes, you. And your brother; he too. That was what you wanted to talk to me about . . . your brother.

MATTHEW: Adam.

TYRANT: It is written: he who struggles against Tyranny unmasks me. All the better. I, Tyrant, I too need people who understand and can work with me. You do understand now, don't you, Matthew?

(*Silence.*)

Well, then, I will teach you.

MATTHEW: You killed my brother.

TYRANT: Tut . . . Tut.

MATTHEW: Can you teach me how to bring my brother back to life?

TYRANT: It was all a mirage, a dream; no one wanted your brother.

MATTHEW: You lie! The people loved him.

TYRANT: What do they want, the people? A little place to call their own in which to cheat and lie — little dreams to retire on and live out their allotted lives. And I, Tyrant, am their greatest invention. Each man who cannot rule himself seeks me to rule him. A little tyrant inside each of them to call their own. I will show you people. Look.

(*Enter Big Ten, running in from all directions.*)

WOLF: Yes, we killed him, but what could we do? Try to understand.

FOX: We had great hopes in him, but he disappointed us. He failed us. He had to go.

LEECH: A terrible tragedy; he had such great promise. He could have been the greatest president we ever had but he wouldn't listen to us. In the end we had to kill him. We didn't want to but he forced us to. What else could we do? Try to understand . . . try to understand . . . please . . . please . . .

TYRANT: Sweet things, aren't they; murderers, and they want to be understood. Detestable!

SHARK: In the end it was better this way. We built monuments to him — named airports, museums, freeways. His pain was little. He died quickly. He lies in peace.

MATTHEW: But the agony you caused.

WOLF: Matthew . . . Matthew . . .

MATTHEW: The agony to the world.

PIG: We did what was best. What had to be done. His pain is over. It is we who suffer. It is we who should be pitied.

MATTHEW: Oh my God.

(*Exit Big Ten.*)

TYRANT: Horrible, isn't it? Weaklings! I'm ashamed I had to use them. I, who have walked with man on all the continents of the earth since the beginning, can tell you — man will never change. Capable of no great evil, he no sooner commits a murder, than he gets on his hands and knees and begs forgiveness. And I, who had such great hopes for him in my youth!

MATTHEW: Why did you do it?

TYRANT: Boredom.

    I am Nothingness.
    I desire the abyss.
    I am made of the wishes of billions.
    The rage, frustration, hatred and pettiness
    Of the world collect in me.
    As long as men shall live,
    I shall live.
    I am hidden behind every noble gesture,
    Every tender smile.
    Every act of kindness
    Must pay me its due.
    I hide; I wait.
    I am the shadow of life.
    I am all the misery of the world.
    Kill that and you kill me.
    I am man's escape from freedom.
    The absence of the self they fear to face.
    I am the proof
    That man will never change.
    What chance had your brother
    Against me?

CHORUS: (*All chanting offstage.*)
    We want Tyrant!
    We want Tyrant!
    We want Tyrant!

TYRANT: Hear them. They're bored again, the little darlings.

CHORUS: (*All chanting offstage.*) We want Tyrant! We want Tyrant!

TYRANT: I'll have to grind out some novelty to amuse them. But what exactly? Ah, yes, I have it. The marriage feast of hell.

    (*Tyrant puts on top hat and tails, cane and white gloves. Enter Chorus tap dancing to "Tea for Two," followed by "Ain't She Sweet," with balloons, masks; women in wedding dresses, men in*

formal attire.)
Come to me all maimed,
Diseased, deformed creatures.
Pray to me.
In me you live and breathe,
And have your being.
I am life's revenge upon life.
The black sickness that ravages health.
The corruption that waits
To steal upon each flower.
Give me your minds,
Your souls, your hearts.
Come to the wedding feast of hell.
(*Enter Vanity and The Greek in wedding attire. They are escorted by the Big Ten who are dressed in formal attire, with top hats, and carry luminous umbrellas. The scene is done in black light. Tyrant directs Big Ten and Chorus in tap dance routine.*)
Once every thousand years, hell rises up and swallows the earth in greed. This world's a bargain basement. There's not a thing that can't be bought. Liberty, who will buy Liberty?
(*During the next few speeches, the Big Ten rip Matthew's clothes off, piece by piece in slow motion: coat sleeve being torn from his arm, pants leg being pulled off his leg, etc.*)

LEECH: She's mine.

TYRANT: Liberty to Leech. Justice?

WOLF: I'll have her.

TYRANT: Justice to the Wolf. Truth?

FOX: I'll take her.

TYRANT: Truth to the Fox. What am I offered for Honor?

PIG: Everything I have.

TYRANT: Throw Honor to Pig. Who will have Beauty?

WEASEL: Me.

TYRANT: Beauty goes to Weasel. And last but not least — Goodness.

SNAKE: Since the beginning of time Goodness is mine.

TYRANT: Of course, my favorite, Snake. How could I be so forgetful? Goodness has always been your favorite, Snake. What comes next? The human mind.

VULTURE: That's mine.

TYRANT: Vulture claims the mind of man. Let him have it. Very little is left.

CHORUS: (*All chanting.*) We want Tyrant! Tyrant! Tyrant!

TYRANT: You see, Matthew?

WOLF: Hey, Tyrant, you left something out.

TYRANT: What's that?

WOLF: The soul.

TYRANT: Oh, that belongs to me.

WOLF: Did you hear that? Tyrant gets the soul. Ha, ha.

FOX: Everyone knows the soul doesn't exist.

SHARK: There's no such thing. You told us so yourself.

BIG TEN: Can you touch it, taste it, see it, smell it? Who's ever weighed it? Can we bottle, package or contain it? No!

CROCODILE: Then by all means, give our souls to Tyrant. Let him take what we do not have.

PIG: What a joker you are, Tyrant. Ha, ha, ha.

TYRANT: Let it be my private joke. Ha, ha, ha.

ALL: Ha, ha, ha.

MATTHEW: Oh God, not your souls.

TYRANT: It's no use, Matthew. They're deaf, dumb and blind. The fools. You see, Matthew?

(*All freeze except Matthew and Tyrant.*)

MATTHEW: Yes, I see.

TYRANT: Everything is working out just as I told you.

MATTHEW: Everything is working out just as you told me.

TYRANT: The people have made their wants clear.

MATTHEW: The people have made it clear.

TYRANT: Now you see at last.

MATTHEW: Now I see at last.

TYRANT: Don't be sad, Matthew. That's the way life is. It will never change.

MATTHEW: Yes, that's the way life is.

TYRANT: And now you'll join us. Your education is complete.

MATTHEW: And now I'll . . .

SPIRIT OF ADAM: (*Calling from offstage.*) Matthew . . .

MATTHEW: Adam! Adam! Is that you?

(*Enter Adam. All freeze except Adam and Matthew.*)

SPIRIT OF ADAM: Hello, Matthew.

MATTHEW: Oh, thank God you're here. I thought I had lost you.

SPIRIT OF ADAM: You can never lose me, Matthew.

MATTHEW: I've missed you, Adam.

SPIRIT OF ADAM: Yes. 'Til we meet again, brother.

MATTHEW: 'Til we meet again, brother. Adam . . . Adam . . . I need
   you.
SPIRIT OF ADAM: I'll always be with you.
MATTHEW: Don't go. I don't know what to do.
SPIRIT OF ADAM: Remember. Remember. Remember me.
   (*Exit all, except Matthew.*)
MATTHEW: Corruption breeds like maggots
   In the noonday sun.
   Justice slinks and hides in cellars
   Like a cur beaten to an inch of his life,
   While men in fear and trembling pray
   To that black power that beats them
   For their little portion of life.
   Life's a madhouse, and all are inmates in it,
   Chained to that imposter, life.
   God must have hated men,
   He made them so badly.
   After the Deluge, they turned out apes,
   To see them mince and amble
   'Round the earth, slithering on their bellies
   To lick the fingers of corruption;
   Each one a whore to his dream of glory,
   Hatching mischief, anguish, discord, gloom,
   Who must forever and forever and forever
   Turn 'round the spindle of his unborn self.
   Has anyone confessed it? Life's a dream,
   A shadow play without an ending,
   A tyrant who gives us birth
   And at death squeezes us back to dust.
   How does that bright angel, the Earth,
   Bear this scheming race,
   These petty two-legged creatures of a day,
   Grasshoppers hopping to and fro,
   Piping their shrill songs of righteousness
   Sure to poison the ear of God.
   The Earth's a patient saint
   To bear such calamitous music
   Or is this, too, a part of
   The Song of Creation?
   The Earth's penitence or her mercy,

For look how she observes
In silent meditation
Her rape; the generations of men
Clambering over her mountains and valleys,
Trampling over her meadows and brooks,
Oblivious to her presence
Their heel breaking the long-stemmed flower,
Bruising her holy flesh.
Or does she remember the first man
Who drank her sacred water,
Inhaled her perfumed sky,
Looked with astonishment
At her blue-green sea?
And does she hope for his return . . . ?
That golden race of men
Who bowed down to Earth
And reverenced her as mother.
For the sake of that first man,
Does she put up with this
Leaden race of men?

SCENE 6: THE CAMPAIGN

(*Enter Joseph Man.*)

JOSEPH MAN: I've been waiting for you, Matthew.

MATTHEW: Joseph Man.

(*Enter Farmer.*)

FARMER: We all have.

(*Enter Blackman.*)

BLACKMAN: Been a long time waiting.

(*Enter Chorus, in locomotive tap, with Tyrant disguised as campaign supporter.*)

CHORUS: (*All in syncopated rhythm.*)
Been waiting for you! Waiting for you!
Waiting for you! Waiting for you!
Waiting for you! Waiting for you!

(*The crowd hoists Matthew on its shoulders.*)

CHORUS: (*All in syncopated rhythm.*)
Matthew King for president!
Matthew King for president!

Matthew King for president!
Matthew King for president!
(*Enter Nurse, Topman in wheelchair, and Destiny.*)

MATTHEW: I've made my decision, Dad. I'm sure this is the right thing
to do.

(*Topman turns away; Destiny freezes in horror.*)

Wish me luck. Pray for me, Mother.

(*Chorus speaks as individuals.*)

CHORUS: He's won the primaries.

CHORUS: Matthew can't be stopped.

CHORUS: Victory!

CHORUS: Better hop on the bandwagon.

CHORUS: To the next president: Matthew King.

CHORUS: Matthew, he'll make everything right.

MATTHEW: I will finish what my brother set out to do.

CHORUS: (*All.*) Hurrah! Hurrah!

(*Enter Araby Araby. Tyrant hands him a gun and points his arm in
direction of Matthew; three shots ring out. Matthew, crying
"Brother," falls dying into Adam's arms.*)

CHORUS: (*Chanting in syncopated rhythm.*)

Keep cool! Keep cool! Keep cool!

PRUDENCE: (*Running to him.*) Matthew! Matthew!

CHORUS: (*All in syncopated rhythm.*)

Oh, no! Oh, no!

BLACKMAN: All hope gone now. All hope gone now. The bastards!
The dirty, filthy bastards!

(*Enter Big Ten, smiling, in limousine. Tyrant joins them. All
freeze.*)

(*Blackout.*)

SCENE 7: ARLINGTON CEMETERY

(*Enter Luke.*)

LUKE: You came a long hard way, my brothers,
Blessing the land that bred you;
Here you lie in silent benediction,
Blessing the land that cursed you.

Our country's a graveyard
Our dreams twisted goblins in the night,

A junkyard filled with the rot and debris
Of a million murdered promises.
Oh night, tender night,
Swallow me up with my brothers.
Murderous night, cover me up
Let me lie with my brothers.
The ground is cold tonight
I'll drink myself to stupefaction.
The living are not as happy as the dead;
No one mourns for them,
And yet they're halfway
On the road to death.
Poor fools that cannot see their end
In their beginnings;
Runaways from the grave . . .
Still, they must come to this.

What's a man?
The after-leavings of Creation.
A piece of dust
In the eye of God;
The mortal remnants
Of an immortal dream.

(*Exit.*)

SCENE 8: A CORPORATE BOARD ROOM

(*Enter Big Ten in limousine, laughing.*)
CROCODILE: The world is ours.
PIG: Yes, the world is ours.
FOX: At last.
WOLF: And what a beautiful world it is, Pig.
PIG: Most beautiful. Is it not beautiful, Leech?
LEECH: Yes, most beautiful.
SHARK: Nothing to stand in our way ever again.
VULTURE: The field is clear, so to speak.
JACKAL: And now for the spoils, gentlemen.
WEASEL: Ah, yes, the division.

WOLF: As you know, gentlemen, I own fifty percent of our great nation, and so I shall take the largest share. Fox, who owns twenty-five percent, is next.

THE OTHERS: I want mine! I want mine!

WOLF: Gentlemen, you shall have it. Five percent for you Pig, and you Crocodile, and you Shark. A magnificent three percent each for Snake, Jackal and Weasel. A handsome two percent for Leech and a fertile one percent for Vulture.

VULTURE: The division is unfair.

LEECH: Grossly unfair.

VULTURE: One percent? Why, that's nothing!

WOLF: It's billions.

VULTURE: Yes, but your wealth is untold, Wolf.

WOLF: As it should be. Mine was the planning, the design; I thought it out.

FOX: With the help, of course, of Fox.

WOLF: With Fox's help, of course.

SHARK: But we were in on this from the beginning.

PIG: I hate to say this, Wolf, but you're making a killing.

SHARK: I want a larger cut.

WOLF: Gentlemen, I see no reason for dissension.
(*Draws revolver from briefcase and places it on table.*)
Each according to his nature. Since mine is a large and generous nature, I am perfectly satisfied with the division.

JACKAL: You won't accommodate us then?

WOLF: How can I? The structure of power prohibits it. As long as I am the head of this organization, things will remain as they are.

SHARK: You're ravenous, Wolf.

PIG: You're stuffing yourself on our share.

LEECH: Sucking the blood out of us.

SNAKE: Squeezing us dry.

WOLF: I am as God made me. Gentlemen, that will be all.

WEASEL: No further discussion?

WOLF: No further discussion. I see no point in it. Not if we are to remain one happy family. We are one happy family, are we not, gentlemen? (*Silence.*) Excellent! Let us go on to the next point of business.
(*Exit Big Ten in limousine.*)

SCENE 9: THE KING FAMILY SUMMER HOME

(*The living room.*)

LUKE: They tried to kill me, Mother.

DESTINY: What are you talking about, Luke?

LUKE: They tried to kill me, Mother.

DESTINY: You're drunk again, Luke.

LUKE: Can't you hear me? They tried to kill me!

DESTINY: Stop it at once. Your father's upstairs.

LUKE: I won't stop it. Listen to me.

DESTINY: I won't listen to you. Do you want to drive me mad?

LUKE: Mad, mad . . . the whole world is mad. Look at me, Mother. I
haven't long to live. I'm your last remaining son. Then all your
sons will have been murdered. You'll be all alone then, Mother;
all alone.

DESTINY: Where have you been? What's happened to you?

LUKE: At the bottom of the sea, but it was cold down there and I came
up for air. But the girl, she's a mermaid, singing wildly in my ear,
"I want to live, I want to live." But she can't, poor girl. She's dead.

DESTINY: LUKE!!!!

LUKE: We were alone in the car, just the two of us. I was driving her
home. We crossed the bridge. A car pulled out and forced us off
the road into the river.

DESTINY: Oh, my God! Oh God! And the girl, the girl?

LUKE: She never came up again.

DESTINY: You left her there? How could you do that!

LUKE: I couldn't find her. I dived in the darkness after her a hundred
times, but I couldn't find her.

DESTINY: You were drunk!

LUKE: I wasn't drunk, Mother. I told you those men tried . . .

DESTINY: Stop it, Luke. Stop it at once! Do you expect me to believe
that insane story? No one would believe it! A girl died tonight
because of your weakness. Have you taken leave of your senses?
(*Pause.*) Who was she?

LUKE: My secretary.

DESTINY: Rosemary? Oh, what are we to do . . . Rosemary . . . that
poor girl . . . what am I to tell her family . . . the scandal . . .
You're all I have left, Luke. What will happen to you now?

LUKE: What will happen to any of us?

(*Goes upstairs to his son's bedroom; Peter is in bed.*)

PETER: Tell me more about the giant, Daddy.

LUKE: The Tree of Life stretches from heaven to earth. The giant guards the Tree and blocks the way, and he challenges anyone who tries to reach the top to overthrow him. Only a hero can beat the giant.

PETER: Is the giant very big?

LUKE: As big as the world.

PETER: What happens to someone who can't beat the giant?

LUKE: Then he crushes you and hurls you to your death.

PETER: Is that what happened to Uncle Adam and Uncle Matthew?

(*Silence.*)

They met the giant, and the giant crushed them?

(*Silence.*)

Did you climb the Tree, Daddy?

LUKE: I tried.

PETER: And you beat the giant?

LUKE: No, I didn't beat the giant.

PETER: Why?

LUKE: I turned back, I was afraid.

PETER: I don't believe it. You could never be afraid. You just pretended to turn back to fool the giant, until you could get past him.

LUKE: No, I will never meet the giant, now.

PETER: I will. When I grow up, I'll climb the Tree and I'll beat the giant. I'll throw him down, and then you and Uncle Adam and Uncle Matthew and anyone else who wants to, can climb to the top of the Tree with me.

LUKE: Perhaps you will, my son . . . perhaps you will.

(*Luke goes to Topman's bedroom; Topman is in wheelchair.*)

Oh, my father, I have failed you.

Forgive me. Oh, my father, help me.

I don't know how to live,

And I don't know how to die.

What are you thinking behind your eyes

When you see your sons butchered?

What's inside you left to call your own?

Do you long for death,

That great release which quells all woes?

Or are you standing on the other side of life,

Looking through the eyes of death
At what we call life?
Your soul's immense with dying
And does it grow with feeding on death?

SCENE 10: JOSEPH MAN'S HOME

JOSEPH MAN: Adam King, dead; Samuel Y, dead. Now Matthew King, dead. My time will soon be over.

MARTYR: Oh, Lord!

JOSEPH MAN: Matthew . . . Our last chance, gone. They've murdered the mind, the spirit, and now, the heart of the country. I'm next.

MARTYR: No.

JOSEPH MAN: They won't stop now.

MARTYR: I won't let them! It doesn't have to be.

JOSEPH MAN: It has to be. We've always known it. We don't want to start lying to each other now, do we?

MARTYR: No.

JOSEPH MAN: That's right.

MARTYR: You're all I got.

JOSEPH MAN: There's the children.

MARTYR: It's different.

JOSEPH MAN: This is for them. I've been saving it against the time. (*Hands her a sealed letter.*) I tried to be a good father. I could have done it better.

MARTYR: You're the best man I've ever known.

JOSEPH MAN: I've done the children one good turn though. I've loved their mother.

CHORUS: (*All chanting offstage.*) Joseph Man! Joseph Man! Joseph Man!

JOSEPH MAN: They've come.

MARTYR: It's too soon.

JOSEPH MAN: Yes. (*Silence.*)

MARTYR: Life comes down to a few precious moments.

JOSEPH MAN: Yes.

CHORUS: (*All chanting offstage.*) Joseph Man! Joseph Man! Joseph Man! Joseph Man!

JOSEPH MAN: I've got to go.

MARTYR: I know. Oh, if the earth would only stop and we could stand like this forever.

JOSEPH MAN: But the earth is turning. And we must turn with it.

MARTYR: I've never seen a man bear so much pain. What keeps you going?

JOSEPH MAN: The same thing that keeps you going: God. Promise me you'll be steady to the end.

MARTYR: I don't know . . .

JOSEPH MAN: Set my mind at peace.

MARTYR: Yes.

CHORUS: (*All chanting offstage.*) Joseph Man! Joseph Man! Joseph Man!

MARTYR: They're calling. You've got to go. Oh, someone help.

JOSEPH MAN: For thirteen years we've been waiting for help. But the help has not been forthcoming. It's too late now. It won't come now.

MARTYR: I want you to know . . . I . . . I won't be with another man.

JOSEPH MAN: It's all right if you do.

MARTYR: I won't be. Don't forget your muffler, baby.

(*She freezes as Joseph Man leaves her. He slowly ascends to the upper stage and becomes a silent witness to all that follows. Lights slowly fade out on Martyr as the next scene begins.*)

SCENE 11: KNOCKSIN AND THE VICTORY CELEBRATION

(*Chorus and Big Ten enter tap dancing in a victory celebration. Confetti and noisemakers. Tyrant in their midst leading Knocksin on a leash. Chorus and Big Ten freeze intermittently as the celebration and dialogue alternate in a stop/start manner.*)

TYRANT: Well, what is it, Knocksin? Speak up.

KNOCKSIN: I want my chance . . . to serve you.

TYRANT: He has spent a lifetime scraping off any semblance of manhood. Haven't you, Knocksin?

KNOCKSIN: Yes.

TYRANT: No scruples.

KNOCKSIN: No scruples.

TYRANT: No hope.

KNOCKSIN: No hope.

TYRANT: No beliefs.

KNOCKSIN: No beliefs.

TYRANT: Pliable, flexible, easy to manage.

KNOCKSIN: Easy to manage.

TYRANT: There you are, ladies and gentlemen. Nature's revenge against God for daring to produce man. The triumph of mediocrity. Could we ask for anything more? . . . And he won't get out of line, will you, Knocksin?

KNOCKSIN: I won't get out of line.

TYRANT: He'll be very grateful.

KNOCKSIN: Very grateful.

TYRANT: The country wishes to hide its guilt. Knocksin will help you. The country wishes to bind up its wounds, its bleeding heart and return to business as usual; who better than Knocksin? A people deserve the president they get . . . Knocksin is clearly the people's choice. Hooray!

(*As Chorus exits in one direction, Big Ten exits in opposite direction, pulling Knocksin on leash. Tyrant remains, smiling.*)

SCENE 12: THE KING FAMILY HOME

LUKE: You and I are the last ones left, Mother.

DESTINY: I go on, Luke.

LUKE: I go on too, Mother.

DESTINY: With a bottle.

LUKE: I drink so I can bear the smell of the other animals around me.

DESTINY: Be kind, Luke.

LUKE: I had a brother killed by kindness . . . two brothers.

DESTINY: You must forget the past, my son.

LUKE: Sometimes I hear Adam and Matthew calling to me . . .

DESTINY: I know. I hear them. You must not listen.

LUKE: Their lives cry out for justice.

DESTINY: They are with God, and a far greater life.

LUKE: And we are with . . . where are we?

DESTINY: You think it was the evil of the world that killed your brothers; it was the mercy of God. They had a dream that lives in men's hearts, and which by their actions, men always betray. But Adam and Matthew lived their vision. Had they lived to see what men did to it, it would have broken their hearts. Now you must live your life, Luke.

LUKE: Live . . .

DESTINY: Does that terrify you, my son? Listen to me. Your brothers lived and died like men. I want you to live your life as they lived theirs, not in regret for the past but in pride of manhood for the future that must come into being.

LUKE: What future can there be for us?

DESTINY: There's your family. And Adam and Matthew's children. You're all the father they will know. You're the head of the family now. There is much to do.

LUKE: You don't want me to run.

DESTINY: You're a man. You must decide.

LUKE: But the debt I owe my brothers . . .

DESTINY: I think the debt you owe your brothers can best be paid by looking after their children.

LUKE: You're a grand lady, Mother.

DESTINY: Rubbish! I've simply told you the truth.

LUKE: That's what I mean.

SCENE 13: THE JIG IS UP

(*Big Ten rush in; Wolf stands while the others sit down in a row cross-legged on upper stage, frantically sucking their thumbs.*)

FOX: Caught, caught, caught!

WEASEL: I told you we shouldn't have killed him!

WOLF: Shut up, all of you!

SHARK: You got us into this, Wolf. Now you get us out of it!

VULTURE: Fox too! Fox too!

JACKAL: Wolf and Fox have betrayed us!

WOLF: We're all in this together! If I go down, you go down with me.

FOX: Count me out, Wolf!

CROCODILE: Not me! Not me! Not me! I didn't mean it! I didn't mean it! I didn't know what I was doing. I was misled.

FOX: Crocodile tears at this late hour?

CROCODILE: My intentions were good!

WOLF: Put that bottle down.

CROCODILE: What's wrong with a little drink?

FOX: You're a mess, Crocodile!

WOLF: Drunkard!

CROCODILE: Now, don't be disagreeable, Wolf, just because you're a teetotaler! Have a drink, fellahs. Drinks on the house . . . Ha, ha. You're paying, Wolf . . . You hear that, boys, Wolf is gonna pay for . . . doing this to us . . .

JACKAL: Ha, ha, ha . . . Wolf is going to pay. Wolf is going to pay.

CROCODILE: 'Cause I didn't mean it! I didn't mean it . . . Mother. I'm a nice boy.

VULTURE: You make me sick!

CROCODILE: OHHHHHH!

WOLF: You're making an exhibition of yourself.

CROCODILE: I can't help it!

PIG: What is it, Crocodile?

CROCODILE: My conscience is hurting.

WOLF: SHHHHHH!

VULTURE: Mine too!

WEASEL: Mine too!

SNAKE: Mine too!

JACKAL: Mine too!

PIG: Mine too!

LEECH: Mine too!

SHARK: Mine too!

WOLF: Tell them about conscience, Fox.

FOX: Conscience! Ha! What is it? Has anyone felt it? Seen it? Touched it? Tasted it? No.

CROCODILE: Then it doesn't exist?

WOLF: It doesn't exist.

CROCODILE: Then what am I feeling?

WOLF: Scared, Crocodile, scared.

LEECH: Scared.

SNAKE: Scared.

JACKAL: Scared.

SHARK: What are we going to do?

WOLF: Keep quiet, all of you! We'll find a way out of this.

FOX: We always do.

WOLF: Tyrant . . . He'll help us. We can count on Tyrant!

ALL: Tyrant, Tyrant . . . We want Tyrant!

(*Enter Tyrant tap dancing.*)

TYRANT: You called for me?

JACKAL: Oh, Tyrant. Thank God you're here.

VULTURE: Help! Help! We need help!

PIG: You see, Tyrant, it's like this . . .

WOLF: Shut up. I'll handle this. (*To Tyrant.*) Some of the boys have got themselves into a little jam.

TYRANT: What has that to do with me?

WOLF: Well, we knew we could count on you to pull a few strings.

TYRANT: Why?

WOLF: Why?

TYRANT: Yes, why?

WOLF: Well, uh, you see . . . uh . . . you tell him, Fox.

FOX: We're in the soup. The organization is being exposed.

TYRANT: That's a matter of indifference.

FOX: You don't understand.

TYRANT: I understand.

FOX: But we're your buddies. Your pals!

TYRANT: And you were caught?

WOLF: Well . . .

TYRANT: And you talked?

WOLF: Oh, no, no. Not a word . . .

FOX: Extenuating circumstances.

SHARK: A matter of time.

PIG: It will soon blow over.

TYRANT: But —

WOLF: A small misunderstanding.

PIG: It'll soon blow over.

TYRANT: Yes—

WOLF: Some of the others, they lost their heads, and they . . .

TYRANT: And they talked?

FOX: We were betrayed by the people we loved.

TYRANT: They've found you out?

FOX: In a word, yes.

TYRANT: Then you are useless to me.

WOLF: But you need us, Tyrant.

TYRANT: Not anymore.

WOLF: Look here, Tyrant, you can't do without us!

TYRANT: You fools!

SNAKE: But we're the Big Ten!

TYRANT: You're a slot in the universe.

WOLF: I'm Wolf!

FOX: I'm Fox!

SHARK: I'm Shark!

LEECH: I'm Leech!

PIG: I'm Pig!

JACKAL: I'm Jackal!

SNAKE: I'm Snake!

WEASEL: I'm Weasel!

VULTURE: I'm Vulture!

CROCODILE: I'm Crocodile!

TYRANT: Exactly! Easily replaceable. There are millions like you waiting to take your place. Now a King . . . If I could get a King, that would be something worthwhile. But they're the kind I never get. Your time is up, gentlemen.

JACKAL: You can't do this to us!

LEECH: We're members in good standing of the Church of Universal Matter!

TYRANT: Yes, and to her you will go.

WOLF: Where are you taking us?

TYRANT: To matter's final resting place,
   The inert center of the earth.
   And there you shall serve me faithfully,
   Endlessly, eternally, all the rest of your days.
   Come gentlemen, you are mine.

CROCODILE: Nooooo!

TYRANT: Yessss!

CROCODILE: What will you do with us?

TYRANT: Why, eat you, of course!

   (*Tyrant grabs Wolf's wrist. They all grab each others' wrists in an effort to resist Tyrant. He drags entire chain of Big Ten screaming down to hell.*)

SCENE 14: THE KING FAMILY HOME

(*Topman lying on his deathbed, Cardinal Common Tribute and Luke with him. Throughout scene Topman makes effort to communicate.*)

CARDINAL COMMON TRIBUTE: And do you think they'd let a scoundrel like you into heaven?

TOPMAN: Ahhhhh . . .

CARDINAL COMMON TRIBUTE: (*Repeating after Topman.*) For money? Not even after all you've given the church.

TOPMAN: Ahhhhh . . .

CARDINAL COMMON TRIBUTE: Oh, visiting rights? That's different. (*Enter Nurse.*)

TOPMAN: Ahhhhh . . .

LUKE: God keep you from seeing your sons, Dad? No, He wouldn't be so unkind.

TOPMAN: Ahhhhh . . .

CARDINAL COMMON TRIBUTE: Heaven? I think there is. I'm not sure. I've lived too long in this world to . . . be sure.

TOPMAN: Ahhhhh . . .

LUKE: You've killed your sons? You sent them into a world of wolves? All your fault? No, Dad! You've sacrificed them to your ambition? Too late to make up for what you've done? Don't say that, Dad. You can never be forgiven? Never? No, Dad, no.

(*Topman struggles to rise.*)

CARDINAL COMMON TRIBUTE: And where do you think you're going? (*To Nurse.*) Better get the family.

(*Nurse exits.*)

Oh, you want to die on your feet like a man. (*Exit Cardinal Common Tribute.*)

(*Enter Adam and Matthew. As Topman crosses to meet his sons, Luke reaches after him, in a posture, frozen in time.*)

SPIRIT OF ADAM: Hello, Dad.

TOPMAN: Adam . . . Matthew . . . is that you?

SPIRIT OF MATTHEW: Yes, Dad.

TOPMAN: I knew you'd come. I was expecting you. I was coming to you, but I had . . . trouble . . . walking . . . no one . . . to give me a hand.

SPIRIT OF ADAM: We're here now, Dad.

TOPMAN: Where . . . are you? It's cold and dark.

SPIRIT OF ADAM: We're right here, Dad.

TOPMAN: I've waited so long for you; neither living nor dead. We'll always be together now, won't we boys?

SPIRIT OF MATTHEW: Always.

TOPMAN: Oh, my sons! My sons!

SPIRIT OF ADAM: Come on, Dad.

SPIRIT OF MATTHEW: Lean on us, now.

TOPMAN: Where are we going?

SPIRIT OF MATTHEW: We can't be loafing around here.

SPIRIT OF ADAM: We've got to get moving.

TOPMAN: Yes, yes, there's work to be done.

SPIRIT OF MATTHEW: Can you walk, Dad?

TOPMAN: I can walk. It's just like old times. If only Mark were . . .

SPIRIT OF ADAM: Mark is waiting for us, Dad.

TOPMAN: Mark . . . I always knew we'd make it. Didn't I tell you boys that a man can't be beaten. That if only we stuck together we'd be sure to win, that nothing on earth could stop us.

SPIRIT OF MATTHEW: Whatever you say, Dad.

TOPMAN: Ah, my proud eagles. You've flown high.

SPIRIT OF ADAM: We've got to fly higher.

SPIRIT OF MATTHEW: And yet a little higher.

SPIRIT OF ADAM: And then we're there.

TOPMAN: Will we find Mark?

SPIRIT OF MATTHEW: Mark is there.

SPIRIT OF ADAM: He's waiting for us, Dad.

TOPMAN: I'm dying.

SPIRIT OF ADAM: Yes.

TOPMAN: I'm glad. Will it be long?

SPIRIT OF MATTHEW: Just a moment.

TOPMAN: And then?

SPIRIT OF ADAM: You begin to live.

TOPMAN: You die and then you live. Strange . . .

SPIRIT OF ADAM: Yes.

TOPMAN: I'll be free then, won't I? Ohhh . . . boys. There's something I've learned while you've been gone. They can have the world. We've got each other.

(*He collapses, Luke and Blackman carry him to his bed.*)

(*Joseph Man descends from the upper stage as Chorus enters, single file, in locomotive tap, and moves in serpentine fashion around the stage, Tyrant disguised among them. Joseph Man intermingles with Chorus. During his speech individual members of the Chorus cry out in a gospel response.*)

JOSEPH MAN: (*To audience.*) Well I don't know what will happen now. We've got some difficult days ahead. But it really doesn't matter with me now, because I have been to the mountaintop. I don't mind.

Like anybody, I would like to live a long life; longevity has its place. But I am not concerned about that now.

One day we will have to stand before the God of history and we will talk in terms of the things we've done.

Yes, we will be able to say we built gargantuan bridges to span the seas, we built gigantic buildings to kiss the skies. Yes, we made our submarines to penetrate oceanic depths. We brought into being many other things with our scientific and technological power.

It seems that I can hear the God of history saying, "That was not enough! But I was hungry and ye fed me not. I was naked and ye clothed me not. I was devoid of a decent sanitary house to live in, and ye provided no shelter for me. And consequently, ye cannot enter the Kingdom of Greatness. If ye do it unto the least of these, my brethren, ye do it unto me."

We must learn to live together as brothers, or we will all perish as fools. We are tied together in the single garment of destiny, caught in an inescapable network of mutuality. And whatever affects one directly, affects all indirectly. For some strange reason I can never be what I ought to be until you are what you ought to be. And you can never be what you ought to be until I am what I ought to be. On the day I die, I'd like somebody to mention that Joseph Man tried to give his life serving others. I'd like for somebody to say that day that Joseph Man tried to love somebody. I want to be able to say that day that I did try to feed the hungry. I want you to say on that day that I did try in my life to visit those who were in prison. And I want you to say that I tried to love and serve humanity.

I just want to do God's will. And He's allowed me to go up to the mountain. And I've looked over. And I have seen the promised land.

I may not get there with you. But I want you to know tonight that we as a people will go to the promised land.

So I am happy tonight. I am not worried about anything. I am not fearing any man. Mine eyes have seen the glory of the coming of the Lord![11]

(*Enter Washout. From a distance he raises rifle. Tyrant guides his hand. Two shots ring out. Joseph Man falls into arms of Adam and Matthew. As he dies, he cries "Oh Lord, help me." A third shot rings out. Members of Chorus raise umbrellas forming funeral dirge. As they exit, humming "We Shall Overcome," the King family and Tyrant, disguised as a friend of the family, gather around Topman's deathbed.*)

DESTINY: So many years . . . so many years. Goodbye, Topman.

PRUDENCE: Our Father which art in heaven,

DESTINY: Hallowed be thy name.

LUKE: Thy kingdom come.

VANITY: Thy will be done.

NURSE: On Earth.

CARDINAL COMMON TRIBUTE: As it is in heaven.

FASHION: Give us this day our daily bread.

DESTINY: And forgive us our trespasses,

LUKE: As we forgive those who trespass against us.

VANITY: And lead us not into temptation,

TYRANT: But deliver us from evil.

CARDINAL COMMON TRIBUTE: Amen.

(*All freeze.*)

(*Enter Storyteller.*)

STORYTELLER: And now our story's ended. They dared the ancient dream, the age-old dream: to change the world, 'til in the end tyranny rose up and slew them. Why do we worship our great men and then murder them? Sometimes of an evening, I look up in the sky and see them there, eternal as the stars, immortal as the dream they gave us which seared and burnt our hearts. This earth's a sorry place, rarely touched by greatness. They walked with us a brief time, but we shall remember a long time the legend of Adam King and his band of brothers.

(*Storyteller begins to ascend stairs to upper stage during his speech. The Spirit of Joseph Man has joined Adam and Matthew on the upper stage. They turn their backs to the audience, kneel down on one knee and at the moment the speech ends, reach upward and release from their hands three white doves which soar freely over the audience.*)

MUSIC

BY DAVID LITWIN

ADAM KING'S THEME

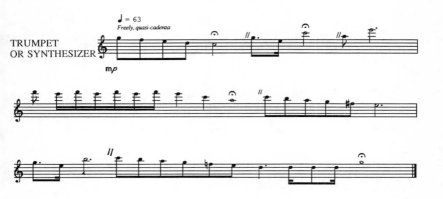

A reminder of this theme may be played at appropriate moments during the play.

TYRANT'S ENTRANCE

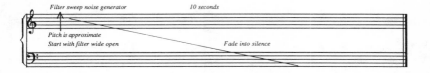

FIRST CHORUS ENTRANCE

BACKGROUND FOR TYRANT'S SPEECH

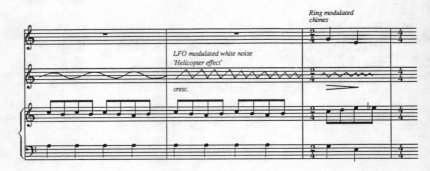

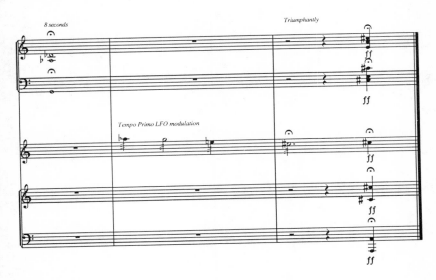

THE MAGICIAN

A Play in Two Acts

1978

For George Ivanovitch Gurdjieff

He who knows the World
Knows a corpse
And of him the World
Is not worthy.

The Gospel of Thomas

CHARACTERS

The Magician
Tyrant

King Family
Luke, a Senator
Pearl, his sister
Destiny, his mother
Fashion, his wife
Heather
Peter } children to Luke and Fashion

Frank
The Big Ten, bankers and industrialists
Their Clones
Luke Clone
The Great Beast
The Prophet of Blasphemy
The Great Whore of Babylon / Robot Computer
Scientists and Assistants

The Figure of a Dancer
The Hound of Hell

The Horse 'Til We Meet Again

Security Guard
Chess Pieces

PROLOGUE

TYRANT: In this foul, depraved and bestial age
  When obscenity triumphs over Eros
  And Vice sends Virtue packing,
  When Shadow devours Substance,
  And Lies, the Truth,
  And humanity like a distempered dog
  Biting its tail in madness
  Crawls toward darkness,
  Who but I, Tyrant, shall be the savior of the age?
  See how my shadow falls across the Sun
  Giving men refuge against the unbearable light.

  Do I detect a flutter?
  A secret excitement in your loathing?
  The thrill of recognition as you disclaim me?
  Who seeks me must open the door of his mind
  And there he'll find me.
  Confess . . . you're happy with me.
  Am I not the apt and perfect symbol of your fantasy?
  Your faithful servant?

  But I mustn't linger.
  The play's about to begin.
  Now open wide the mouth of Hell.
  Come, every loathsome creature and my trusted aides.
  For I have sworn an eternal vow against the Light of Heaven.
  That Earth shall darken, darken,
  Until . . . ha, ha, ha!
  All Light is out.

  (*Blackout.*)

ACT I

SCENE 1: LUKE AND DESTINY

(*Tyrant watching from afar.*)

DESTINY: So pale, my son. You who were always so filled with joy and laughter.

LUKE: I have dark dreams.

DESTINY: Dark dreams . . . ?

LUKE: They came again last night. The ghosts of my brothers, like dark apparitions, urging me to my revenge.

DESTINY: Don't speak of this.

LUKE: The shots . . . the shots . . . keep ringing in my ears.

DESTINY: Oh, my son, my son.

LUKE: Must I always hear their voices crying out in the night? Always hear Pearl crying out as their blood-stained bodies pass before us, her cries mingled with theirs, broken by that vile assassin, Life. Oh, it's all mixed up in my mind. What evil thing inhabiting our house sent my brothers to their death? This star-crossed house that sent them to their doom, while I, protected by my mother, sit home and hide from every passing shadow. Why don't I stand and fight?

DESTINY: Oh, my son, I have seen your suffering. I have seen your life wasting away under a burden too great to bear. And through the years I have been filled with a secret pride that you are my son. An immense love that makes you dearer to me than all the world. The Earth is green and beautiful, but it has not been beautiful for you.

LUKE: Oh the shame of it! And Pearl . . .

DESTINY: Enough! Enough! You have done what you had to do and because of that our house has stood.

LUKE: Stood on the ruins of a last enfeebled son, too cowardly to take action against the evils of the age.

DESTINY: What can you do?

LUKE: Anything is better than this waiting. Day in and day out seeing my life drained away.

DESTINY: Luke . . .

LUKE: Don't pity me, Mother. I've pitied myself long enough.

DESTINY: Things will change. They have to. Be patient, Luke.

LUKE: Nothing will change. Unless men change it. I've been thinking of running again.

DESTINY: No!

LUKE: Yes.

DESTINY: They'll kill you as surely as they killed your two brothers.

LUKE: Let them. I'm past caring.

DESTINY: You'd leave me and the children?

LUKE: Hire a nursemaid for them.

DESTINY: We've been over this a thousand times, Luke.

LUKE: Let me go, Mother.

DESTINY: You made a promise.

LUKE: I can't keep it.

DESTINY: Do you want to break my heart?

LUKE: Let me go.

DESTINY: And send you to your death?

LUKE: Perhaps you'd be doing me a favor. I'd be with Adam and Matthew then.

DESTINY: Oh, my boy. What can I say to you?

LUKE: You can say, "Take your life, Luke, and live it," as you once said. But you didn't mean it, Mother. Did you?

DESTINY: I meant it.

LUKE: Then . . . ?

DESTINY: Is this what you really want to do?

LUKE: I . . . I think so.

DESTINY: And your wife . . . your family? Your duty to them?

LUKE: And what of my duty to myself?

DESTINY: Who has given you that duty but your family? We are nothing by ourselves.

LUKE: "He who hath wife and children hath hostages to fortune."

DESTINY: Is that so bad, Luke?

LUKE: It's horrible.

DESTINY: Where are you going?

LUKE: Out!

DESTINY: But where?

LUKE: To take the children to the park. That's my life, isn't it, Mother? To take the children to the park.

(*Blackout.*)

SCENE 2: THE PARK

(*People in the park, Tyrant disguised among them. Enter Luke, Heather, age seven, and Peter, age eleven, followed by Security Guard.*)

MAGICIAN: (*Enters singing.*)*

Balloons, balloons, to take you to Heaven . . .

Who will take a ride to Heaven?

PETER: I prayed for you last night, Daddy.

HEATHER: I did, too.

LUKE: Prayed for me? Why?

PETER: You're always so sad. I don't want you to be sad, Daddy.

HEATHER: Don't cry, Daddy. We love you.

MAGICIAN: (*Singing.*)*

Four brothers: one was slaughtered in the War.

The second murdered on the Road.

The third followed in his brothers' wake.

While the fourth stayed home and lived.

Four brothers went on the Way.

The first was murdered by the War.

The second slaughtered by the hand of man.

The third's blood soon was spilled.

Three brothers struggled and died.

While the fourth stayed home and lived.

LUKE: What are you singing?

MAGICIAN: An old tune. Old as the hills.

LUKE: Yes, but . . .

MAGICIAN: If applies to you, you must sing it, too. Come.
(*Singing.*)

Four brothers to the Wars did go.

One fell, and now there're three.

Two fell, and now there're two.

Three fell, and now there's . . .

LUKE: Stop it!

MAGICIAN: But you know it. Come sing with me.

LUKE: Stop it!

MAGICIAN: Come. It do you good. I promise you. Sing!

*Music p. 161

LUKE: Who are you?

MAGICIAN: A friend.

LUKE: You're no friend to me. I've never seen you before. I don't know you.

MAGICIAN: Strange. You sure you don't know me? I know you very well. Come, look closer.

LUKE: Who sent you?

MAGICIAN: Oh ho, you think I one of those government spies that follow you around night and day. No such luck, my boy. That's not my business. The ones you're looking for, they over there . . . and there.

LUKE: Who are you?

MAGICIAN: I am what I am.

LUKE: What do you want with me?

MAGICIAN: Why, to sing with me, my boy, to sing with me.

LUKE: You're mad.

MAGICIAN: You not say that when you get to know me better. Why you not blow whistle on them?

LUKE: What did you say?

MAGICIAN: All these years you think about it but never do it. And for same reason Matthew not do it.
(*Singing.*)*
So the country wouldn't go up in flames.
He sat on his ass and looked away.
So the country wouldn't go up in flames.

Yes, this how Matthew felt about it, too.

LUKE: Matthew . . . What do you know about my brother?

MAGICIAN: Everything. He and I good friends. Adam, too.

LUKE: Are?

MAGICIAN: Are.

LUKE: You're crazy. Get away from me. They're dead.

MAGICIAN: The dead are always with us. They as alive and kicking as . . . you. Maybe more alive. Who knows?

LUKE: Is this somebody's idea of a joke?

MAGICIAN: It makes my heart sad to hear you talk this way when I bring you messages from your brothers.

LUKE: Messages from my . . .

*Music p. 162

MAGICIAN: The same messages you get from them. But is hard for you to hear them. And then again, you not always listen. That's why I come. To help you.

LUKE: Listen! If you don't leave, I'm going to call a policeman.

MAGICIAN: A policeman! A policeman? What for? Why you call a policeman? To guard you from me? You a funny man. This is best joke I hear in years. Here. I call one for you. Oh, Mr. Policeman!

LUKE: Never mind.

MAGICIAN: What?

LUKE: I said never mind.

MAGICIAN: You sure? I call one for you. No trouble at all.

LUKE: No . . . forget it.

MAGICIAN: Oh, you just make joke. You not really want someone to guard you from me. Just making fun. Very good. I know you have good sense of humor. Now it come out. See, we becoming good friends already. Here, have candy.

LUKE: I can't believe this is happening.

MAGICIAN: Oh, is happening. That's the trouble. Whole world is happening. But nobody doing anything about it.

SECURITY GUARD: (*Approaching.*) Is everything alright, Mr. King?

LUKE: It's alright, George.

MAGICIAN: Fine and dandy. Great big wonderful world. You happy, I happy, and Senator King, he happy.

SECURITY GUARD: I thought there might be trouble.

MAGICIAN: Plenty big trouble unless you have cigarette. Why you think I call you over, for health? Must smoke. Doctor's orders. Senator King, he no have cigarette, but he say, "Why not ask George, he nice fellah." You big strapping guy, good family man, don't tell me you no have one little cigarette. And in return, I give you good tip on horse this afternoon.

SECURITY GUARD: (*Laughing.*) Oh, is that all?

MAGICIAN: Hey, you call this cigarette? This no cigarette. This filter. How am I to smoke filter?

SECURITY GUARD: I'm sorry.

MAGICIAN: Why do you smoke filter? You crazy? Want to get cancer? I ask for cigarette and you give me cancer. What a pickle. Never in whole life do I need friend so badly to share smoke with me, but now I all alone.

(*Singing.*)*
Alone as a wave on a sea am I.
Alone as a wave on a sea.

Just goes to show can never tell what will happen next. Well, must rely on self as usual.
(*Singing.*)*
One little cigarette.
Where are you, one little cigarette?
I know you 'round here somewhere.

Ah, here you are. You have real thing all the time and you pretend you not know. You great kidder. Maybe ought to go on stage.

SECURITY GUARD: Well, I'll be damned.

MAGICIAN: Ah, ah, ah! Don't say that. Maybe come true.

SECURITY GUARD: You're a magician.

MAGICIAN: You speak right. How you know that?

SECURITY GUARD: That was a hell of a trick.

MAGICIAN: You speak better than you know. (*To Luke.*) See, even he know who I am. Now this real cigarette, but now have problem. Have no light. Man must have light in this dark world.

SECURITY GUARD: That I can do.

MAGICIAN: That no light. That torch.

SECURITY GUARD: What the hell?!

MAGICIAN: Try again. Nothing coming out. Not even a spark.

SECURITY GUARD: For Pete's sake.

MAGICIAN: Empty! Never mind. You good man. You try. And just to show there's no hard feelings, remember that horse I tell you about?

SECURITY GUARD: Yeah.

MAGICIAN: I going to give him to you.

SECURITY GUARD: What's his name?

MAGICIAN: "'Til We Meet Again."

SECURITY GUARD: Where's he running?

MAGICIAN: In the seventh.

SECURITY GUARD: There ain't no horse running by that name in the seventh.

MAGICIAN: Sure there is. What kind of guy you think I am? I not tout you wrong.

*Music p. 163

SECURITY GUARD: (*Taking sporting page out of pocket.*) I tell you there is no . . . for Christ's sake, there is! "'Til We Meet Again!" I must be getting blind.

MAGICIAN: See. It turn out just like I say.

SECURITY GUARD: Can I bet him all the way?

MAGICIAN: Would I give you nag? This horse champion. I know him personally. We good friends, like you and me.

SECURITY GUARD: I can count on it?

MAGICIAN: Hey, come here. Does your mama love you? Well, this horse and me, we like this. He tell me he gonna win. You think he gonna disappoint me? Never. He never let me down yet. He have great stuff. Maybe he start slow, but he finish strong in the end. At the finish he come in first. And you know why? Because he know I no monkey around with losers. He know I only interested in winners, and if he lays down on job and no run good race, I never talk to him again, and what's more, I walk away and never see him again. And maybe I even send him to glue factory. And this would break his heart. Know why? Because he got nobody else to talk to. Other horses won't talk to him. Is true. And why? Because envy. Horses just like people. But you know that. That's why this race sure thing. Understand?

SECURITY GUARD: Well, I'll be damned.

MAGICIAN: Hey, I warn you 'bout that already. Don't look now, but I think your friend is waiting for you.

SECURITY GUARD: My friend . . . ?

MAGICIAN: The one that's waiting to take bet.

SECURITY GUARD: Oh yeah . . . Hey, how did you know?

MAGICIAN: Try lighter now. Maybe it work better.

SECURITY GUARD: Lighter?

MAGICIAN: Now that we have good heart to heart talk and straighten everything out, maybe light, how you say . . . recuperate?

SECURITY GUARD: For Pete's sake . . . how in the . . . ah . . . ah . . . ah . . . You did it. Say, who's your friend, Senator? He's quite a magician.

(*Security Guard withdraws.*)

MAGICIAN: How come everybody knows me but you? He try to give me light, but it hopeless. How can man who put himself first give anybody light? This light no good to me. I need different kind of light. Light that comes from man who put himself last. Maybe you have that kind of light, eh?

LUKE: Who are you?

MAGICIAN: You not know yet? But maybe you have that kind of light, huh?

LUKE: (*Taking out lighter.*) "The Last shall be First." How did you know Adam gave this to me? How could you know? I've never shown this to anyone.

MAGICIAN: Adam and me good friends. I already tell you this. Why you not listen? Adam and Matthew want you to understand something. They want to help you. You have big problem. Quiet now. Be still. Hear them. Here, deep inside you.

LUKE: Who are you?

MAGICIAN: You still not know? Is alright. Patience. One day you will know.

LUKE: And everything else you said. It's not possible. You couldn't have known it. No one could have. It's not possible.

MAGICIAN: Everything is possible. That's what I've come to teach you. See the Sun . . . it say that everything is possible. Hear the wind . . . it says, "Yes, everything is possible." And the children. Hear their laughter . . . it says, "Oh yes, all is possible."

LUKE: But . . .

MAGICIAN: And, oh yes, you and I, here and now, this too is possible.

LUKE: WHO ARE YOU??!!

MAGICIAN: A little while and you will know.

LUKE: I don't think I will ever want to see you again.

MAGICIAN: Oh, yes, you will want to see me again.

LUKE: Come children, let us go.

MAGICIAN: And on the day you wish it, I will be there.
(*Singing.*)*
Balloons, balloons, to take you to Heaven.
Who will take a ride to Heaven?

PETER AND HEATHER: Me! Me! Me! Me!
(*Blackout.*)

SCENE 3: THE LEGACY

LUKE: The lights are going out all over the world.

FASHION: Yes . . .

LUKE: One good man after another murdered. Not a single real leader

*Music p. 161

left. They've murdered them all. Nothing but puppet governments all over the world.

FASHION: What's left?

LUKE: Nothing. I'm to go to the Senate every day of my life and make a public showing, in a haze of publicity, my picture on the front pages. I'm to pose as the friend of man. God, what a mockery. I'm to fight for the poor, oppressed and downtrodden against the monopolies, pollution, nuclear armament, war — all for the rights of man. While every bill I introduce, every measure, is secretly defeated or so watered down, it makes no difference.

FRANK: That's the scenario.

LUKE: What a farce.

FRANK: It could be worse.

LUKE: Nothing could be worse.

FRANK: They could have killed you.

LUKE: Are you sure that would have been worse?

FRANK: Maybe not.

LUKE: I won't be used this way.

FRANK: It's either that, or retire from public office.

LUKE: I can't do that.

FRANK: Well, you can always make a deal with them.

LUKE: For Christ's sake, Frank. You're supposed to be my friend.

FRANK: Yeah, that's why I'd like to keep you alive. You're crazy enough to get yourself killed.

LUKE: Sell out . . . ?

FRANK: That's the idea.

LUKE: No.

FRANK: Then stay the way you are and pretend you don't know what's happening, or retire.

LUKE: No other options?

FRANK: Not in this life, not in this time.

LUKE: There must be another way.

FRANK: Don't bet your life on it. We're on the Dreamland Express. The Twentieth Century Unlimited. Everything goes today.

LUKE: But to whore my life away . . .

FRANK: All politicians are whores. You know that.

LUKE: All?

FRANK: No one knows better than you what happens to the few who aren't.

LUKE: I can't live that way.

FRANK: Sure you can. We all do. Just lay down and spread your legs like the rest of us.

FASHION: Frank, you're a bastard!

FRANK: He should know what he's getting into. It's easy once you get into the swing of it. Just close your eyes and look away and have a drink. When things get tough say, "This is no concern of mine," and have a couple of drinks. When you start to shake, stop up your ears and quietly finish off the bottle. And for those nights, those intolerable nights when you can't sleep because you can't shake it off and you begin to tremble and break out in a cold sweat, why that's simple — just go on a two-day binge until you pass out. And all your troubles are over. It's not so bad, really.

FASHION: Oh, Frank . . .

FRANK: It's a good recipe. I've always used it when I've had to witness the murder of a country or the murder of a man.

FASHION: You're the best reporter in Washington.

FRANK: Was. When we still had newspapers. That's why I came to work for you, kid. Still want me to talk to them?

LUKE: You don't want me to. Do you?

FRANK: No.

LUKE: Why not?

FRANK: For old times' sake. For sentimental reasons.

LUKE: Yes . . .

FRANK: I remember your brother.

LUKE: Go on.

FRANK: I remember when he first came to office. His first press conference. There we all were, sitting there. Myself . . . I was stoned in anticipation of the usual garbage, and then he came breezing in. I couldn't believe it. First thing out of his mouth was a joke. And it was funny! And then another one. First thing you know we started laughing, and before you knew it we were rolling in the aisles. And cuss . . . why the man could outswear a Marine sergeant. It was unbelievable! The way he answered questions . . . you saw the whole goddamn world for what it was. He knew the name of every reporter in that room — every reporter! There were dozens of us! And not only the names, but the newspapers we worked for, our relatives, even the whiskey we liked. I never saw anything like it. You felt like you knew him your whole life; we all did. And then they killed him. And it was over. All over. The world went to hell. The rest is history. I didn't know Matthew very well. I didn't want to know him. It was the end of the line for me. I just wanted to close my eyes and go to sleep.

FASHION: Like everyone else?

FRANK: Like everyone else. Funny though, I didn't count on the nightmares.

LUKE: Why did you come to work for me, Frank?

FRANK: You seemed . . . so . . .

FASHION: Unprotected . . . ?

FRANK: Unprotected.

LUKE: Like Adam the day he went to Dallas.

FRANK: Yes . . . only worse. For him it was quick. For all your brothers. But for you it's a slow death. I hate to see what's happening to you. You're eating your heart out in constant torment, and for what? For nothing. It could have been a beautiful world but it's not. And there's nothing you or I or anyone can do about it. It's too late. Camelot will never rise again. It's over. Forget it and get out. You can't bring back the dead again.

LUKE: You forget. I'm a King, too.

FRANK: Yes . . . I guess you are.

LUKE: I'll talk to them.

FRANK: You're sure you know what you're doing?

LUKE: I have to. I have no choice. It won't hurt to talk to them. Maybe I can find a way . . . to do some good.

FRANK: A man can rationalize anything.

LUKE: I have to try, Frank.

FRANK: O.K., kid. It's your funeral.

(*Frank and Fashion exit.*)

SCENE 4: A CRY FOR HELP

LUKE: You can't bring back the dead again. What did he say? The dead are always with us. No! I mustn't think of him. That way lies madness. But how did he know? How did he know? I feel like I'm going to break. I've got to stop this . . . get a grip on myself, or . . . if only I could know if it happened or not. Maybe I'm mad already. No, it's not possible. It was only a dream. And yet he seemed so real.

(*Enter Magician.*)

MAGICIAN: Hey, why you sit in dark like Hamlet? Want to go crazy?

LUKE: Huh . . . !

MAGICIAN: Maybe you crazy already.

LUKE: What . . . ! Who is it?

MAGICIAN: Me.

LUKE: You!!

MAGICIAN: Naturally. Why? You expect someone else?

LUKE: I can't see you.

MAGICIAN: That's 'cause you in dark. Here, I turn on light.

LUKE: My God! How did you get here?

MAGICIAN: I walk here.

LUKE: Who let you in?

MAGICIAN: You let me in.

LUKE: No!

MAGICIAN: Sure. I already tell you, the day you want to see me, I be there. Well, here I am, my boy. What you want?

LUKE: What do I want?

MAGICIAN: Yes, what you want? Every man want something. One man want to be general. Another man want to masturbate in closet. This sound very crazy, but some man even want to be president. Is so. Some people have strange tastes. Me, I want glass of water. You have? Very thirsty.

LUKE: Over there.

MAGICIAN: Thank you, my boy. This very good thirst quencher. Hits the spot. Better even than how you say, Seven-Up. But why you not drinking?

LUKE: I don't care for any water, thank you.

MAGICIAN: You not care for any water? But this very bad! Must have. Water very good for man. He die without it. Once I lost in wilderness. All alone. Not know which way to turn. All I have is little water to show me way out. Nothing else. But is enough. For this water teach me how to find my way. That's why I say water is best friend to man, (*laughing*) except for wine which is even better friend. So now we drink water together like good friends. Maybe later drink wine and become best friends. But now water, she bring us together. Here, we drink from same glass and make water toast. Don't be shy. Drink deep, deep, deep. Is good for you. Clear head. Have more. (*Spills water over Luke's head; laughing.*) Now you baptized in Holy Spirit. No more dead man. Feel good, huh! Like man reborn. Now we sober. Later, maybe, we get drunk. But now sober, so we can have good talk. See, I as real as this water. Why you doubt evidence before your eyes like dead man, huh?

Doubt also very bad for man; many things bad for him, but water, she wash it all away. Hey, I almost forget. You no tell me. How are children?

LUKE: The children are fine.

MAGICIAN: And wife, she fine, too?

LUKE: Yes.

MAGICIAN: And the mama? You not mention the mama. Why you not mention the mama? You holding out on me. Ohhh, I think you not treat her so good. That mean next time you be in ass's womb and you be born jackass. You not like that, huh! Got to change! Man have only one mama. And your mama very good lady. Stop you from making jackass of yourself. She your guardian angel. You be dead without her. Think. She very old and tired. She ready to die long ago. She live good life; she earn good death. Why you think she still hanging around? Because she know you crazy. Must protect big idiot like you. And this very hard for her, for she very old. Why, she almost as old as me, and that very old indeed, 'cause I almost as old as God. (*Laughs.*) Everbody knows that. I tell you what you need. (*Holds water in front of him.*)

LUKE: Ohhh, my sister! Pearl's face . . . in the water.

MAGICIAN: Sure, she upstairs, waiting for you.

LUKE: Waiting for me . . . my sister?!

MAGICIAN: Sure. She been waiting a long time. You go and see her now. She upstairs waiting.

LUKE: Upstairs? But there is no upstairs.

MAGICIAN: What are you talking about? There's always upstairs.

LUKE: But this is the last floor.

MAGICIAN: No, you make mistake. You forget third floor.

LUKE: The third floor?

MAGICIAN: Why you act so dumb? Every house got third floor. Remember you used to go up there all the time to talk with Adam and Matthew.

LUKE: Adam and Matthew . . . ?

MAGICIAN: And when you little boy, you spend all your time up there in one special little room. Pearl waiting for you in that room now.

LUKE: No!

MAGICIAN: What's the matter, you not want to go?

LUKE: I can't go. There is no such room. There is no such floor! It doesn't exist!

MAGICIAN: It's right above you. All you got to do is go through that door.

LUKE: That door?! What door?

MAGICIAN: That one. Then you find out for yourself.

LUKE: Oh my God!!

MAGICIAN: That's right. That's a good boy.
   (*Sound of a heartbeat.*)

LUKE: Oh, what's that pounding? Is it my heart that's pounding?

PEARL: (*From a distance.*) Luke! Luke!

LUKE: Someone's weeping. Is it my heart that's weeping?

PEARL: I want to live! I want to live!

LUKE: Someone's calling. Is it my heart that's calling?

PEARL: I love you, Luke.

LUKE: Pearl?

PEARL: I prayed so hard for you to come. I missed you so. Open the door, Luke.

LUKE: I can't.

PEARL: Open the door. Open the door!

LUKE: It's bolted.

PEARL: Break it down.

LUKE: I'm trying.

PEARL: Try harder . . . harder.

LUKE: The bolt is off.

PEARL: Let me out!

LUKE: I can't open the lock.

PEARL: Yes, you can. I know you can.

LUKE: Help me.

PEARL: It was you who locked me in, Luke.

LUKE: No!

PEARL: Only you can open the door.

LUKE: How?

PEARL: Use the key.

LUKE: The key?

PEARL: The one I gave you.

LUKE: I don't know where it is.

PEARL: You've thrown it away.

LUKE: No.

PEARL: You've lost it. (*Weeping.*) I'm lost . . . lost. Never to see you again . . . never.

LUKE: Forgive me, Pearl.

PEARL: Now I'll have to stay here 'til the day I die. It's so lonely without you. Oh, why didn't you come back for me sooner, while you still had the key? You promised you would. You would have told me funny sad stories the way you used to. And we would have danced and sang, and taken long walks in the woods. But you never came.

LUKE: Pearl.

PEARL: Daddy used to visit me all the time after he had his stroke. Mommy used to bring me flowers. She doesn't come much anymore. I still have Adam and Matthew, though. They visit me. Sometimes Mark is with them. They make me laugh. They're so funny.

LUKE: Adam and Matthew are dead, Pearl.

PEARL: No, they're not.

LUKE: Mark, too.

PEARL: I see them all the time.

LUKE: It's your imagination.

PEARL: If you had the key you could see them for yourself.

LUKE: Stop it!

PEARL: You think I'm crazy, don't you? That's why you locked me in here. You're ashamed because all those people call me crazy: "Your crazy, retarded sister." You mustn't listen to people. They don't know any better. We know, don't we, Luke? Open the door now. I want to hug and kiss you and hold you in my arms forever.

LUKE: I can't.

PEARL: You could if you wanted to.

LUKE: I told you I lost the key.

PEARL: Then you must find it. Luke? Can you hear me?

LUKE: Yes.

PEARL: You don't want me to die, do you?

LUKE: No.

PEARL: Are you afraid?

LUKE: Yes.

PEARL: There's nothing to be afraid of.

LUKE: What do you want, Pearl?

PEARL: I want myself.

LUKE: Where will you find it?

PEARL: Don't you know? In you. I'll find myself in you. You must bring me into the light.

LUKE: Into the light?

PEARL: Yes. Don't be ashamed. Promise me that you will.

LUKE: I . . . must find the key.

PEARL: Promise me.

LUKE: I promise.

PEARL: Ohhh . . . you've made me so happy . . . so happy.

LUKE: Have I, Pearl?

PEARL: Oh, yes . . . yes. Now I've a reason to live. I can't wait to be with you again. Hurry! Hurry!

LUKE: I will.

MAGICIAN: Well, my boy . . . what you find?

LUKE: A ghost.

MAGICIAN: Sure, a living ghost. But this very good for you. Put color in cheeks. Before you pale as ghost yourself. Now you green. (*Laughing.*) But is O.K. We gonna put rosy red color back in cheek, and make you healthy as apple Adam eat.

LUKE: I think I'm going to get sick.

MAGICIAN: What you talking about? This no time to get sick. Must run for President of America. (*Laughing.*) What would country do without you?

LUKE: President?

MAGICIAN: Sure! Every boy want to be president when he grow up . . . no?

LUKE: Well . . . yes. But . . .

MAGICIAN: No buts about it, my boy. When duty calls must go. Everybody running around. You got to run around too. Besides, this your dream, no? Everybody got to live out his dream. Otherwise, how he become real man? This important. To be man! Understand? Otherwise, how can let skeleton out of closet?

LUKE: I'm shaking.

MAGICIAN: Everybody got skeleton in closet. Must let out, so skeleton can dance.

LUKE: I'm going to faint.

MAGICIAN: Faint! Why you not tell me this before? This very inconsiderate of me. Here, lie down. Go to sleep. Then all your troubles be over. (*Luke lies down.*) But first you have key? So skeleton can dance?

LUKE: Key?

MAGICIAN: Must have key. Where is key?

LUKE: Sleep . . . let me sleep.

MAGICIAN: Sure, sleep. You think you sleep life away, huh? No such luck, my boy. (*Snaps his fingers. Sound of a heartbeat again.*)

PEARL: (*From a distance.*) Luke!! Luke!! Let me out! Let me out!
(*Luke jumps bolt upright.*)

LUKE: The key . . . the key.

MAGICIAN: What key? What you talking about? Go back to sleep.

LUKE: I must find the key.

MAGICIAN: What you want to find key for? Maybe better go back to
sleep and have pleasant dreams, no? Except, then maybe you have
nightmares.

PEARL: Promise me, Luke. Promise me!

LUKE: No, no, I must wake up!

MAGICIAN: First you want to sleep, then you want to wake up. Hey,
Hamlet, what's the matter with you? Why you no make up your
mind?

PEARL: I'll die, Luke. I'll die.

LUKE: Pearl!

MAGICIAN: Oh! A woman. Why you not say so before. That explains
everything. This why you in fever. This Pearl, she driving you
crazy: you all shook up. This only prove man do anything for
woman, even wake up out of sound sleep. Now I understand. She
give you key to her room, and you lose, huh? What a dope! Man
who can do that, I don't think he can ever amount to anything. I
think I wash my hands of you.

LUKE: (*Grabbing him.*) No! No!

MAGICIAN: Well, what you want me to do about it?

LUKE: Help me.

MAGICIAN: Help you find key and become President of United States
all at once?

LUKE: No . . . yes.

MAGICIAN: No . . . yes. Which is it, you crazy man?

LUKE: Yes. Yes! Both!

MAGICIAN: This is tall order. O.K. If I help you, what you pay me?

LUKE: Pay you?

MAGICIAN: Sure. What you think. I work for nothing?

LUKE: I'll pay you money.

MAGICIAN: I got all the money I want.

LUKE: I'll make you a rich man.

MAGICIAN: I a rich man now.

LUKE: I'll . . . I'll give you a cabinet post.

MAGICIAN: Cabinet post?! (*Laughing.*) This is second funniest joke I
hear in years. Me, cabinet post! Make me minister of munitions

maybe. Give me privilege of blowing people up, 'specially ones I don't like. You crazy?

LUKE: I'll give you anything you want.

MAGICIAN: Better. What you got?

LUKE: I've got . . .

MAGICIAN: Yes . . .

LUKE: I've got . . .

MAGICIAN: Plenty of nothing. That's what you got, my boy. And the blues besides, isn't that so, my friend?

LUKE: Well then, there's nothing I have to offer you.

MAGICIAN: Pay me with that.

LUKE: Pay you with that . . . ?

MAGICIAN: Your nothingness.

LUKE: My nothingness?

MAGICIAN: Your poverty. Give me that.

LUKE: I don't understand.

MAGICIAN: You will, my friend. You will.

LUKE: But it doesn't make sense. You're to give me everything, and in return I'm to give you nothing? It doesn't make sense.

MAGICIAN: Your poverty, yes. Well, is it a bargain? Yes or no, for that's all I'll take.

LUKE: I have to say yes.

MAGICIAN: Come then, I have good friend. He going to make you President of United States, and through him you maybe find key, too.

LUKE: Do I know him?

MAGICIAN: No, but you will.

LUKE: What's his name?

MAGICIAN: Tyrant.

(*Magician takes bottle of liquor from his person and spills it around the floor in a circle.*)

LUKE: What in the world are you doing?

MAGICIAN: What you think I doing? Making hole in floor.

LUKE: Making a hole in my floor?!

MAGICIAN: Sure. This powerful stuff. Burn through anything. Make nice, big hole.

LUKE: What on earth for?

MAGICIAN: Must get to basement.

LUKE: But there is no basement.

MAGICIAN: You going to start that again? Of course there is

basement. Every house have third floor and basement.

LUKE: What do you want to go to the basement for?

MAGICIAN: How else you going to find key?

LUKE: The key is in the basement?

MAGICIAN: Sure.

LUKE: Well then, let's use the stairs.

MAGICIAN: There are no stairs. Must make.

LUKE: No stairs?

MAGICIAN: Of course there are no stairs, you idiot. You think I go to all this trouble if there are stairs? You think anybody can go to bottom of Earth any time he feel like it?

LUKE: The bottom of Earth?

MAGICIAN: Sure. That's where key is, where Tyrant lives. You drop it there long time ago. Remember?

LUKE: Tyrant lives at . . .

MAGICIAN: Naturally. Where else you think he live? O.K. Let's go.

LUKE: Go where?

MAGICIAN: Into the hole.

LUKE: I'm not going into any hole.

MAGICIAN: Sure you are. Just jump into that hole now.

LUKE: I can't.

MAGICIAN: How you know that 'til you try?

LUKE: I don't want to try.

MAGICIAN: Hey, you ask me make you president, right?

LUKE: Yes.

MAGICIAN: You beg me to help you find key, right?

LUKE: Yes.

MAGICIAN: Well, how I gonna help you if you not give me penny's worth of trust?

LUKE: I trust you, but I'm not going to jump in that hole.

MAGICIAN: Don't worry, you not get dirty.

LUKE: I'm afraid I'll be killed.

MAGICIAN: Not a bad idea. It might do you some good. But no such luck. You gonna land safe and sound. Go ahead.

LUKE: I won't.

MAGICIAN: Oh, so that's the kind of guy you are, huh? You make deal with me and then you welch. You one bad guy! So long.

PEARL: (*From a distance.*) You must, Luke! You must!

LUKE: Wait!

PEARL: I'll die if you don't!

LUKE: I'll jump if you jump with me.

MAGICIAN: You one big baby. Can't do anything by yourself. Want me to take you down in my arms.

LUKE: I won't go unless you come with me.

MAGICIAN: When you gonna get weaned from mama's milk? O.K., baby, gimme hand. Let's go.

LUKE: The hole's too small.

MAGICIAN: What?

LUKE: The hole's too small for the two of us. You only made it big enough for one.

MAGICIAN: Is so. Hey, this real problem. How I going to fit you into hole?

LUKE: Us.

MAGICIAN: Sure, us. What you think I mean?

LUKE: Make the hole bigger.

MAGICIAN: What you want hole bigger for? Is nice the way it is.

LUKE: Yeah, but . . .

MAGICIAN: I got it. This no problem. I make you smaller.

LUKE: You can't do that.

MAGICIAN: Hey, dumbbell, what you talking about? If can make hole to bottom of Earth, then can make you smaller.

LUKE: The house is getting larger.

MAGICIAN: Oh, no, you getting smaller.

LUKE: Oh God!

MAGICIAN: And smaller. Soon you be so small that you float down hole, light as feather, in mama's womb . . . down, down, down to the bottom of the Earth. Here we go . . .

(*Blackout.*)

SCENE 5: TYRANT

LUKE: Where are we?

MAGICIAN: In mama's arms. In bowels of Earth. You have good trip?

LUKE: I feel as though the life were sucked out of me.

MAGICIAN: Mother Earth, she hold on tight. You breathe deep . . . deep. Good boy.

LUKE: I can't see.

MAGICIAN: What are you talking about? You have good light.

LUKE: I have no light . . . Oh . . . Adam's light.

(*Gasps, whispering to himself.*)

Tyrant!

MAGICIAN: Yes.

(*Luke watches as if in a dream as Tyrant's realm emerges from the darkness: spectral, cold, hypnotic. Darkness beneath the deepest trench in the darkest ocean, blindness closer than taste or bone. Droning music vaguely liturgical, a choir of computers searching for a holy lullaby. Faces appear. They are blurred as if unborn. Hands in surgical gloves. Human body parts landing in a tubular metal chamber — they ring. Marching and shuffling feet. The Big Ten are there: Wolf and Fox lead; Snake, Weasel, Leech, Jackal, Shark, Pig, Crocodile, Vulture follow. Teams of scientists in surgical masks and swarming assistants in white. Tyrant is smiling down benevolently. At his side a Robot Computer in the seductive shape of the Whore of Babylon.[1] He squeezes her bottom. With the other hand he blesses his congregation's work, over and over and over. They are making the Great Beast.*)

TYRANT: Was not I destined to preside at the birth of Antichrist?
(*Chanting.*)
Now is the hour of our deliverance.
Banished be all light.
Banished be that emissary of the stars.
The Son of Light, the hated Jesus Christ.

The Great Beast is loosed upon the Earth.
Under the Star of David he slithers
A second time toward Bethlehem,
To maim and crucify again the Son of Man
And shame Him and His God upon the Cross.
I will not rest 'til Man is extinct.

GREAT BEAST: We!

PROPHET OF BLASPHEMY: (*Played by Frank.*) His first word.

GREAT BEAST: We . . . We.

PROPHET OF BLASPHEMY: His second word.

GREAT BEAST: WeWe.

TYRANT: All hail the Great Beast. This creature, made of lead and dust, one part beast, one part plant, one part mineral, but no part of Man or Holy Ghost, shall devour man. The creature that cannot say "I."
(*Tyrant lifts one forefinger above his head. The Great Beast twists one of its seven heads, with a razor sharp beak, toward Tyrant.*

The Big Ten shudder, back away. Wolf raises a finger; so do the others. The Great Beast pricks a drop of blood from the finger of each. From each drop of blood a clone is born. Their eyes are dead; the mark of the Great Beast. Otherwise they are exact copies, moving as if in the mirror with their originals. Lewd kissing and fondling between each original and his clone. The Prophet of Blasphemy pounds a hard rhythm with his staff. The Whore of Babylon laughs, sending clones and originals into an obscene, serpentine dance, stalking, groping, caressing. All collapse in a heap at the feet of the Prophet of Blasphemy.)

LUKE: They're committing suicide.

MAGICIAN: Whole world committing suicide, my boy.

(*The hands of the Big Ten originals take on a life of their own and rise into the air, pulling their owners to their feet. They strangle themselves to death and collapse. Clones leap up, laughing.*)

TYRANT: (*Embracing Luke.*) Luke, say hello to your old friend, Frank.

LUKE: Frank, how could you do it?

PROPHET OF BLASPHEMY: It's better this way, kid. Better. Now you're one of us.

TYRANT: (*To Magician.*) He has a full understanding of the situation?

MAGICIAN: A full understanding.

TYRANT: Do you?

(*Luke looks at the Magician, then back to Tyrant.*)

Perhaps you'd best meet some of your constituents. The people have decided to elect Luke King for President.

CLONES: The people have decided to elect Luke King for President.

TYRANT: We'll want to shake hands with Luke King.

CLONES: We'll want to shake hands with Luke King.

GREAT BEAST: WeWe.

TYRANT: You seem to have made a great hit with the people.

LUKE: They're clones.

TYRANT: Precisely. Far more adaptable than their originals. A new kind of constituency.

LUKE: But . . .

TYRANT: You're the right man for the job.

LUKE: Why me?

TYRANT: You're highly inspirational. You needn't worry. Frank will give you all the help you require. Won't you, Frank?

PROPHET OF BLASPHEMY: Of course.

TYRANT: And I will guide you.

LUKE: I can't do it.

TYRANT: Of course you can. I have the greatest faith in your capability.

GREAT BEAST: WeWe.

TYRANT: And so does everyone else.

(*The Great Beast swoops down and pricks Luke's finger.*)

LUKE: What have you done?

TYRANT: Insured your survival, Luke. Just a precaution. In case of injury to the original. I like to have a copy of everything on hand. In any case, you now have a kind of biological immortality. Lucky man.

(*Luke Clone appears.*)

LUKE: Oh my God!

(*Luke Clone reaches toward Luke as he advances on him.*)

LUKE: (*Screaming as lights fade out.*)

MAGICIAN: (*In the dark, whispering to Luke.*) The key! The key! Don't forget the key!

ACT II

SCENE 1: PEARL

LUKE: Was it a dream?

MAGICIAN: A dream? Hey, what's the matter? You think I go to all this trouble to put you in dream? No, I go to all this trouble to take you out of Dreamland. And this is thanks I get.

LUKE: I'm sorry. It was . . . a nightmare.

MAGICIAN: You telling me. I never run so fast in whole life. Must have lost five pounds. You know something, I don't think those fellahs like us.

LUKE: I can't believe it was real.

MAGICIAN: Is real, alright. As real as key in your hand.

LUKE: (*Unclenches fist.*) The key. Oh . . . oh . . . I'm going to . . .

MAGICIAN: Throw up. (*As he pounds him on the back.*) That's right, my boy, vomit up your life. You feel much better afterwards. What's this? Look what come out. Like Jonah out of belly of whale. Key! You must have swallowed when you face Great Beast. Now you keep in hand. Don't lose. Now you believe is real?

LUKE: Yes, yes.

MAGICIAN: But maybe want to go back and check it out . . . just to make sure.

LUKE: I don't want to go back there.

MAGICIAN: You no want to go back?

LUKE: I won't go back.

MAGICIAN: But how you going to become president?

LUKE: I'm not.

MAGICIAN: You not want to become president anymore?

LUKE: No.

MAGICIAN: America is big country.

LUKE: I'm done with all that.

MAGICIAN: Maybe want to become leader of undiscovered country.

LUKE: What are you talking about?

MAGICIAN: Is time to become leader of free world — your self.

LUKE: My self?

MAGICIAN: Only world you can make free.

LUKE: Free world. What a mockery. I'm a slave.

MAGICIAN: First thing you ever say in whole life that's true. Is hope for you. Maybe you done being boy now. Ready to become real man.

LUKE: How? How?!

MAGICIAN: Must become President of self.

LUKE: President of self . . .

MAGICIAN: Good idea, huh? I thought you might like. Sure, whole of America inside Self. Congress, Judiciary, Senate, House of Representatives, millions and millions of people. All the highways and byways, hamlets, cities, towns, everything — they all there inside you. You come with me, and I show you real America. Everything outside just reflection of what's inside.

LUKE: Just a reflection . . . ?

MAGICIAN: Sure. Self very great. Contain everything. Not only America but whole continent. Earth. Solar System. Universe. You not only in Universe, but Universe in you, too.

LUKE: That's impossible.

MAGICIAN: Oh, no, very possible. Is all done with mirrors. One day, I show you, maybe. Oh, oh, here comes someone else inside you — wife.

(*Enter Fashion.*)

FASHION: Luke, where have you been? Mother and I have been so worried about you. You've been gone three days. What happened?

LUKE: I've been gone three days?

FASHION: I know that. Where have you been? I was out of my mind with grief. I thought you'd been killed. I didn't know what to tell the children. Well, answer me.

LUKE: I . . . I . . . was . . . Fashion, you haven't met . . . Let me introduce you to . . .

FASHION: To whom?

LUKE: To this gentleman.

FASHION: What gentleman?

LUKE: Why, this man right here. (*Magician remains seated in chair.*)

FASHION: Luke, what are you talking about? There's no one here.

LUKE: No one here . . .

FASHION: Luke, what's come over you? Are you alright?

LUKE: Of course I'm alright.

FASHION: Why do you pretend there's someone there? Oh God, you're mad! You're having hallucinations. You're mad!

LUKE: Fashion, control yourself.

FASHION: You talk to me about controlling myself.

LUKE: Yes, I do.

FASHION: Keep quiet. The children will hear you.

LUKE: I don't care if the whole world hears me.

FASHION: Oh yes, big man, make a stir. Run, run . . . go ahead, run. But make sure you lose, or you'll end up in the gutter with a bullet in your head like your brothers.

LUKE: I don't give a damn about any of that.

FASHION: You don't give a damn about anything. Not me, or the children, or anyone. You can't even face your own kids.

LUKE: How can I face them.

FASHION: You're becoming twisted and mean.

LUKE: I loathe myself.

FASHION: If you got off the bottle long enough . . .

LUKE: When it comes to that, you're no slouch yourself.

FASHION: And who forced me to it?

LUKE: Yes, blame me when things get too tough to handle.

FASHION: Oh, Luke, I love you but . . .

LUKE: Maybe you'd better go away.

FASHION: What good would that do?

LUKE: I'm not fit to live. Shall I tell you about your husband? Shall I tell you what I'm really like? I used to sit in my room and say: "I'll get them now . . . shall it be by hanging, or fire, or the gun? Who will be first? Wolf? Fox? Crocodile? Leech? Pig? Or will I strangle the Snake and the Weasel?" But I couldn't do it. I knew if I did, I'd become an animal like them. And so I'd get potted to the gills and pass out. And then the dreams, the terrible dreams; I'd wake up in the middle of the night screaming — strangling the Wolf and the Fox and the Shark; chopping them into little pieces.

FASHION: I know, Luke, I know.

LUKE: Murdering them as they murdered us: killing them all for what they did to Adam and Matthew, and Dad, and me . . . and you, and all of us. For what they did to the world. And I couldn't stop the dreams. I couldn't stop them. It got so I was afraid to go to sleep. I used to play tricks on myself to stay awake. I was in the middle of a terrible nightmare and I couldn't get out. I still can't. Oh baby, help me. Help me!

FASHION: I want to, Luke. I want to.

LUKE: And then the women, one after another. I couldn't stop. And then you began to drink. I broke your heart, Fashion. God help me. And then I saw I had to pull myself together. I had to run. It was my duty. The country . . . my brothers, the world, were counting on me. I had to run. I would stand shoulder to shoulder with my brothers. I would redeem the past. Despite all the slander. There was still something I could do . . . Oh, why wouldn't you let me run when there was still a world to save?

FASHION: You know why.

LUKE: You called me a murderer. You threatened to leave me. I didn't know what to do.

FASHION: They would have murdered all of us.

LUKE: You don't know that.

FASHION: After what they did to Adam and Matthew, and all the witnesses. You knew they were capable of doing it. They were capable of anything.

LUKE: I should have taken the chance.

FASHION: At the price of your own children's lives? They threatened to wipe out the entire family.

LUKE: And what have I done to Heather and Peter by not running? My poor kids. What kind of a world have I brought to them? I wanted to protect them and instead I've thrown them to the wolves. They and millions of other kids. I should have taken my stand. I should have been willing to die for the Truth like my brothers had. They were men. But I couldn't do it . . . couldn't do it. I never knew how to fight for principle. I . . . I . . . let them break me . . . those bastards. They whipped me. All of us. And I stood for it. It was all my fault . . . my fault. I shouldn't have listened to you. You, and my mother and Vanity and Prudence. I shouldn't have listened to you. I knew the truth but I hesitated and I was lost. After that I was never the same. Nothing was ever any good any more.

FASHION: You were trying to throw your life away. You still are, because of some misplaced sense of honor. All these years I've been fighting to save you and whatever little is left of us.

LUKE: By threatening to leave me? By boozing, boozing! By constant hysteria? Driving me crazy?

FASHION: Driving you crazy?!

LUKE: Yes, by every form of blackmail in your power.

FASHION: So, you're going to run now. You've decided. After everything.

LUKE: It's too late now. There's nothing I can do. It's all gone. Did you know I wanted to die?

FASHION: Stop it Luke!

LUKE: I've prayed for death. Poor boob, I didn't even have the courage to kill myself.

FASHION: Stop it!

LUKE: I've failed at everything. My life's complete. I'm a useless appendage.

FASHION: I won't hear you. (*She starts to go. Luke grabs her. She puts her hands over her ears.*) I won't hear you!

LUKE: You will hear me. This man came and has been teaching me to live again.

FASHION: Stay away from me. You're insane and you want to drive me insane. Ahhhhhh! (*She runs screaming to the window.*) Stay away from me. I'm going to jump!! I'm going to jump!!

LUKE: Fashion!

(*Magician puts hand on Fashion's shoulder.*)

FASHION: Let me go, Luke! Let me go!

LUKE: I'm not touching you.

(*Magician passes hand three times quickly across her face. She suddenly calms down.*)

FASHION: Oh, I'm tired. So very tired. I think I'll lie down and rest. I don't know what's come over me. Did you have a good day at the office, dear?

LUKE: Yes . . .

FASHION: That's nice. The children missed you. They send their love. (*Kissing him.*) I'll see you at dinner.

(*Exit Fashion.*)

LUKE: Fine . . . Why couldn't she see you?

MAGICIAN: She wasn't ready to.

LUKE: She almost jumped.

MAGICIAN: Almost.

LUKE: She could have killed herself.

MAGICIAN: Yes.

LUKE: You're dangerous.

MAGICIAN: Very.

LUKE: What will happen to her now?

MAGICIAN: She'll forget.

LUKE: Everything?

MAGICIAN: Everything.

LUKE: But why?

MAGICIAN: She doesn't want to remember.

LUKE: You forget when you don't want to remember?

MAGICIAN: That's right. And yourself?

LUKE: I want to remember.

MAGICIAN: Then you must use the key. Pearl is waiting for you.

LUKE: Pearl . . .

MAGICIAN: Where you going?

LUKE: To her.

MAGICIAN: Wait! Before you go there's something you must know. I'm going to tell you something that very few men ever hear. If you use that key your life can never be the same. If you open that door you can never return to what you are.

LUKE: Why not?

MAGICIAN: Because you won't be able to find your old life again. It will be gone.

LUKE: Gone?

MAGICIAN: You will have died to it.

LUKE: And if I don't go through that door?

MAGICIAN: Then you be like everyone else. Live make-believe life here in Dreamland. Cover up fact you don't exist.

LUKE: I know too much.

MAGICIAN: You will forget, and you will never see me again. Think. It's not too late to turn back. But once you open that door you can never come back. There'll be nowhere to come back to. You'll have to go on, whether you want to or not.

LUKE: And if I fail . . . ? (*Goes to window and looks out.*) I can always jump.

MAGICIAN: Such things happen. One last thing. A man only hears this once in a lifetime. Such an opportunity never recurs. Perhaps you will want to be alone and think it over. It's a very important decision.

LUKE: To face the specter of nothingness all the rest of my days. Somewhere out there a clone is seeking my existence. Perhaps he will succeed in becoming me . . . impersonating me . . . Or perhaps I'll live a life of cover-up like everyone else, a life of make-believe here in Dreamland. (*Laughing.*) Who would know the difference?

MAGICIAN: God.

LUKE: Yes. God . . . He would know . . . and so would I.

MAGICIAN: You will always be alone if you go this Way.

LUKE: This Way . . .

MAGICIAN: The Way of the Immortals.

LUKE: It begins in nothingness. This is your payment.

MAGICIAN: Yes.

LUKE: And it ends . . .

MAGICIAN: As a citizen of reality.

LUKE: Then an end to this fictitious existence. I'm ready.

MAGICIAN: Are you sure?

LUKE: Yes. (*Starts to go.*)

MAGICIAN: I'll always be with you.

LUKE: You said I'd always be alone.

MAGICIAN: That's why I'll always be with you.

> (*A long look. Luke goes towards Pearl. Magician follows at a distance. Sound of a heartbeat.*)

LUKE: Pearl . . . Pearl . . . Oh, answer me, Pearl!

MAGICIAN: Use the key, quick. No time to waste.

PEARL: (*Faintly.*) Luke! Luke!

LUKE: It won't work.

MAGICIAN: Of course it will work. Use elbow grease. Turn! Turn!

LUKE: It's beginning to turn.

MAGICIAN: Keep turning. Harder! Harder! Work harder. Put shoulder behind it.

PEARL: Where are you, Luke?

LUKE: I'm coming, Pearl. It won't . . . turn anymore.

MAGICIAN: Must turn! Is just rusty. Closed for long, long time. Must open.

LUKE: I can't do it.

MAGICIAN: Must do it. Must open.

PEARL: I can't wait any longer, Luke.

LUKE: Hold on, hold on. Can't . . . can't.

MAGICIAN: Can do! Can do!

LUKE: I've no more strength. I can't go on.

MAGICIAN: Must go on.

LUKE: God!

MAGICIAN: God damn. What you call on God for? Call on every devil in hell. You can do anything if you make Devil work for God.

PEARL: Dying! Dying . . .

MAGICIAN: Put whole self into it or Pearl lost and you finished forever.

PEARL: Going . . .

LUKE: No! Ahhhhhhh . . . It's OPEN!

PEARL: Luke!

MAGICIAN: What you waiting for? You as bashful as bridegroom. Cross threshold.

LUKE: It smells like . . . like . . . death.

MAGICIAN: Tomb of death. Go in.

LUKE: Don't die, Pearl, Don't die!

(*Luke goes in.*)

PEARL: Oh, Luke!

(*Luke carries Pearl out.*)

Is it your face? Do I hold you in my arms once more?

LUKE: Yes, Pearl.

PEARL: Oh Luke, I so want to be beautiful. Make me beautiful.

LUKE: You are beautiful.

PEARL: I'm ugly. And cold . . . I've waited too long.

LUKE: Shhh. Don't say that.

PEARL: Too long . . .

LUKE: Oh Pearl.

PEARL: Kiss me, kiss me.

LUKE: With all my heart.

PEARL: Oh . . . ohhh. I feel your warmth touching me. (*Crying.*) It's such a long way home. (*Laughing.*) I'm home. I'm home!

LUKE: Yes.

PEARL: Oh God! Is it true?

LUKE: Yes, beloved.

PEARL: Why can't I stop crying? You're crying too.

LUKE: I'm happy.

PEARL: Open the curtains. I want to see the Sun.

LUKE: You must rest.

PEARL: Please . . .

(*He opens the curtains.*)

The day . . . the day's on fire. It burns. The sunbeams . . . burn. I want to reach out and touch them. Oh, how many days have passed me by.

LUKE: Close your eyes.

PEARL: No. I want to remember this . . . your face filled with light against the Sun. Light upon light. I will keep my eyes open and open and open every moment of my life. No more darkness for me. I'm alive! I'm alive! Oh, I want to live. Open the window. I'm mad to feel the wind on my face. Oh, what is this ecstasy? The brightest day, the darkest night, the Sun, the Moon, the stars. I want them all, all. The sky above, the Earth below, the bell that tolls for me, the clock upon the church top spire, the honey bird fluttering in the wind, the rivers, the woods, the damp dark marshes, the lakes washing the Earth in the cool of dusk, the train whistles in the night . . . all, all. I want to leave my footprints on the sand and sound the ocean's depths, hug the Earth, fling myself from the highest heights and . . . fly. Oh, take me to the rooftop. I can walk.

LUKE: But . . .

PEARL: I can walk! Oh happy day . . . with you here beside me. Take my hand and never let me go.

LUKE: I won't.

PEARL: Remember when we were children? We used to come up here and look upon the Earth and shout from the rooftop. But no one could hear us.

LUKE: All the people down below . . . so little.

PEARL: Like tiny ants.

LUKE: And we two giants, alone on the face of the Earth.

PEARL: You promised you would conquer the world and lay it at my feet.

LUKE: How good life was then.

PEARL: And is now. And always shall be.

LUKE: No more pain.

PEARL: Pain, pain, go away. Come again some other day. Remember?

LUKE: I remember.

PEARL: Old Man Pain, he gone away, he never gonna come back again. And if he do we break his back. (*Laughing.*)

LUKE: And if he does we break his bone. If only it were true.

PEARL: We'll make it true. Dance with me.

LUKE: Pearl, you can't dance.

PEARL: I will.

LUKE: But your . . .

PEARL: I won't be crippled if you dance with me.

(*A magnificent waltz is heard as Magician begins playing harmonium from a distance. First very softly, tenderly, slowly, then ever faster and faster until it mounts into a majestic and triumphant crescendo.*)

LUKE: My Lady, may I have this dance?

PEARL: You may, Sir, if your intentions be honorable and your purpose true.

(*They begin dancing.*)

You see. I can do anything when you hold me in your arms.

LUKE: Yes.

PEARL: Faster. Faster! The world is singing. Hear it? Pearl can dance. She can dance! Circling, circling, ever circling in your arms. (*End of dance.*) Oh Luke, will every star in Heaven come out tonight and bless us? Will they know that you and I are here? Will they whisper all their secrets in our ear?

LUKE: Night is falling.

PEARL: Falling softly . . . over the rooftops and window panes. Night is huddling over all the buildings. One by one, the lights in the houses are going on. How beautiful . . . the city is . . . glowing in the night.

LUKE: As beautiful as the glow in your cheek, and as soft.

PEARL: Is my cheek soft?

LUKE: As soft as the stars. And as bright. You've got your wish, Pearl.

PEARL: My wish?

LUKE: The stars have come out to greet you.

PEARL: Oh! Star light, star bright, first star I see tonight . . .

LUKE: Blazing diamonds in the night. I'll steal a fistful and place them 'round your neck.

PEARL: Don't move a star in Heaven, oh, not for me. They're perfect the way they are, but . . .

LUKE: But . . .

PEARL: Take me to them.

LUKE: What . . . ?

PEARL: I want to go to the stars. Take me there.

LUKE: That's not possible.

PEARL: Silly, don't you know everything's possible?

LUKE: But I don't know the way.

PEARL: Find the way. You have a friend.

LUKE: A friend?

PEARL: Yes, ask him. If you don't ask for the stars how can you ever hope to get them?

LUKE: He'll tell me I'm crazy.

PEARL: Then be crazy enough to ask. They're just within our reach. We'll leap off the rooftop and plunge into the sky.

LUKE: Pearl, what am I going to do with you?

PEARL: Give me what I pray for. Love me, love me, love me, and take me to the stars.

MAGICIAN: (*Approaching them.*) Lady want to go to stars. Must take. What kind of lover are you? Is this the way to celebrate reunion?

LUKE: Easier said than done.

MAGICIAN: You man or worm? Must make up mind. Worm, he crawl on the earth. Man, he live in the stars.

LUKE: Let's go downstairs.

MAGICIAN: Is no downstairs.

LUKE: No downstairs?

MAGICIAN: Is disappear. Too late to turn back now. I tell you that before.

LUKE: What am I to do?

MAGICIAN: Why you not hide in closet? Pretend this not happening.

PEARL: Go on!

LUKE: Where?

PEARL: Right through the sky.

LUKE: Next thing you know you'll have me walking on water.

MAGICIAN: Oh, that comes later.

LUKE: You're too much.

PEARL: I believe in you, Luke. You can do it.

LUKE: If only I could believe in myself.

MAGICIAN: You all uptight. You want to, but you not know how. You just scared.

(*Magician takes out flask and three wine glasses.*)

LUKE: What is this?

MAGICIAN: Necessary to relax if you want to go to stars. Is for relax. This very good stuff. Loosen you up. Remember I tell you one day maybe we drink wine and become best friends. Taste.

PEARL: It bubbles.

LUKE: Champagne . . . ?

MAGICIAN: Champagne for pikers. Only good for after-dinner speeches. This maybe two thousand years old. Come from ancient vineyard, brewed by monks.

LUKE: Monks?

MAGICIAN: Sure, they best drunkards in world. What you think they do in monasteries? Make tea? This potent stuff. Take you to the stars. Drink up. O.K., what star you want to go to?

LUKE: Oh, any one will do.

PEARL: No! That one.

MAGICIAN: This very good. This best star in sky. Our very own. O.K. Let's go.

LUKE: How are we going to get there?

MAGICIAN: How you think? Step on sunbeam.

LUKE: But the Sun's not shining.

MAGICIAN: What are you talking about? Sun is always shining.

LUKE: But it's night out.

MAGICIAN: Best time to travel. Too hot during the day.

LUKE: You've made this trip before?

MAGICIAN: Sure, I go up and down all the time.

LUKE: How?

MAGICIAN: Walk out of time, step on a sunbeam and she carry you up.

LUKE: But there is no sunbeam. Can't you see it's night?

MAGICIAN: Sure, and next thing you gonna tell me there's not stars up there in Heaven. Better have another drink. You going crazy.

LUKE: Of course there's stars. I'm not blind.

MAGICIAN: I'm glad you admit that. Things not as bad as I thought. And if stars, must be starsbeams, no?

LUKE: Starsbeams . . . ?

MAGICIAN: Starsbeams.

LUKE: Well . . . yes.

(*By this time Luke is tipsy.*)

MAGICIAN: Is called sunbeam during the day and starsbeam during the night, but is same thing, no?

LUKE: Oh!

MAGICIAN: Everybody have beams, connect him with stars. You beginning to get it now?

LUKE: I think so.

MAGICIAN: Good. You not as far gone as I thought. All aboard.

(*Enter a horse, played by an actor carrying a white silk hobby horse with a flowing mane.*)

LUKE: What's this?

MAGICIAN: Looks like a horse to me.

LUKE: A horse!

MAGICIAN: That's what it is, alright. No doubt about it.

LUKE: What's a horse doing in my house? What's he doing here?

MAGICIAN: Where else you expect him to be? Is your horse, you tell me. You no like?

LUKE: My horse?

MAGICIAN: Sure. 'Til We Meet Again. He come to take you on journey to the stars.

PEARL: 'Til We Meet Again . . .

LUKE: Oh God! That was the horse that was running in the seventh.

MAGICIAN: This horse always running between Heaven and Earth. Only trouble is you always keep him tied up. Now you untie him. He take you anywhere you want to go. Like I say, he champion. He go the distance. He rare breed. One of horses of the Sun. Here, give sugar. Make friends. He love sugar. Now we gonna be three men on a horse. Get on. Me up front, Pearl in the middle, and you take the rear end.

LUKE: I thought we were going to ride on a sunbeam.

MAGICIAN: That's right. Horse ride on sunbeam, and we ride on him. Ready?

PEARL: Ready.

MAGICIAN: Fly! (*Pause.*) Fly! (*Pause. Magician looks at Pearl.*)

PEARL: Fly! (*Pause.*)

MAGICIAN: This horse no fly.

PEARL: He's not moving.

LUKE: Some horse.

MAGICIAN: Huh?

LUKE: Nothing.

PEARL: Oh, he's never going to fly!

MAGICIAN: Lovely girl, don't cry. I fix. Hey, 'Til We Meet Again, why you no fly? What's that? Oh, you don't say. Oh, no wonder. He say you too heavy. Must take off clothes. Hey, what you taking jacket off for? This no nudist colony.

LUKE: You said I should take off my clothes.

MAGICIAN: So why you take clothes off body? Body not you. You not need all this self-importance you carrying. All this doubt and fear weighing you down. These are the clothes you must leave behind. Become like little child, innocent, naked, like sister, Pearl. She teach you. And then we rise, light as feather, to Papa Sky. Give him kiss, honey, and maybe he leave all his misery behind. This wonder horse. He not going to move unless you have faith in him. What's the matter, you think he ride for nothing?

PEARL: I believe in you, 'Til We Meet Again. Say it, Luke.

LUKE: Pearl . . .

PEARL: For me, say it.

LUKE: Until We Meet Again, I believe in you.

PEARL: Again.

LUKE: I believe in you.

PEARL: Again.

LUKE: I believe in you!

PEARL: Now . . . fly, fly.

(*A black velvet sky with iridescent stars sweeps across the stage and floats underfoot during the remainder of the scene. Music begins* as the Figure of a Dancer carries above her symbols of the planets.*)

MAGICIAN: Oh, oh. I think he hear you now. We going light as feather up to Father Sky.

PEARL: Free! Free! Oh Luke, we're free!

LUKE: Leaving Earth behind!

MAGICIAN: Into waiting arms of Papa Sky.

LUKE: The Earth is getting smaller.

PEARL: Oh, don't look back. I never want to turn back.

MAGICIAN: Earth not getting smaller. You getting bigger.

PEARL: And bigger! Oh ride, ride us to our star! Adam and Matthew are up there waiting . . . waiting for us, Until We Meet Again. I know it. I feel it.

LUKE: Are you so sure, Pearl?

PEARL: I hear them crying inside of me.

LUKE: It's the wind crying.

PEARL: No, it's them. They're crying for you and me. They'll never be at peace 'til we find them, Luke.

MAGICIAN: Smart girl, your sister. She going to put hair on your chest. Oh, oh, duck!

LUKE: What was that? Flying saucers?

MAGICIAN: You see too many movies. Those meteorites.

LUKE: They almost took my head off.

MAGICIAN: Tyrant's plan. He lay in ambush for you. He not give up so easy.

LUKE: What's he doing up here?

MAGICIAN: Up, down, all the same to him.

LUKE: But he lives down there.

MAGICIAN: He live up here, too. These crazy meteorites, his second home. They as hysterical as a bunch of hens in heat. Lots of big

*Music p. 163

trouble for everybody on Earth. Drive everyone nuts.

PEARL: Is Tyrant everywhere?

MAGICIAN: Everywhere, sweet girl . . . except stars.

PEARL: Why?

MAGICIAN: Only one thing he afraid of . . . light. (*Pearl laughs.*) Is funny, no? (*Laughing with her.*) Hey, why you no laughing?

LUKE: It's not funny.

MAGICIAN: Oh, beg pardon, sourpuss. (*Gales of laughter between Pearl and Magician. Then Luke breaks and joins in.*) Hey, look out, you gonna have nervous breakdown. You actually happy. Boy, you one stubborn guy. Did mule kick you when born?

(*All laughing. Suddenly Luke and Pearl fall asleep.*)

MAGICIAN: Hey, wake up. This no time for you to fall asleep. Miss beautiful scenery. Not every day in week can see Saturn and Jupiter.

PEARL: Where . . . where are we?

MAGICIAN: Going past planets.

LUKE: What happened?

MAGICIAN: You dreaming. Soporific Man, he throw dream dust in eye.

LUKE: Soporific Man?

MAGICIAN: Sure. Planets, they put you to sleep.

PEARL: Why?

MAGICIAN: So everybody stay on Earth. If people wake up, they all want to go to Sun. And this not allowed. Only for few. For people with big ache in heart . . . Desperate people who have nothing else to live for. People . . . like you.

PEARL: Why can't everybody go?

MAGICIAN: Mother Earth, she get very lonesome and die of broken heart if all her children desert her. So Soporific Man throw dream dust. Some have pleasant dream, some have nightmare, but all snore soundly. That way only few wake up and leave her. Is arranged that way.

PEARL: Who arranges it?

MAGICIAN: Oh, somebody.

PEARL: This is not a dream. I'm awake and free, riding through the silver silence of the midnight sky, riding on my wonder horse, riding to the stars. What's that music I hear, so far, yet so near?

MAGICIAN: The harmony of the spheres.

PEARL: He hears, my magic horse, he's prancing, prancing, nostrils flaring, wings outstretched, racing swiftly, leaping upward on a beam of light. How strange and awesome. Oh, there's a shooting star.

LUKE: There goes another. It's eerie.

MAGICIAN: And another. Lots of fireworks around here.

PEARL: How fearful this journey of myself through this dark immensity. And yet I'm not afraid at all.

LUKE: It makes me dizzy. This emptiness . . . I think I'm going to fall.

MAGICIAN: You think you going to fall. What about fish?

LUKE: Fish?

MAGICIAN: Sure, Fish. He swimming in ocean. He look down into depths one day. "Oh, oh, I gonna fall," he say. "I not know it so deep." Ocean call to him, "Hey, Fish." But Fish say, "Pft . . . pft." He too important to listen. "Hey, Fish, better listen to me," Ocean say. Fish say, "Can't now, I going to drown." Ocean, he just laugh and say, "You not going to drown. Who you think support you all this time? And who you think support you now?" This very good story.

PEARL: Yes. Oh, what star is that?

MAGICIAN: Star of Love.

PEARL: Brightest star in Heaven.

MAGICIAN: You like?

PEARL: It's divine.

MAGICIAN: My good friend live there. You heard of him, maybe?

LUKE: Who?

MAGICIAN: Jesus Christ. I, his follower.

PEARL: Will we go on like this forever?

MAGICIAN: Nothing to stop us but ourselves.

PEARL: Ourselves . . . Who is God?

MAGICIAN: Who are you?

PEARL: I don't know.

MAGICIAN: Maybe God, He not know who He is either. Maybe He wake up from sleep one day, scratch head, and say, "Hey, who am I?" Some pickle. Maybe He make whole Universe just to find answer to this one question.

PEARL: Will He ever find out?

MAGICIAN: Who knows . . .? But maybe you find out who you are, it help Him find out who He is.

PEARL: Is that what I was born for?

(*Magician plays harmonium; hums quietly.*)

Is God lonely?

MAGICIAN: What you think, angel?

PEARL: I think He must be very lonely. Are you?

MAGICIAN: Sometimes I lonely.

PEARL: Sometimes I'm lonely, too. What do you do when . . .

MAGICIAN: I make song:

(Sings.)*
Oh Sun be my Brother,
Oh Moon be my Sister.
Oh Heaven and Earth
Be my Father and Mother.

How long must I wander,
Nameless am I,
Homeless and free as the sky.

PEARL: Promise me you'll always be my friend.

MAGICIAN: I promise.

PEARL: I'm glad.

MAGICIAN: Me, too.

PEARL: It's good to have a friend.

MAGICIAN: Now we pals 'til the Earth and Moon collide.

PEARL: Something's entering my eyes and mouth, my lungs and heart.
I feel . . . so strange . . . so beautiful. The radiance of . . . the
Sun! The Sun! Oh God, it's milky white! When will we arrive?

MAGICIAN: Now!

PEARL: Where are we?

MAGICIAN: Here and now.

PEARL: With everyone we love. Oh, how precious.

LUKE: They knew you. They greeted you as a friend.

MAGICIAN: Yes.

LUKE: Oh . . . oh . . . I'm being pulled . . . down.

PEARL: Mother is calling to you. You must go.

LUKE: I don't want to go.

PEARL: She needs you.

LUKE: I want to stay here with you, Pearl.

PEARL: Don't be silly. I'm coming with you.

LUKE: You are?

PEARL: You know wherever you go, I go with you.

*Music p. 163

LUKE: (*Gasps.*) I almost forgot.

PEARL: Look, there's a glob of light coming our way. Duck!

LUKE: It's a galaxy.

PEARL: No, no, it's a star cluster, throbbing and bubbling with life. Billions of tiny seed points of light. Quick, let's jump on one.

LUKE: Oh! We're inside it. Inside a little tiny seed of light. I'm swooning. Hold me tight.

PEARL: A billion tiny stars are dying to the light, plunging to their death with a billion little lives.

LUKE: Why must we die?

PEARL: So we can be conceived.

LUKE: And then?

PEARL: We're entombed in flesh and blood.

LUKE: Is that why it's so dark?

PEARL: Yes.

LUKE: And then?

PEARL: We're born.

LUKE: Why?

PEARL: I don't know.

LUKE: It's so strange to be conceived.

PEARL: I know.

LUKE: You won't ever leave me?

PEARL: Oh, no.

LUKE: (*To Magician.*) Forgive me. I didn't know.

(*Blackout.*)

SCENE 2: A CASE OF MISTAKEN IDENTITY

(*The two children in the front yard, sitting in the garden gazing at one another. Tyrant watching from a distance.*)

HEATHER: Wasn't she beautiful . . . ? A beautiful lady, and she's shining in Daddy's eyes.

PETER: They're coming home now.

DESTINY: Children, children . . .

PETER: Here comes Grandmother . . . Run!

DESTINY: Come back here! Peter . . . Heather! Oh . . .

(*Enter Luke.*)

LUKE: Hello, Mother.

DESTINY: My God, Luke, how you frightened me. I didn't expect . . . You weren't at dinner. Fashion is so anxious about you. I don't know what to do about her. You . . . you mustn't treat her this way . . . any of us. Luke, I . . .

LUKE: I've been with Pearl.

DESTINY: It was so embarrassing. The Ambassador was waiting. And you didn't appear. It's no way to conduct . . .

LUKE: I said, I've been with Pearl.

DESTINY: No way . . . to conduct your life.

(*Silence.*)

LUKE: Did you hear me, Mother?

DESTINY: Pearl is dead.

LUKE: She's alive and well. She's with me now.

DESTINY: It took a long time for you to learn not to talk that way. You mustn't.

LUKE: I mustn't act that way.

DESTINY: Yes . . . no!

LUKE: Or lie as I always have. Our life's a fiction. Pearl's not crippled.

DESTINY: She's crippled . . . crippled . . . and dead!

LUKE: She's alive.

DESTINY: You're frightening me, Luke.

LUKE: You think I'm mad, Mother?

DESTINY: You've been under too much strain. Too much unhappiness. I don't recognize you. You're not yourself.

LUKE: I will show you myself, my real self. I'll show you Pearl.

(*Exit Luke, then enter Fashion.*)

FASHION: Was that Luke?

DESTINY: Do you love my son?

FASHION: Love him? I don't even know who he is. Sometimes I want to go a long way away and never see him or you or the children again. And then there are the nights I cry myself to sleep for what we've missed. I suppose I love him.

DESTINY: You must be strong.

FASHION: How long can I love a man who's not there for me.

DESTINY: He needs time and patience and then he'll heal. He'll be himself again, you'll see.

FASHION: When? When there's nothing left of me. I can't go on this way. I just can't. We pass each other like two ships in the night sending out distress signals to one another that are never answered. Oh it's madness to stay together.

DESTINY: Don't leave him. I beg you.

FASHION: As if I could. It's impossible to part. I've tried. Oh Mother, what should I do?

DESTINY: You must reach him.

FASHION: I can't get to him.

DESTINY: But you do love him?

FASHION: Of course I love him. But I'm afraid I'm going to lose him. I'm going crazy.

DESTINY: I fear for his mind, Fashion.

FASHION: If only I could help him.

DESTINY: We must bring him back to us. If only there were someone we could turn to . . . someone who . . .

PEARL: (*Enters and calls softly.*) Destiny . . .

DESTINY: . . . someone who . . . Pearl . . . ?

FASHION: What is it, Mother?

DESTINY: It's nothing . . . I thought I heard . . .

PEARL: Destiny . . .

DESTINY: Oh, it's . . . there's someone here . . . in the garden.

FASHION: There's no one here.

DESTINY: Yes, yes, I can feel . . . her presence. Pearl . . .

FASHION: Pearl! But she's . . .

DESTINY: Shhhhh. Can't you feel her with us . . . now . . .

PEARL: Destiny . . .

DESTINY: She's calling to us. Oh, my baby . . . my baby! (*She becomes faint.*)

FASHION: Mother!

DESTINY: I'll be alright.

FASHION: Let me get you into the house.

DESTINY: I must . . . (*Begins sobbing.*)

FASHION: You must lie down, Mother. (*Leading Destiny into house.*) (*Peter, Heather, and Magician appear on the rooftop.*)

PETER: Will Tyrant swallow up the whole Earth and everything on it?

MAGICIAN: He going to try. How we going to stop him?

HEATHER: He's like a big black cloud covering the whole world.

PETER: We're going to stand so still, he won't find us. Then we'll wait 'til he passes us by.

(*Luke Clone enters the garden from the house.*)

LUKE CLONE: Pearl . . . psst . . . over here.

PEARL: Luke . . . what are you doing in the shadows? Come into the light . . . You're not Luke. You're dead!

LUKE CLONE: I am Luke.

PEARL: Oh my God, your eyes are dead!

LUKE CLONE: You're coming with me. (*He grabs her.*)

PEARL: You've murdered Luke.

LUKE CLONE: I am Luke.

    (*Heather enters the garden.*)

HEATHER: Daddy, you're hurting the beautiful lady!

PEARL: Let me go!

LUKE CLONE: Quiet! You'll disturb Mother.

    (*Luke Clone throws Heather to the ground, puts hand over Pearl's mouth and carries her off. Luke and Peter run into the garden and find Heather weeping on the ground.*)

LUKE: PEARL!! PEARL!!

HEATHER: You hurt her.

LUKE: Hurt who?

HEATHER: My beautiful lady!

LUKE: No, darling! No!

HEATHER: Yes, you did. I saw you. And then you took her away.

LUKE: No, Heather, it wasn't me. It . . . Oh God . . . Baby, listen to me. It wasn't Daddy. It was . . . PEARL!!

    (*Enter Fashion as Luke rushes past her.*)

FASHION: What is it?

HEATHER: (*As she runs to her mother weeping.*) Mommy . . .

FASHION: (*Taking both children in her arms.*) Heather . . . Peter . . . What's happened? What's going on?!

MAGICIAN: A case of mistaken identity.

SCENE 3: A WAGER

TYRANT: We meet again.

MAGICIAN: You haven't changed a bit, brother. Up to your old tricks, I see.

TYRANT: Nor you, brother. Shall we continue our game?

MAGICIAN: Sure, is good game. The Game of Life.

TYRANT: High stakes.

MAGICIAN: The Soul of Man. You really think you going to win this game?

TYRANT: I always have.

MAGICIAN: You think so.

TYRANT: Atlantis, Egypt, India, China, Babylon, Carthage, Rome, all mine.

MAGICIAN: Oh, I don't know. A few good men and women escape.

TYRANT: We'll see . . .
MAGICIAN: We'll see at dawn.
TYRANT: At dusk.
MAGICIAN: Naturally, at dusk.
(*Blackout.*)

SCENE 4: A GAME OF CHESS

(*A chessboard covers the entire stage.* * *The chess pieces are played by actors and actresses among whom are Heather, Pawn of Prayer; Peter, Pawn of Humility; Fashion, Pawn of Sadness; Destiny, Pawn of Destiny; Frank, Pawn of Blasphemy. The Magician and Tyrant appear and face each other across the board. They are served by chessmasters — Figure of a Dancer for the Magician and the Hound of Hell for Tyrant.*
Luke enters, looking for Pearl who is the Castle of Despair. Unable to discover her he assumes his place as the Knight of Faith. Luke Clone shadows him throughout the game. The chess pieces move, as if magically, enacting the struggle of will between the Magician and Tyrant. The tempo is fast ** *— the scene is a dance.*)
TYRANT: I'll take black.
(*Tyrant's force fills the Black pieces with life.*)
MAGICIAN: As usual.
TYRANT: White for you?
MAGICIAN: As usual.
(*The Magician radiates life into the White pieces.*)
TYRANT: Your move.
MAGICIAN: My move?
TYRANT: Your move.
MAGICIAN: I guess it my move then, huh? I move, let me see. I move the Pawn of Common Sense. (*He nods and the Pawn of Common Sense moves forward one square.*) Hey, you no mind if I smoke . . . drink?
TYRANT: I'd rather you wouldn't.
MAGICIAN: But I no be able to concentrate on game . . . no drink . . . no smoke. Have a heart.
TYRANT: Every man to his own whim. The Pawn of Folly. (*The Pawn*

*See pp. 156-7 for character names and chess moves.
**Music p. 163

of Folly moves forward one square.)

MAGICIAN: Hey, that good move, that Pawn of Folly. I like that move. That girl, Folly, she stop my Common Sense.

TYRANT: You like it?

MAGICIAN: Yes. I like it so much I going to give you the Pawn of Laughter.

TYRANT: The Pawn of Ridicule.

MAGICIAN: Oh, oh. I stop laughing now. You play tough game, brother.

TYRANT: Your move.

PAWN OF HUMILITY: Humility. *(Played by Peter.)*

(The chess pieces call out their names while moving throughout the scene.)

BISHOP OF DESTRUCTION: Destruction.

(The Hound of Hell trots behind the Bishop of Destruction who meets the dancer escorting the Magician's Bishop of Creation.)

BISHOP OF CREATION: Creation.

PAWN OF MALICE: Malice.

PAWN OF HEALING: Healing.

TYRANT: The Castle of Despair. *(Moves Pearl, Castle of Despair.)*

MAGICIAN: Hey, something wrong here. Why such a beautiful girl caught in Castle of Despair? This I no understand. Must send Knight of Faith to rescue. *(Moves Luke, Knight of Faith.)*

TYRANT: You will find Despair very elusive. I move her there. *(Moves Castle of Despair.)*

MAGICIAN: No sense she run away. Faith, he coming after her. *(Moves Knight of Faith.)*

PEARL: Luke! oh, Luke . . .

LUKE: Pearl!

TYRANT: Come and get her if you can. *(Moves Castle of Despair.)*

PEARL: Don't let him do this to me, Luke.

LUKE: I won't.

MAGICIAN: No sense hiding Despair. Faith going to conquer her. *(Moves Knight of Faith.)*

(From this point on in the game, the tempo quickens. During the following dialogue 30 chess moves are made arising out of the conflict between the Souls of the Magician and Tyrant.)

TYRANT: You wouldn't care to make a little side bet on that, would you, brother?

MAGICIAN: Sure, what you want to bet?

TYRANT: America.

MAGICIAN: America? You want to bet America?

TYRANT: I do.

MAGICIAN: Home of the brave and land of the free?

TYRANT: That's right.

MAGICIAN: Anything you say. You're on, brother.
(*Pause in dialogue for the remaining moves.*)

KNIGHT OF SLAVERY: Slavery. (*Strikes at Freedom and misses.*)

TYRANT: All the pieces are out.

KNIGHT OF FREEDOM: Freedom. (*The Dancer glides lightly alongside him.*)

MAGICIAN: All the pieces are out.

KNIGHT OF SLAVERY: Slavery. (*Coils and strikes Freedom who collapses onto the board. The Hound of Hell drags him away.*)

TYRANT: My Knight of Slavery takes your Knight of Freedom. Ha, ha.

MAGICIAN: Sometime must be slave like Chosen People before can reach Promised Land. Meanwhile, I take your Ridicule. (*Takes Pawn of Ridicule.*)
(*Several moves are made.*)

TYRANT: My Folly eliminates your Sadness. Weep your eyes out, brother, if you can.

MAGICIAN: What I going to do now? Oh, I guess I take your Bishop of Corruption. (*With his Knight of Faith.*)

TYRANT: My Bishop of . . . (*Moves his Knight of Slavery.*)

KNIGHT OF SLAVERY: Slavery. (*Marching on the Queen of Love.*)

MAGICIAN: And now my Knight of Faith, he threaten your Queen of Crime and your Castle of Despair.

TYRANT: I cannot give up my Whore . . .

PAWN OF BLASPHEMY: Blasphemy. (*Played by Frank; mumbling drunkenly he threatens the Queen of Love.*)

PEARL: (*To the Magician.*) No, not the Queen of Love . . . not for me.

MAGICIAN: Must make sacrifice.

PEARL: It's too big.

LUKE: Pay it! She's beyond all price!

PEARL: Forget me. I'm not worth it.

LUKE: You're worth the world and all that's in it.

MAGICIAN: You hear! No sacrifice too big for Faith to make. My Knight of Faith, he got to ransom lady in distress.

(*Luke and Luke Clone join Pearl on her square and the three move together hereafter.*)

TYRANT: Very touching.

LUKE: Free her!

TYRANT: Must I be witness to this vile romance?

LUKE: Give her to me!

PEARL: Ohhhhh! You've freed me! I'm free . . . at last.

LUKE: My precious Pearl!

PEARL: I thought I'd never see you again. I'd given up hope. But we're together again.

LUKE: I'll never let you go.

PEARL: Take me with you.

LUKE: I will.

TYRANT: One moment, my knight in shining armor. You've ransomed the Queen of Love. Who will protect you now? (*Knight of Slavery overwhelms the Queen of Love. Hound of Hell drags her off.*)

MAGICIAN: The Pawn of Prayer. (*Played by Heather.*)

BISHOP OF DESTRUCTION: Destruction.

KNIGHT OF FAITH: Faith. (*He smashes the Pawn of Blasphemy to the ground.*)

(*Several moves.*)

PAWN OF SPITE: Spite. (*The Hound of Hell snarls and drags the Pawn of Spite forward.*)

KNIGHT OF FAITH: Faith. (*The Dancer delicately leads the Magician's Faith to end Tyrant's Bishop of Destruction. She snaps her fingers in his face.*)

MAGICIAN: Check. (*Laughing.*)

(*Dance halts momentarily, all watch as Tyrant strides over to his King of Degeneration, played by the Great Beast, and surveys the board. The Magician stands firm. Then . . .*)

KING OF DEGENERATION: Degeneration. (*Released by the Hound of Hell.*)

(*Several moves.*)

KNIGHT OF SLAVERY: Slavery. (*Tyrant's will drives Slavery toward the King of All.*)

KNIGHT OF FAITH: (*Faith stands in Slavery's way.*) Faith.

QUEEN OF CRIME: (*The Great Whore of Babylon.*) Crime. (*Clicking like an insect, Crime poisons the Bishop of Creation on her way to the King of All.*)

PAWN OF PRAYER: Prayer. (*Advances on bended knee.*)

KNIGHT OF SLAVERY: Slavery.

PAWN OF PRAYER: Prayer.

QUEEN OF CRIME: Crime.

TYRANT: Check. (*Fondling his Queen.*)

KING OF ALL: King of all. Regeneration.

QUEEN OF CRIME: Crime. (*Smiles at the Dancer as she stings the Pawn of Common Sense to death.*)

PAWN OF PRAYER: Prayer. (*The Magician guides her steadily, deeper into Black territory.*)

TYRANT: My trusted Knight will end your game plan. (*Moves Knight of Ignorance to block Pawn of Prayer.*)

MAGICIAN: Just a square away.

TYRANT: It might as well be a million miles when Ignorance blocks the way. Submit, brother. You're vanquished.

MAGICIAN: How I going to submit when I have my Knowledge . . .

CASTLE OF KNOWLEDGE: Knowledge. (*Knowledge breaks Knight of Ignorance, frees Pawn of Prayer.*)

TYRANT: You won't get away with this . . .

KNIGHT OF SLAVERY: Slavery. (*Arrives within striking distance of the King of All.*)

TYRANT: Check.

KING OF ALL: King of All. (*Frees himself.*)

PAWN OF INDOLENCE: Indolence.

MAGICIAN: Too late. I redeem my Queen. This little Pawn of Prayer you scoff at . . .

PAWN OF PRAYER: Love. (*Heather, reaching the last rank, is transformed from the Pawn of Prayer into the Queen of Love. The Dancer helps her into a robe and a crown and places a star in her hand.*)

MAGICIAN: Check. (*He kisses Heather on the cheek.*)

KING OF DEGENERATION: Degeneration. (*Tyrant sends the Hound of Hell to guard his King as he escapes.*)

KNIGHT OF FAITH: Faith. (*Risks a lone attack on Tyrant's King.*) (*Several moves.*)

CASTLE OF RECOLLECTION: Recollection.

TYRANT: I was waiting for that.

QUEEN OF CRIME: Crime. (*She reaches Luke, the Knight of Faith. The Hound of Hell tears him away leaving Pearl alone with Luke Clone.*)

CASTLE OF KNOWLEDGE: Knowledge. (*The Magician recovers with his Knowledge and ends Tyrant's Pawn of Waste.*)

PAWN OF INDOLENCE: Indolence. (*Spits on the board.*)

TYRANT: Check. (*He embraces Indolence.*)

KING OF ALL: King of All. (*Moves out of check by brushing the Pawn of Indolence off his feet.*)

QUEEN OF CRIME: Crime. (*Hypnotizes the Castle of Knowledge.*)

(*In a fury, Tyrant sends the Queen of Crime and the Knight of Slavery to attack the King of All. With a simple gesture of his hands the Magician summons the Queen of Love to protect Him.*)

QUEEN OF LOVE: Love.

KNIGHT OF SLAVERY: Slavery. (*The Hound of Hell races to Tyrant's side.*)

TYRANT: Check. (*He strokes the Hound who licks his hand.*)

KING OF ALL: King of All. (*He steps away.*)

KNIGHT OF SLAVERY: Slavery. (*The Hound of Hell leads Slavery to the kill.*)

QUEEN OF LOVE: Love. (*The Magician's Love shields his King.*)

QUEEN OF CRIME: Crime. (*Aiming her left hand with a triumphant smirk.*)

TYRANT: Check. (*The Hound of Hell howls while the Dancer kneels and prays.*)

KING OF ALL: King of All. (*Raising His eyes.*)

KNIGHT OF SLAVERY: Slavery. (*Takes Pawn of Humility.*)

TYRANT: Check again, brother. One more move to checkmate, and your King falls into the hands of the Great Beast. Get out of this one if you can.

KING OF DEGENERATION: WeWe. WeWe. (*Not a move.*)

TYRANT: What's the matter? You're trembling. Confess, the day belongs to the Antichrist. You're hopelessly trapped.

KING OF DEGENERATION: WeWe. WeWe.

TYRANT: Meanwhile, I'll take your Knight of Faith and run.

PEARL: Put him down.

TYRANT: Ha, ha!

PEARL: Put him down. He belongs to me.

MAGICIAN: The game's not finished.

TYRANT: But you are, brother. You've got 'til morning to make your move. If by the first cock crow, you're still stuck, the game is lost. Time is running out. You're in a terrible plight. The King of Degeneration is wearing down the Universe's life.

KING OF DEGENERATION: WeWe. (*Not a move.*)

TYRANT: Eternal darkness will always conquer the light. Now let's see your King of All, your Jesus Christ, get off the cross and put to flight the Antichrist. Ha, ha, ha, ha! A pleasant night! And remember, 'til the first cock crow.

(*Tyrant exits with Luke leaving Luke Clone in his place with Pearl.*)

MAGICIAN: We in an awful fix.

PEARL: What are we going to do?

MAGICIAN: I not know, little one, but somebody up there better like us or we dead.

PEARL: It's going to be a terrible night.

(*Blackout.*)

SCENE 5: THE MAGICIAN

LUKE: I'll never serve you!

TYRANT: Ha, ha. Why you fool. Look upon the Earth. What do you see? Billions of little grey mice, cannibals devouring one another in their greed.

LUKE: They're lost. Men would leave you in a moment if they could find the way out.

TYRANT: That's enough!

LUKE: That's why you build cities of terror and greed — to shut out the Light.

TYRANT: I'll silence you.

LUKE: But not the truth. I've seen a Power greater than you, Tyrant. If you want my life, take it. The God of Light will take care of my family.

TYRANT: You'd like to die. But I have a worse fate for you.

LUKE: I won't submit.

TYRANT: Big words, little man. You'll rot in the dungeon of despair. I'll crucify you on the rack of life, and grind you down on the teeth of time.

LUKE: You have no power over my immortal part. (*Laughing.*)

TYRANT: You nothing . . . !

LUKE: Yes. I am nothing and therefore I have everything.

TYRANT: You???!!! Ha, ha, ha, ha, ha.

LUKE: I.

TYRANT: We'll see what you say when you have to live with . . .

(*Family tableau on chessboard. Luke Clone replaces the Knight of Slavery and masquerades as Luke.*)

DESTINY: Son. (*To Luke Clone. She is playing the Pawn of Destiny.*)

FASHION: Darling.

DESTINY AND FASHION: You've come back!

TYRANT: Ha, ha. This is what all your talk amounts to . . . what all your dreams . . . your struggles . . . were for: the clone. The Second Creation that will wipe you off the Earth. Is your heart breaking? So much for your God of Light. Your life is forfeit. How does it feel to have lost your identity? Where are your friends now? I'll tell you what I'll do . . . Find someone who would die for you and you'll be free to go . . . Ha, ha. Not a one? What a pity.

MAGICIAN: Oh, I wouldn't say that.

TYRANT: You!

MAGICIAN: It ain't Aunt Sally. Release him. I take his place. Always at your service, brother. You have me. Let him go.

TYRANT: Not on your life.

MAGICIAN: A small price.

TYRANT: Do you think so brother? You're mine. (*To Luke.*) You're free.

LUKE: Not free until . . .
    (*Cock crow.*)

TYRANT: The first cock crow. (*To Magician.*) You're caught. The game is lost.

MAGICIAN: Not so fast, brother. (*Without yet moving her.*) The Pawn of Destiny.

LUKE: There's no such move!

MAGICIAN: Look again, brother . . . Queen of Love, bring on the morn.
    (*Heather, Queen of Love, raises her arm, holding a shining star which illuminates the chessboard.*)

PEARL: The Star of Love . . .

TYRANT: Take that light away!
    (*Magician snaps fingers; all freeze except the Magician and the children. The Magician calls them to him.*)

MAGICIAN: Tyrant. His black cloud still hanging over us.

HEATHER: Will it ever go away?

MAGICIAN: Up to you. You and all the kids. How you say? Your generation, this your task. It's your world. You got to fight hard for it. Fight hard enough and you win and make cloud go away.

PETER: We'll beat Tyrant.

HEATHER: And then we can go to the stars.

MAGICIAN: That's why I send you Hero.

HEATHER: Who is he?

MAGICIAN: You find out when he comes.

HEATHER: Do we know him?

MAGICIAN: Maybe.

HEATHER: I know who it is.

PEARL: No you don't. Nobody can know who it is. Right?

MAGICIAN: Well, he not Hero yet. But he will be.

PETER: What do you want us to do?

MAGICIAN: Swear you be his true friend to the death.

HEATHER: I swear.

PETER: I swear.

MAGICIAN: You give word. This your real oath now. On this, friend of Hero can never go back.

HEATHER: I promise.

PETER: I'll never forget.

(*End of freeze.*)

DESTINY: (*Making her move.*) Take THAT!! (*She slaps Luke Clone.*)

LUKE: (*Battles with his clone and kills it.*)
   I've killed the corpse that was myself.
   (*Blackout.*)

TYRANT: My God!

MAGICIAN: Careful brother, you're going to convert yourself.

SCENE 6: THE PARK

(*The park is empty and darker. Luke is seated at the bench where he first met the Magician. The children play silently. Pearl enters walking slowly toward Luke. She stops, draws up her veil. She and Luke gaze at one another.*)

MAGICIAN: (*Sings.*)*
   Balloons, balloons, to take you to Heaven . . .
   (*Tyrant, disguised as an ordinary person, draws near, studies them and moves away. Pearl withdraws. A few moments later Luke follows her with the children.*)

*Music p. 161

(*Singing.*)*
See how the morning puts darkness to flight.
At the invincible Sun's arising, ignorance flees.
What is shall always be.
What has never been can never be.
The Sun's all-seeing eye gladdens men's hearts.
His eternal light will always conquer night.
His herald of the morn puts Tyrant to flight.
(*Tyrant bows to the Magician. A moment of recognition.*)

*Music p. 163

CHESS GAME

CHESS GAME MOVES

White (Magician)	Black (Tyrant)	White	Black
1. P-K4	P-K4	31. P-B4	B-K3
2. P-KB4	P-Q4	32. N × P	Q-N3
3. P-KN3	B-KN5	33. B × QP	Q × B
4. B-QB4	P-QR4	34. QR-Q1	Q-K6
5. P-QR3	R-R3	35. N-Q4	P-QB4
6. N-K2	R-K3	36. N × B ch.	K-N1
7. N-Q4	R-Q3	37. R-Q6	N-B4
8. N-B5	B-K2	38. P-K5	R-Q2
9. P-N3	P-Q5	39. R × R	RP × P
10. B-N2	P-KB3	40. P-R5	N × RP
11. B-K2	P-R3	41. N × BP	N-N6
12. P-N4	N-R3	42. N-K6	Q × B
13. N-B3	R-R2	43. P-B5	N-Q7
14. N-N5	N-B4	44. P-B6	Q-K5 ch.
15. P-B3	P-QN3	45. K-N1	Q × KP
16. N-R7	P-R4	46. P-B7	N-Q3
17. R-QB1	N-KR3	47. R × N	N-B6 ch.
18. O-O	P-KN4	48. K-N2	P-R5
19. Q-N3	Q-N1	49. P-B8/Q ch.	K-R2
20. N-N5	K-B1	50. N-Q4	Q × P
21. K-R1	Q-R1	51. Q-N4	K-N2
22. P-Q3	P-B3	52. R-B2	Q × N
23. P-QR4	N-R3	53. R × P	P-R6 ch.
24. N-B7	N × N/7	54. K × P	Q × R/6
25. N × P	N-R3	55. Q-B5	N-N8 ch.
26. N-B5	Q-R2	56. K-N2	N-K7
27. P-Q4	P × QP	57. Q-R5	Q-B3 ch.
28. N × B	N-QB4	58. K-B1	N × P ch.
29. N-B8	P-N4	59. P × N	
30. N × R	N × Q		Draw

Pearl, Castle of Despair	Knight of Slavery	Bishop of Destruction	Queen of Crime	King of Degeneration	Bishop of Corruption	Knight of Ignorance	Castle of Disbelief
Pawn of Malice	Frank, Pawn of Blasphemy	Pawn of Spite	Pawn of Ridicule	Pawn of Folly	Pawn of Waste	Pawn of Idolatry	Pawn of Indolence
Pawn of Healing	Pawn of Work	Heather, Pawn of Prayer	Fashion, Pawn of Sadness	Pawn of Common Sense	Pawn of Laughter	Peter, Pawn of Humility	Destiny, Pawn of Destiny
Castle of Knowledge	Knight of Freedom	Bishop of Law	Queen of Love	Christ, King of All	Bishop of Creation	Luke, Knight of Faith	Castle of Recollection

MUSIC

BASED UPON RUSSIAN
AND LITHUANIAN FOLK SONGS

ADAPTED AND ARRANGED BY SHARON GANS
LYRICS BY A. F. HORN

Songs to be performed *a capella* or with guitar accompaniment.

BALLOONS

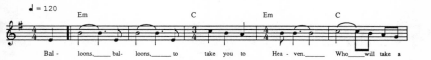

FOUR BROTHERS

bro-thers_____ to the Wars did go. One fell, and now they're three.

Two fell and now there're two. Three fell and now there's...

SO THE COUNTRY

♩ = 116

So the coun-try would-n't go up in flames. He sat on his ass and looked a- way. So the

coun-try would-n't go up in flames._____

ALONE AS A WAVE

♩ = 96

A - lone as a wave on the sea am I. A - lone___ as a wave___ on the sea.

ONE LITTLE CIGARETTE

♩ = 88

One lit-tle cig-a-rette. Where are you, one lit-tle cig-a-rette? I know you're 'round here some-where.

SKY SCENE

A piece such as "Events in Dense Fog" from
Brian Eno's *Music for Films* to be used.

HOW LONG MUST I WANDER

CHESS GAME

Underscore scene with ominous, sparse, pulsating music.
Gradually build dynamics and density to climax.

SEE HOW THE MORNING

164 THE MAGICIAN

Sun's all see - ing eye glad-dens men's hearts.___ His e- ter-nal light__ will al-ways con-quer night. His

her - ald of the morn puts Ty - rant_____ to flight.

I

A Play in Three Acts

1981

To Peter Demianovich Ouspensky

Behold, I send you into a world of wolves.
Be ye therefore as innocent as the dove,
And as wise as the serpent.

The Gospel of Matthew

For the children of the Earth
That they may protect themselves against
The powers that seek to destroy them.

CHARACTERS

Storyteller

The Magician

King Family
Daniel, son to Adam and Vanity
Topman
Destiny, his wife
Luke
Fashion, his wife

Paul, son to Matthew and Prudence
Peter, son to Luke and Fashion
Heather, daughter to Luke and Fashion

Joshua Man, son to Joseph and Martyr

Spirit of Adam King
Spirit of Matthew King
Spirit of Joseph Man

Vanity, his wife
Prudence, his wife
Martyr, his wife

Cardinal Common Tribute, friend to the King family

Grace

Higher Animals
Lion
Eagle
Horse
Elephant
Bull
Phoenix
Dove

Tyrant

Clones of the Big Ten, bankers and industrialists
Wolf
Fox
Snake
Weasel
Leech
Jackal
Shark
Pig
Crocodile
Vulture

Senator Moskins
Senator Jollit
Youngman of the State Department

Chorus
Children's Chorus

ACT I

SCENE 1: VENGEANCE

STORYTELLER: Out of the dark Abyss
  A solitary light shining in splendor
  Splits the womb of primordial night.
  All existence steps forth
  Hanging on a thread of light
  The worlds like golden lamps
  Turning round the boundless light.
  All Creation sings to God
  Every winged creature that frolics in the sky
  Every fish that leaps for joy,
  Lives in Heaven's clear transparent light.
  All the Earth is one delight.
  Now the music has stopped.
CHORUS: Why? Why?
STORYTELLER: Portents fill the sky
  And stars fall from the Heavens.
CHORUS: Where? Where?
STORYTELLER: The Earth bleeds, her waters
  Flooded with a crimson stain.
  Earthquakes devastate the land.
  All Creation cries out for deliverance.
  Now Tyrant rides the Beast of Shame.
  The Great Beast, up from the mouth of Hell.
CHORUS: Killers stalk the land,
  The time of the assassins is at hand.
  Who will save man from man?
  Oh for another Adam.
STORYTELLER: Oh for a solar hero to pluck fire from the sun,
  A light bringer to deliver us from darkness.
  (*Enter Daniel, Magician, Bull, Dove, Lion, Eagle, Horse and Elephant.*)

MAGICIAN: Now, my boy,* I think you ready to play your part. For ten years I teach you all the magic that you need. The rest is up to you.

DANIEL: I'm ready.

MAGICIAN: They can't see me. They'll see what you can do.

STORYTELLER: Who will play Adam in this sorry time?

DANIEL: I will.

CHORUS: A mere boy.

DANIEL: Who calls me boy? Did you cry "boy" when David saved you from Goliath? I feel like Adam, carrying the hump of Creation on my back, bent and bowed with the weight of a thousand generations. I was there with Abraham and Isaac, stood with Moses at the foot of Sinai, drove my chariot with Elijah to the throne of God, suffered all oppression and injustice with Isaiah. I fathered the race of man and I am their only begotten child. As Joshua I crossed the Jordan. Fought the Great Beast with Solomon and David. Thrown into the fiery furnace of God, I come again as Daniel. In every age I come with my coronets and my drums.

CHORUS: You're mad.

DANIEL: The maddest fellow that ever lived. Did ever a man live who wasn't mad? Why, to be alive is to be mad.

CHORUS: Who are you?

DANIEL: I am myself alone. Star-driven, wind-whipped, the blood of all Creation in my bones. Thunder fathered me. Wind mothered me. Fire and water nurtured me. I am one with the elements. And you? Who are you? Are you the Devil?

CHORUS: We are honest God-fearing men.

DANIEL: The same old lie. (*Enter Wolf and Fox.*) You've lived with the Devil all your lives. Direct me to him.

CHORUS: He's raving.

DANIEL: Where is Tyrant?

CHORUS: We know no such man.

DANIEL: You live with him, breathe his air, eat the food he gives you.

WOLF/FOX: We are honest God-fearing men.

DANIEL: Amen. Witnesses to the ritual murder of a King.
 (*Silence.*)

WOLF/FOX: That was a long time ago.

DANIEL: You saw my father murdered and yet you said nothing.

*This play has a score written for electronic and ancient oriental temple instruments.

WOLF/FOX: We know nothing of it.

DANIEL: He who can protest and does not is an accomplice to the crime.

CHORUS: We are innocent of your father's blood.

DANIEL: And of the blood of all the good men who followed after him? You are guilty. Your silence condemns you.

CHORUS: Oh Son of Adam! Go away. Leave us in peace. What do you want with us?

(*Daniel opens his mouth in a silent scream forming the word "revenge."*)

STORYTELLER: A son's revenge. That's my story. On a grey November day, on a mournful Sunday afternoon, a little boy not more than three comes to see his father buried by the men who knew him best. Who knows what goes on in the mind of a child when he sees his father slain . . .

DANIEL: (*To Chorus.*) I know you . . . you good and righteous men. (*Crying out.*) Where is that Old Slanderer and Hinderer, He Who Limps, that Old Devil, Tyrant?

CHORUS: He is hidden from our sight.

DANIEL: But not from mine. Out into the light, then.

TYRANT: Who dares to call my name?

DANIEL: The Son of Man.

TYRANT: What do you want with me?

DANIEL: To even an old score. I've come to give you fair warning. Your time is up.

SHARK: Shall I kill him now, Tyrant, or later?

TYRANT: No, let him live for a while. He amuses me. You're insolent.

DANIEL: He who made my inmost parts composed me equally of Arrogance and Wrath, Patience and Receptivity. Call it insolence if you will. My grandfather danced with you but broke his promise. I will fulfill it. Here's the contract. His sons in return for the world.

TYRANT: You.

DANIEL: Yes, I.

TYRANT: What can you do for me? Can you murder, loot, steal?

DANIEL: Mere hack work. Save it for your underlings. I understand you have designs on Heaven. I can arrange it.

TYRANT: What have you to offer me?

DANIEL: Your inmost desire. Thou shalt be God.

WOLF: Who are you?

DANIEL: You will soon know. Look carefully, Wolf, don't you recognize me?

WOLF: Adam King!

DANIEL: His son.

WOLF: He's risen from the dead!

FOX: Stay away from me you evil spirit!

DANIEL: You're speaking of yourself, Fox. You killed my father. Your lives are forfeit to me.

WOLF: We are the ruling class. We counselled him in war and peace. Why should we wish to hurt him?

DANIEL: Greed. You vultures, you jackals. All that took part in my father's murder shall die! None shall live.

SHARK: I'll kill him now, Tyrant.

TYRANT: No! He begins to interest me.

DANIEL: Why do you waste your time with this scum? They're worse than useless. I will deliver Heaven to you, or you to Heaven. Think, Tyrant, your deepest dream come true. That's my end of the bargain.

TYRANT: And mine?

DANIEL: I alone shall have authority over all the Earth.

TYRANT: The Earth is mine.

DANIEL: A mere speck of dirt. I can make the Universe yours.

TYRANT: Give me the contract.

DANIEL: (*Hands him the contract.*) You see, Tyrant, all conformable to law.

TYRANT: Hmmm.

WOLF: Don't sign it, Tyrant, it's a trick.

FOX: Look at the small print! Look at the small print!

TYRANT: Shut up!

DANIEL: Of course Wolf, Fox, and the rest shall be under my dominion — the dominion of man. That's in the contract, too.

WOLF: Never. We will never serve man. The Earth is ours and everything that's in it. You promised it to us, Tyrant.

TYRANT: Keep quiet, you fools. Can't you see I'm concentrating?

DANIEL: Why do you hesitate, Tyrant? They've tried and failed. Think of the eternal torment that awaits you if you miss your one chance, your only chance, to be God.

TYRANT: And if you fail?

DANIEL: I'll give you my life.

TYRANT: I'll sign! Give me the pen.

DANIEL: In blood.
WOLF/FOX: No, no, no!
TYRANT: Out of my way.
DANIEL: A blood covenant. Now you are bound to me, and I to you.
TYRANT: Now, show me the way.
DANIEL: Follow.

SCENE 2: ARLINGTON

HEATHER: He's come back. Oh, Peter, he's come back.
PETER: Who's come back?
HEATHER: Daniel.
PETER: Daniel! Here?
HEATHER: Yes, yes!
PETER: You've seen him?
  (*She nods.*)
  I must go to him at once.
HEATHER: Wait!
PETER: But does Mother know?
HEATHER: No. Only you and I.
PETER: The whole family must know.
HEATHER: They'll know soon enough. He's coming this evening.
PETER: To Father's party? The Presidential Ball?
HEATHER: Yes.
PETER: Ten years . . .
HEATHER: Ten years . . .
PETER: What does he look like?
HEATHER: Like a man absent from himself.
PETER: And you could recognize him after all these years?
HEATHER: There's only one Daniel.
PETER: How did you meet him and where?
HEATHER: I was sitting in the study watching the fire and then . . .
PETER: Yes . . .
HEATHER: He was there.
PETER: There?
HEATHER: I saw . . . his face.
PETER: His face?
HEATHER: Yes, in the fire.
PETER: An hallucination.
HEATHER: No, he was there, I tell you. It was a terrible shock. I

looked away. And when I turned back he was gone. Then I grew terribly restless. I began pacing back and forth. It was as if something stronger, something that couldn't be resisted was forcing me out of the house. Then I heard a voice . . .

PETER: Inside your mind?

HEATHER: I don't know . . . but the voice was saying, "Go to Arlington. Go to Arlington . . . "

PETER: Arlington!

HEATHER: Yes. And then I was out in the street half walking, half running and when I arrived . . .

(*She steps downstage into spotlight.*)

Daniel.

DANIEL: Hello, Cuz.

HEATHER: Daniel . . . ?

DANIEL: It's me, Heather.

HEATHER: Oh, Daniel, Daniel, Daniel. (*Embracing him.*) We all thought you were dead.

DANIEL: All?

HEATHER: I didn't believe it.

DANIEL: You got my message.

HEATHER: Yes.

DANIEL: I knew you'd come.

HEATHER: Oh where have you been? We turned the world upside down looking for you.

DANIEL: On a journey to the stars. I flew with the Great Eagle to the North Star. Traveled with the Bull to Orion.

HEATHER: Why didn't you take me with you?

DANIEL: One day I will.

HEATHER: We searched the Earth for you.

DANIEL: Why didn't you try Jupiter and Mars?

HEATHER: I did. But you weren't there either.

DANIEL: I was lost at sea. Captured by pygmies. Devoured by giants.

HEATHER: That's what Peter said . . . How did . . . you know?

DANIEL: It doesn't matter now. There's something I want you to do.

HEATHER: Anything.

DANIEL: Do you mean that?

HEATHER: You know I do.

DANIEL: Good. Alright then. Listen . . .

(*He puts his arm around her and they begin to walk upstage as the lights fade out.*)

As soon as you get home . . .

HEATHER: Yes . . .

DANIEL: You're to tell Peter of our meeting.

HEATHER: Alright.

DANIEL: And then, here's what I want you to do . . .

SCENE 3: THE PRESIDENTIAL BALL

(*Destiny is costumed as Abigail Adams; Luke as James Madison; Fashion as Dolly Madison; Peter as Benjamin Franklin; Paul as Abraham Lincoln; Heather as Mary Todd Lincoln; Senator Moskins as Alexander Hamilton; Senator Jollit as George Washington. Other guests.*)

(*Prudence and Vanity, costumed as two ladies, enter on either arm of Ben Franklin as he makes his entrance. The scene opens with a bare stage, revealing the Storyteller. Destiny, Luke and Fashion receive each guest. Tyrant, disguised as the butler.*)

STORYTELLER: Ladies and Gentlemen . . . The President of the United States, George Washington, accompanied by Benjamin Franklin, our Ambassador to France . . . Ladies and Gentlemen . . . I have the honor to present the President of the United States, Thomas Jefferson, accompanied by Alexander Hamilton, the Secretary of State . . . Ladies and Gentlemen, the President of the United States, Abraham Lincoln . . . Ladies and Gentlemen, may I present the President of the United States, William McKinley, accompanied by President James Garfield . . . Ladies and Gentlemen . . .

(*Enter Daniel. The Magician appears.*)

DANIEL: I'll announce myself, thank you. Ladies and Gentlemen, I'm the dead President you've heard so much about — killed before my time.

(*They all turn in consternation.*)

MOSKINS AS HAMILTON: Adam King!

DANIEL: Exactly.

JOLLIT AS WASHINGTON: What is this? A joke?

DANIEL: That remains to be seen.

MOSKINS AS HAMILTON: What bad taste.

DANIEL: For the dead to rise again? Hardly. I'm in good company, am I not? With Mr. Lincoln, Mr. McKinley, Mr. Garfield, all murdered.

LUKE AS MADISON: Murdered . . . !

DANIEL: Assassinated if you prefer. And by the same forces, I believe.

MOSKINS AS HAMILTON: This is ridiculous.

DANIEL: The truth can never be ridiculous. Only those who hide it.
  (*Heather nudges Peter, who is costumed as Ben Franklin.*)

PETER AS FRANKLIN: You spoke of forces, sir. What do you mean?

DANIEL: Why, the same forces you all work for. The Syndicate, the
  Company, the Trust. A man as wise as you should know these
  things, Mr. Franklin. Did you not warn us of the Great Beast in
  your day? Well, here we all are. Shall we dance?

VANITY: We shall do no such thing. Who are you?

DANIEL: I might very well ask you the same question. You are not
  what you pretend to be. Any of you.

PAUL AS LINCOLN: This is a masquerade.

DANIEL: Precisely. And we are all here for a little amusement, are we
  not? But at whose expense? What do you say, Mr. Madison?
  (*Gestures to Luke, who is dressed as James Madison.*)

MADISON: I say . . .

DANIEL: That they will never allow a King to become President of the
  United States.

LUKE AS MADISON: Adam . . .

DANIEL: Or if they will, he shall be shot down like a dog in the street.
  My brother and I shall testify to that. Indeed the nation — the
  whole world shall testify to it. What do you say, Mr. Lincoln?

PAUL AS LINCOLN: I say. Here! Here!

DANIEL: What you have meant to me, Mr. Lincoln, I can never say.
  You were the one man who stood in the Company's way. When
  they murdered you they murdered the South and gave the
  Republic a death blow from which it never fully recovered. But I'll
  say this for the Syndicate . . . they gave us both beautiful funerals.
  And McKinley, you signed your death warrant the day you moved
  to break up the big Trusts. And then of course there was that little
  matter of Cuba and the Spanish American War you tried to
  prevent. History does seem to repeat itself, doesn't it. We have a
  lot in common. And Garfield. The Trust again. Always the Trust.
  The Syndicate put you away for the same reason it put us all away.
  We went against them.

VANITY: Will you please leave. Why are you all standing around
  doing nothing? This man wasn't invited here.

DANIEL: I wasn't invited to this world but I came anyway.

VANITY: Will someone shut this man up!?

DANIEL: Since the day I was born, ladies like you have been trying to do just that, but they haven't succeeded.

VANITY: Who are you?

DANIEL: Someone closer to you than you can imagine.

VANITY: How dare you come here and give this cheap imitation of my husband.

DANIEL: No cheaper than the cheap imitation you gave of his wife.

VANITY: Imposter!

DANIEL: Ah, the truth is out. It's time to unmask. (*He does.*)

LUKE: Daniel!

VANITY: My baby!

DESTINY: Daniel! Daniel!

DANIEL: Uncle . . . Mother . . . Grandmother . . . All . . . Good evening.

VANITY: Oh, my God.

DANIEL: Why do you gape? I'm not a ghost. I'm flesh and blood.

DESTINY: You're back from the dead.

DANIEL: You can look at it that way.

VANITY: Oh Daniel, how could you do this to me?

DANIEL: What? Present myself to my family?

PAUL: This is perfect. You're my cousin.

DANIEL: Yes. Unless our mothers lied to us.

VANITY: Daniel!

PAUL: Fantastic.

LUKE: Does my brother come again in his son? Why, this boy must be a duplicate of my brother. Adam has come again in his son.

DESTINY: So fair a lad. The same proud chin. The same resolution.

LUKE: Do the dead return again in the living? Why, this boy has shamed me. And he scarce nineteen years. He's called me forth to battle and I begin to feel again my hot blood rising, healing the old wounds. Why, this must be a second coming.

WEASEL: Luke, we appreciate this little family get together, but why didn't you tell us?

JOLLIT: Yes, if you were going to stage this little family reunion you should have let us in on it.

DANIEL: What have we here?

LUKE: May I present my nephew, Daniel King. Senator Jollit . . . Secretary of the Treasury, Weasel . . . Senator . . .

DANIEL: Moskins. Former Secretary of War, Crocodile. And

Youngman of the State Department.

CROCODILE: You're well informed, young man.

DANIEL: One could hardly fail to be when it comes to men of your stature.

JOLLIT: You flatter us.

DANIEL: One must keep an eye on hypocrisy.

CROCODILE: Hypocrisy . . . ?

DANIEL: Of course one could hardly do without it.

CROCODILE: Without it?

DANIEL: Hypocrisy. It's what makes the world go round.

CROCODILE: How are we to take your meaning, young man?

DANIEL: Any way you like. I presume you intend to do the same job for my uncle as you did for my father.

MOSKINS: We intend to try.

DANIEL: Then he'll soon be in his grave. They say that all politicians are whores.

LUKE: Daniel, I think . . .

DANIEL: Of course, I've never believed that.

WEASEL: Of course not.

DANIEL: Just most of them.

MOSKINS: Luke, I think we'd best be . . .

DANIEL: Of course a politician's job is to serve power. And power is a strange creature to please. One must be properly subservient, one might say almost servile. One must be careful not to offend, shake the boat — disturb the status quo. There's no need for excessive loyalty. In fact, there's no need at all — for loyalty or honor of any kind. And if one gives his allegiance to a man, and he loses power — is murdered for example, why then one simply switches his allegiance to those who murdered him — the new power, that is. It's all very interesting. But these are the rules of power. Wouldn't you say so, gentlemen? And of course one writes books filled with lies celebrating the former, deceased President — preferably best sellers. And not one word of truth . . . not one word of truth.

WEASEL: I think we've heard enough.

DANIEL: You haven't even begun to hear.

MOSKINS: Let's go, Weasel.

DANIEL: What's the matter? Isn't the liquor good enough for you? It's free.

LUKE: Daniel!

WEASEL: Young man, if it weren't for the respect I owe your

family . . .

DANIEL: You'd kill me like you killed my father.

MOSKINS: If it weren't for your extreme youth I'd . . .

DANIEL: If it weren't for your extreme age I'd smash your face in. Swine! Get out of this house.

LUKE: Daniel, what the hell are you doing!?

DANIEL: Uncle, what the hell are you doing?

LUKE: Gentlemen, I'm . . .

MOSKINS: Never mind. We're going.

(*Cabinet members exit.*)

LUKE: This is outrageous conduct. You should be ashamed.

DANIEL: It is you who should be ashamed, Uncle.

LUKE: I . . . ?

DANIEL: For dealing with such time-servers.

LUKE: I needed those men, Daniel.

DANIEL: You need nothing but your own integrity. Fight. Stand up and tell the nation the truth. No man is ever alone if his cause is just.

FASHION: Are you crazy, Daniel? After all your uncle's been through . . . The truth! They'd kill him!

DANIEL: I see in our day men play Judas or Pilate. Either they betray the truth or wash their hands of it. Since my father's death the world's become a foul contagion. And no one to mourn for him.

LUKE: Why, the whole world mourns for him.

DANIEL: But none to take action. Hiding! Hiding! The whole world's in hiding! This mealy-mouthed generation that talks in whispers but cannot act. Oh, to have the blood of the men who killed my father!

LUKE: Violence will not bring back the dead.

DANIEL: Must evil always win the day? In the whole history of the Earth have a dozen battles been won for good?

PRUDENCE: Why yes, of course.

DANIEL: Do you think so, Aunt Prudence? Acquaint me with it. It seems I've been a sluggard in my studies.

FASHION: (*To Luke.*) I want you to withdraw.

LUKE: I can't do that.

HEATHER: Please don't run, Daddy.

PETER: They don't want us. Don't run, Dad. Waiting . . . waiting . . . always waiting for the expected bullet that never comes.

DANIEL: What will you do, Uncle?

LUKE: I don't know.

DANIEL: You'll join the fashionable conspiracy of silence . . . Is that it?

LUKE: I couldn't speak.

DANIEL: You should have spoken. You must speak now! It's your duty.

PETER: No!

DESTINY: His duty is to his family. To you . . . to all of us.

DANIEL: His duty is to the truth. First . . . last . . . and always.

VANITY: You're inhuman, Daniel.

DESTINY: No, not inhuman, Vanity . . . He's just like his father.

FASHION: The truth, the truth. Is that all you know? See how far the truth will get you against Caesar . . . against the power of an armed state.

DANIEL: Try pretence. See where that leads you.

DESTINY: There are worse fates.

DANIEL: Are there, Grandmother? Look at us. We, who should have been the leaders of our generation. To what have we come? We've let them break us.

PRUDENCE: That's not true!

DANIEL: No? You can't live on booze and drugs forever! Look at your own son. Paul's a cynic, his life lost in trivia. And you, Aunt Fashion. What has your son become? Peter has no reason to live or die.

PRUDENCE: You're safe.

DANIEL: Safe!

FASHION: Yes, safe in a dark, cruel world.

DESTINY: We've seen to it that you all have survived.

DANIEL: As what? As mush for the Devil. As cannon fodder for Tyrant. Survived as ciphers in a universal bankruptcy of nature . . . where birth and death are just a clink of the cash register announcing new candidates for the Universal Church of Matter run by the Wolf and the Fox. This is what your philosophy of safety first comes to. No thank you. No.

PRUDENCE: The young man of twenty who sets out to change the world will find at fifty that the world has changed him.

DANIEL: A man creates his own world, Aunt Prudence.

FASHION: Oh Daniel, none of us are free.

DANIEL: What shall we call this? Advice from the dead to the younger generation? For this counsel of Fashion and Prudence much thanks. But I'd rather swim with sharks, or cross swamps with crocodiles. They're ruthless enough to know what they want. But your genteel philosophy will make us their prey. I've misjudged you, Uncle Luke. I had no idea what you were up against. One man is no match against such an array of women. You've held your own. You're a hero after all.

VANITY: Listen to me, Daniel. Even if your Uncle Matthew and Uncle Luke had spoken out and the people had believed them, the powers that be would have brought the military onto the streets and declared martial law. And things would have been much worse. Much worse.

DANIEL: No! Better. At least the American people wouldn't be living in this Disneyland of terror and flattery. Their enemy would be out in the open. They'd be able to fight, instead of living in this schizophrenic horror of now you see it — now you don't.

PRUDENCE: When Matthew died the people knew! They knew! And what did they do about it? Nothing.

DANIEL: Sheep must have shepherds. Or the wolves will eat them.

PRUDENCE: And what if they want to be eaten? Do you have any idea what baseness lies in the heart of these bleating sheep?

DANIEL: It has nothing to do with what sheep want. It has to do with the order of Creation. The rightness of things.

VANITY: And was it right for our husbands to die . . . only to have the people betray them?

DANIEL: What did you expect the people to do?

FASHION: Rise up and avenge them!

DANIEL: When you yourselves were afraid to do so?

DESTINY: We had our family to think of.

DANIEL: And the people did not?

FASHION: No, not in the same way.

DESTINY: You don't know what it was like, Daniel. You were just a babe.

VANITY: It was as if we were hostages in a foreign country, surrounded by the very men who . . .

DESTINY: Vanity! . . . Never mind.

VANITY: What does it all matter, anyway? Our lives are of such little account.

DANIEL: But . . . of account!

VANITY: Who knows? One day we'll all be dead.

DANIEL: Vanity. My mother has taught me all is vanity. Be that as it may, I know what I must do.

DESTINY: What?

DANIEL: You shall see.

FASHION: Why did he have to come back from the dead?

(*Exit Daniel and Magician.*)

SCENE 4: THE COVENANT

(*Daniel discovered on stage. Heather and Peter enter. Heather places a bouquet of flowers on Adam King's grave, as does Peter on Matthew King's grave. Paul enters a few moments later, pauses before Adam King's grave, then goes to his father Matthew's grave. Tyrant, disguised as honor guard.*)

PAUL: (*Softly.*) Hello, Dad . . .

HEATHER: (*Softly.*) Uncle Adam . . . (*A quiet sunny day in April . . . The birds twittering. Slight wind turning up the leaves. A long silence.*)

HEATHER: We're all here.

DANIEL: (*Looking out into the distance.*) Not all. One of us is missing. (*They turn and look in the direction Daniel is looking. Silence. A figure enters and stands at the edge. He looks at everyone. They look at him, then to Daniel.*)

JOSHUA: Daniel King . . .

DANIEL: Joshua Man . . .

JOSHUA: Here I am.

DANIEL: Yes. Paul . . . Senator Matthew King's son. Peter and Heather . . . Senator Luke King's son and daughter.

(*They all nod. Silence. Daniel picks up some dirt and, slowly sifting it through his fingers, he lets it fall back to Earth.*)

DANIEL: Our fathers died for this . . . Some say it's not much to die for, just a handful of dust not worth the trouble. But they didn't feel that way. And now their blood is mingled forever with this good Earth they loved so much. Sometimes I think that every flower that grows, each tree that blossoms . . . has a little bit of them in it. Because it's their spirit that's kept this Earth going. They, and millions of good men and women before and after them who've made it a fit place for human beings to live. I remember one day my father took me on his knee and showed me the glory of the Earth. And as he held me in his arms he whispered that everything was one. The Earth . . . the sky . . . all the men and women . . .

and children . . . one. I never forgot that. As I grew to manhood I thought that was a fair thing to live and die for. I know we all have memories of our fathers . . . terrible memories . . . of the evil men who killed them, and are hurting them now. But we're not children anymore. We must finish the work they set out to do.

JOSHUA: Their work is long gone, man. Forget it. You're a beautiful dude, but you're about fifteen years too late. In my daddy's case, twelve years too late. What they did to him I'll never . . . Man, you realize sometimes I wake up in the middle of the night screaming?

HEATHER: Oh, Joshua, so do I.

DANIEL: Unless we begin to fight, our generation will be the last to know freedom on this Earth and our life will turn into a permanent nightmare.

JOSHUA: Fight! How, man! How?! They got all the guns . . . the media . . . all the power. What've we got? Nothing!

DANIEL: We've got ourselves.

JOSHUA: Ourselves? That's nothing.

DANIEL: In every generation the Great Beast is fought. And in every generation he keeps striking back. And in every generation he must be fought again. Woe to the generation that fails to do that.

JOSHUA: What are you? God's holy messenger? It's too late. They killed my daddy, man. And for me the world will never be the same.

DANIEL: The history of . . .

JOSHUA: History's a deaf mute crying out for justice. All this suffering and not a word from Heaven yet. Oh yes, I used to wait for messages from Heaven. I used to know there was something I had to do. Now I don't want to hear it. The world's gone. The country's gone. And we're gone, man. There ain't nothing left.

DANIEL: Remember . . .

JOSHUA: I don't want to remember. If I remember I'll go mad. I'll kill the men who killed my daddy. And I ain't supposed to do that. I'm a clergyman's son. I'm not supposed to believe in violence. I'm not supposed to murder. Just sit back and let me and my friends be murdered instead.

DANIEL: Twenty brave and free men can change the world.

JOSHUA: You go out and find them, man.

DANIEL: Never ask anyone else to do what you can't do yourself.

JOSHUA: Oh, that's perfect.

PETER: He means we have to make ourselves into those kinds of men.

JOSHUA: I know what he means, but to what purpose? To get our heads blown off like our daddies did?

DANIEL: Sometimes a man has to die for what he believes in.

JOSHUA: I don't have to do nothin'. I don't have to go out and prove I'm a man. I don't have to see my woman's heart broken like my mama's was when they killed my daddy. I'm leaving.

DANIEL: You'll be back.

JOSHUA: You're crazy. I ain't never coming back.

DANIEL: You'll be back.

JOSHUA: (*As he turns his back and starts to go.*) I don't have to . . . I . . . don't have . . . to. (*Daniel gestures and the spirit of Joshua's father enters Joshua and speaks through him. Through the following dialogue, the actor plays both roles: the spirit of his father and himself as a little boy.*)

SPIRIT OF JOSEPH MAN: We must all learn to live together as brothers, or we will all perish as fools. We are tied together in the single garment of destiny, caught in an inescapable network of mutuality. And whatever affects one directly, affects all indirectly. For some strange reason I can never be what I ought to be until you are what you ought to be. And you can never be what you ought to be until I am what I ought to be.[1] (*Freeze; Joshua is thrown back in time to eight years of age; enter his mother, Martyr.*)

JOSHUA: Mama. Mama, they're gonna kill Daddy. They put the dogs on him again. Don't let them kill Daddy!

MARTYR: Hush now, son. Your Daddy's got work to do. You don't want him to see you crying like this. You got to be a brave boy. Otherwise you hurt your Daddy's heart.

JOSHUA: Daddy, you're not gonna die. Promise me you're not going to die.

SPIRIT OF JOSEPH MAN: Why you rascal, you want to make a liar out of your Daddy? Everybody's gotta die sooner or later.

JOSHUA: Oh, Daddy, no.

SPIRIT OF JOSEPH MAN: Why, dying's not bad, son. Not being able to live, that's bad.

JOSHUA: What do you mean, Daddy?

SPIRIT OF JOSEPH MAN: Why, any man who isn't willing to die for what he loves isn't fit to live.

(*End of freeze; Joshua, returning to the present, looks at Daniel.*)

JOSHUA: Who are you?

DANIEL: I am my father's son.

JOSHUA: Then I'm your man.

(*They embrace.*)

STORYTELLER: Ah, fathers and sons,
   Locked in mortal combat,
   In joy and sadness,
   In hatred and in love.

PAUL: I hardly dare to believe what I see, being a natural coward . . .

HEATHER: Hush, Paul.

PAUL: It's true. But before you enlist me in your cause, Daniel . . .

(*Both Daniel and Joshua whirl and say:*)

DANIEL AND JOSHUA: Our cause!

PAUL: Alright, call it what you will. Our cause . . . my cause . . . the cause . . . whatever. I don't think you realize, Daniel, that events unfold independently of man. All the good will in the world won't change that. We have no real control over our destiny. Everything's inevitable. My father had no choice. I was there. I saw it. Given what he was he hadn't a choice in the world. He was totally helpless.

DANIEL: Given the man he was . . . yes. But he didn't have to be the man he was.

PAUL: What!?

DANIEL: You heard me.

PAUL: No, no. That's ridiculous. Of course he had to be . . . the man . . . he couldn't . . . he couldn't . . . he had no choice . . . no choice . . . (*At Daniel's gesture, the spirit of Paul's father enters Paul and speaks through him.*)

SPIRIT OF MATTHEW KING: If we fail to dare, if we do not try, the next generation will harvest the fruit of our indifference; a world we did not want — a world we did not choose — but a world we could have made better. You have been lifted into a tiny, sunlit island while all around you lies a dark ocean of human misery, injustice, violence, and fear . . . In your hands, not with presidents or leaders, is the future of your world. Some men see things as they are and say, why? I dream things that never were and say, why not?[2]

(*Freeze; Paul is thrown back in time to ten years of age; enter his mother, Prudence.*)

PAUL: He knows he's going to die. And he's doing it anyway. Why, Mother, why?

PRUDENCE: Do you want your father to be a different man than he is, son?

PAUL: Oh, but his eyes, death is in his eyes. I can't bear to look at him. He's so scared. And yet he's running anyway. Stop him! You must stop him!

PRUDENCE: No one can stop him.

PAUL: Why?

PRUDENCE: Because that's the kind of man he's chosen to be. Quiet. Here he comes now.

PAUL: Don't do it, Dad. Don't run.

SPIRIT OF MATTHEW KING: I want to tell you something, Paul. Just before your Uncle Adam died, he asked me what I would do if anything happened to him. I said I would carry on. Do you understand?

PAUL: But why you, Dad?

SPIRIT OF MATTHEW KING: Because I made a promise one day to the man I most loved. And it's a promise I must keep . . . or I wouldn't be the man I am.

PAUL: Even at the cost of your life?

SPIRIT OF MATTHEW KING: Yes.

PAUL: You'd leave Mom and the kids and me for a lousy promise?

SPIRIT OF MATTHEW KING: If I have to, Paul. Pray God I don't have to.

PAUL: I'll never forgive you if you do.

SPIRIT OF MATTHEW KING: One day you'll understand, son.

PAUL: I'll never forgive . . . never forgive . . . never forgive. (*End of freeze; a moment of shocked self-perception. He whirls around, crying.*) Daddy, forgive me. (*He breaks down over tombstone on his father's grave.*) I don't know if I should kill you or . . . (*He embraces Daniel.*)

DANIEL: Well, Peter . . .

PETER: Oh Daniel, don't you understand? Our generation's guilty of having seen too much evil.

STORYTELLER: How do you break man's spirit?
  Get a man to betray his comrade
  To betray what he loves.
  That's how you break man's spirit.
  And a country?
  It is the same.

PETER: The people loved our fathers and betrayed them. They should have stood up and fought for them to the very last man, fought to bring their assassins to justice.

JOSHUA: Justice — that's a word that hasn't been heard around here for a long time.

PETER: And what did they do? They just laid down and died. That was our last chance and we blew it.

HEATHER: A few fought.

PETER: And were murdered. What chance have the few ever had against the many?

JOSHUA: The list of the dead is long. Do you think God weeps for his martyred heroes?

(*Enter Chorus in funeral procession.*)

CHORUS: He who stretches out his hand to help another is struck down.
The man who helps his neighbor will be destroyed himself.
Better to remain indifferent.
Unthinking.
Uncaring . . .
Mute . . .

PETER: Now we can't even look one another in the eyes, for we've broken faith with what we love. To hell with this world of lies that makes me want to vomit . . . lies that make me want to die.

DANIEL: Every man has a God. Woe to the man who has a false one.

PETER: Then it's easy for you. For the rest of us life's an intolerable hell.

DANIEL: Fight your way out of Hell.

PETER: In these desperate times, when men are lucky if they're not murdered in their sleep?

DANIEL: We're here to redeem the time. I wasn't born to be time's slave.

PETER: The world will break you if you stand against it.

DANIEL: Will it?

PETER: Yes, as it's breaking my father now.

CHORUS: Give up . . .
Give in . . .
Get out . . .

DANIEL: I was born to bend the world to my will.

CHORUS: Give up . . .
Give in . . .
Get out . . .

DANIEL: The same old cry.

CHORUS: The world is ours, and all that's in it.

DANIEL: The Earth is the Lord's and all that's in it belongs to Him. I won't give it up to dehumanized men.

PETER: Aren't you afraid to die?

JOSHUA: A man has to fight for what he loves.

DANIEL: I am more afraid to go before my Creator and say I cringed on my knees like a dog before the enemy of man.

PETER: But the enemy of man is man himself.

DANIEL: Then you know what you must do.

PETER: What? What?

DANIEL: Redeem your promise.

PETER: I made no promise.

DANIEL: You made a promise a long time ago. Remember.

PETER: No!

DANIEL: Remember.

PETER: No, I . . . (*Daniel gestures. Freeze; Peter and Heather are thrown back in time to eleven and seven years of age. Enter Magician singing.*)

MAGICIAN: Balloons, balloons, to take you to Heaven.* Who will take a ride to Heaven?
You know the world a very dark place.

PETER: Tyrant.

MAGICIAN: His black cloud still hanging over us.

HEATHER: Will it ever go away?

MAGICIAN: Up to you. You and all the kids. How you say? Your generation, this your task. It's your world. You got to fight hard for it. Fight hard enough and you win and make black cloud go away.

PETER: We'll beat Tyrant.

HEATHER: And then we can go to the stars.

MAGICIAN: That's why I send you hero.

PETER: A hero!

HEATHER: What do you want us to do?

MAGICIAN: Swear you be his true friend to the death.

HEATHER: I swear.

PETER: I swear.

MAGICIAN: You give word. This your real oath now. On this, friend of hero can never go back.

PETER: I give you my word. I'll never forget . . . Never forget . . .

*Music p. 234

Never for . . .

HEATHER: (*Whirling around.*) It's you!

MAGICIAN: Yes, little one. It's me. (*She goes into his arms.*)

DANIEL: Godfather ..

MAGICIAN: My boy.

PAUL: Godfather? What's going on here?

JOSHUA: Stick around.

PETER: Now I remember! You're the hero!

(*The spirit of his father enters Daniel and speaks through him.*)

SPIRIT OF ADAM KING: We shall pay any price, bear any burden, meet any hardship, support any friend, oppose any foe to assure the survival and the success of liberty. Only a few generations have been granted the role of defending freedom in its hour of maximum danger. I do not shrink from this responsibility — I welcome it.[3]

HEATHER: (*As they all turn back to Daniel.*) Daniel? Daniel?

(*He and the Magician have disappeared.*)

He's gone.

ACT II

SCENE 1: THE DOVE

STORYTELLER: And it came to pass that all humanity fell under the shadow of Tyrant, and there was every abomination in the heart of man. Fathers turned against their sons; daughters against their mothers; brothers and sisters became strangers and murderers of one another. All had the mark of the Great Beast beween their eyes. The Prophet of Blasphemy broadcast throughout the land; the Great Whore laughed. All were bound for death. Fantasy ate their brains . . . in the City of Man . . . in the City of Depravity . . . in the Land of Dreams.

DANIEL: And it was unbearable and I cried to Heaven.

TYRANT: The Sun! The Sun! You promised me the Sun! Give me the Sun! Pluck it out from the sky.

DANIEL: The Eye of God. You shall have it, Tyrant. And sooner than you know.

TYRANT: Blind Divinity! Limping putrescence. I shall blot You out. None shall ever utter your Name. The world must be prepared for my son. The Antichrist.

CHORUS: Where shall we hide ourselves from the Wrath of God?
We ran to the Earth, but the Earth would not hide us.
We ran to the Valley, but the Valley would not hide us.
We ran to the Rock, but the Rock would not hide us.

STORYTELLER: Oh Man, where shall you go?

DANIEL: And I was lost in the Great City of myself. And I ran out into the street and saw that all men were asleep. And they were like little children who had lost their way . . . whining and whimpering and crying out. And I saw that all pretended to know the Way. And I turned away from their sleep of death so I wouldn't hear the lament to Heaven that stifled in their throats. And every day was the torment of death and every day a drop of blood spilled from my heart.

STORYTELLER: Who shall escape the Wrath of God?

TYRANT: None shall escape.

(*Exit Tyrant.*)

DANIEL: This is damnation.

MAGICIAN: The Judgment of God.

DANIEL: But this is Hell.

MAGICIAN: You must go ever deeper, deeper into Hell; into the darkness of life until your little light is snuffed out.

DANIEL: Or I raise Hell itself into the Light. How long must I live in the belly of this monster whose greed and lust devour the world; this old dragon that swallows the Light of Heaven. How long must I play this double game . . . must I pander to him with my left hand while with my right I seek to slay him . . . must I lie and cheat, mock and slander, murder and advance, like all the rest; in the service of this blasphemous creature? When will it end?

MAGICIAN: When eternity and time are one. Now, my boy, there is a Way narrow and difficult. The Way of Death.

DANIEL: A life for a life.

MAGICIAN: Yes.

DANIEL: I'll take it. I've studied this Tyrant from every angle. He seems invulnerable.

MAGICIAN: You must bring him into the Light.

DANIEL: It's impossible. He lives in the Castle of Time.

MAGICIAN: You must trick him.

DANIEL: How? Nothing seems to work.

MAGICIAN: Ask Heather.

DANIEL: Heather?

MAGICIAN: She will tell you.

(*Lights darken.*)

(*Lights up.*)

HEATHER: What?

DANIEL: He said you would tell me.

HEATHER: He's afraid of the Light.

DANIEL: Nothing more?

HEATHER: I don't know. Unless . . . Unless . . .

DANIEL: Yes?

HEATHER: Once I played a game for Life and Death. And I was the Pawn of Prayer and I became the Queen of Love. Oh, it's all mixed up . . .

DANIEL: Go on.

HEATHER: It was such a long time ago . . . . I remember now. I brought

on the Morn. Oh, but it was more than that . . . I raised my arm
(*she does so as she tells him the story*) and in my hand was the Star
. . . and he went . . . blind.

DANIEL: What kind of star?

HEATHER: (*Looks at him.*) The Star of Love.
(*Heather exits.*)

DANIEL: My heart is strangely troubled. Oh, for the power of Heaven
to wrest the Earth from this monster.
(*The Dove appears.*[4])

DOVE: If you would gain the riddle,
Follow me. Follow me.
There is a man.
　His head is Gold
　His chest is Silver
　His legs are Brass
　His feet are Clay
Who conquers him, conquers all.[5]
If you would know the riddle,
Follow me.

DANIEL: The Dove! The Dove!

DOVE: Follow me. Follow me.

DANIEL: Don't weep, Dove. I will follow, perhaps you will lead me to
the Throne of God.

MAGICIAN: And then?

DANIEL: I will do what you've always taught me, I will kneel and ask.
(*Lights down. Music begins.* * *Grace enters. She is represented by
two women: one is dancing, the other speaks and sings.*)
Is it Heaven?

GRACE: It is I, Grace.

DANIEL: Oh, come to me.

STORYTELLER: Her kiss healed his mouth.

DANIEL: Stay with me.

STORYTELLER: All through the night he held her and in the morning
he would not let her go.

GRACE: I must go.

DANIEL: Stay with me always.

GRACE: You will forget me.

DANIEL: Never. One never forgets what they love.

*Music p. 234

GRACE: Swear.

DANIEL: I swear.

GRACE: Yes, all men make a vow and then they forget. You will forget, too.

DANIEL: There have been others.

GRACE: I come to any man who needs me.

DANIEL: You're a whore.

GRACE: You see? You don't want me.

DANIEL: I want you for myself alone.

GRACE: All men become brothers by possessing me.

DANIEL: Brothers . . .

GRACE: Your deepest wish, and you don't understand. I will go.

DANIEL: No, no. It doesn't matter. Nothing matters as long as you're with me.

GRACE: But you don't understand.

DANIEL: I will understand. I will. But give me something to remember you.

GRACE: Take this ring. It belongs to my Father.

DANIEL: Your Father?

GRACE: The Nameless One. The King of Beauty. If you want me, you must swear eternal allegiance to Him.

DANIEL: What must I do?

GRACE: Fight for Him at the cost of your life.

DANIEL: Blessed Lady, give me the ring.

GRACE: It will bring you much trouble and sorrow.

DANIEL: Nothing of yours can bring me sorrow. Give me the ring.
    (*Daniel dances with one Grace while the other Grace sings.*)

GRACE: It is a ring of fire,
    A ring of gold.
    He who wears it
    Shall become a man of gold.
    I shall walk by your side,
    And no harm shall befall you.
    But if you break faith with me
    I shall be gone.

If the ring once leaves your finger,
You shall never see me again.

But if you pass all the tests

That await you . . .
I'll be yours . . . forever.

And then you can never lose me. And . . .

DANIEL: And will the Dove stop weeping? And will the Phoenix return?[6]

(*Grace nods yes.*)

And will I find my father?

GRACE: If these are the three wishes in your heart.

DANIEL: Yes. Yes. I'll have the ring.

GRACE: You'll have the ring?

DANIEL: Give it to me.

GRACE: As you wish, it's yours. One last thing. When you meet your Adversary you must pray for him.

DANIEL: Pray for him?

(*Grace nods and exits. Lights up.*)

MAGICIAN: What does Heaven say?

DANIEL: I swore an eternal vow to Heaven that I'd cast this Tyrant into Hell. And now Heaven tells me I must pray for him. Pray for this foul monster that murdered my father and is destroying the Earth! Yes, I'll pray for him, after I kill him. I'll encase this Darkness in a bubble of light and send him reeling across the universe in solitary confinement. Or failing that, I'll trick him into the Light and no darkness or trace of darkness shall be left behind.

MAGICIAN: Woe to the man who disobeys Heaven.

DANIEL: Woe to the man who disobeys himself. My father was the prince of peace. His countenance shone as the noonday sun, his inmost parts made for rule. His mind and passion blended in such sweet harmony that men heard angels' voices as he passed. He tuned the discords in men's hearts and made music in their souls. He healed the hostile factions of the Earth and made the warring elements sue for peace, 'til he was struck down and all the world wept. My father's blood cries out for vengeance. We shall see whether the Fox and the Wolf shall inherit the Earth, or Man. Not Heaven or Hell shall stop me.

MAGICIAN: And God?

DANIEL: I'll spit in His eye if He gets in my way.

MAGICIAN: You big devil. Same blood as Grandfather.

DANIEL: Same blood.

MAGICIAN: Maybe is bad blood, huh?

DANIEL: Blood will have blood.

MAGICIAN: Well, if this is the way you feel, maybe is time you see Grandfather. Maybe he help you.

DANIEL: Where is he?

MAGICIAN: In limbo.

DANIEL: Take me to him.

(*Magician nodding, snaps his fingers.*)

Grandfather . . .

SPIRIT OF TOPMAN KING: Daniel . . . little Daniel.

DANIEL: I'm grown now, Grandfather.

SPIRIT OF TOPMAN KING: Yes, grown.

DANIEL: You can rest in peace now. I will avenge my father. I will avenge you all. Give me your blessing.

SPIRIT OF TOPMAN KING: No! No! Not vengeance! What have I done? Will I never be forgiven?

DANIEL: Grandfather . . .

SPIRIT OF TOPMAN KING: Find another way.

DANIEL: But, I thought . . .

SPIRIT OF TOPMAN KING: You will break your father's heart. He will have no rest, nor I, nor any of us 'til there is peace in your heart.

DANIEL: Peace?

SPIRIT OF TOPMAN KING: And I . . .

DANIEL: Yes . . .

SPIRIT OF TOPMAN KING: You are my forgiveness, Daniel.

DANIEL: Your forgiveness?

SPIRIT OF TOPMAN KING: For all my crimes. If you are lost, then I am lost.

DANIEL: Lost . . . ?

SPIRIT OF TOPMAN KING: Promise me, promise me . . . you will find another way.

DANIEL: Grandfather . . .

SPIRIT OF TOPMAN KING: Another way . . . another way.

DANIEL: I must have your blessing!! Grandfather!

MAGICIAN: He's gone.

SCENE 2: WISDOM

(*Five years later.*)

DANIEL: As long as Tyrant casts his spell over humanity he has my father — all our fathers — in his hand. For they believed in man.

Their destiny is connected with humanity.

HEATHER: And we, the grandchildren of Destiny?

DANIEL: Shall correct her mistake.

HEATHER: Change our fates?

DANIEL: Yes. We shall no longer be in bondage to our flesh, but shall follow the spirit of our fathers 'til we redeem the flesh, the world and the Devil.

PAUL: Redeem the Devil!?

HEATHER: It must be so.

DANIEL: Once he, too, was in Heaven and fell from Grace.

PAUL: Then the Devil has been avenging himself on God. But how can we be sure he exists?

DANIEL: Look into your own mind.

HEATHER: Then if we transform our mind, we transform the Devil . . .

DANIEL: Into his opposite.

JOSHUA: Great Lucifer, the brightest star in Heaven before the Fall.

TYRANT: (*Calling.*) Daniel King!

(*Exit Peter, Paul, Joshua and Heather.*)

DANIEL: Here am I.

TYRANT: So young and so attentive.

DANIEL: Always at your service, Tyrant.

TYRANT: Yes, but why?

DANIEL: You know the secrets of Heaven and Earth.

TYRANT: You flatter me.

DANIEL: You're too modest. It's not every day one gets a chance to study with the Devil.

TYRANT: An apt pupil, I see. Like your grandfather.

DANIEL: If you like. My grandfather was ever the child of Fortune. However, I am the child of Wisdom. I'd gladly sell my soul to the Devil to study at Wisdom's feet.

TYRANT: A dangerous game.

DANIEL: And buy it back again with the knowledge that I've purchased.

TYRANT: Ha, ha, ha. You amuse me.

DANIEL: As long as we understand each other.

TYRANT: We do.

DANIEL: Question. How much time does humanity have left on the Earth?

TYRANT: Which humanity? There have been many. I've seen them come and go.

DANIEL: All have failed?

TYRANT: All.

DANIEL: If humanity succeeds you're out of business.

(*Tyrant smiles.*)

There is an ancient legend that the animals were once our brothers.

TYRANT: Who told you that?

DANIEL: Is it true?

(*Tyrant smiles.*)

Why has humanity always failed?

TYRANT: All flesh is grass.

DANIEL: It appears so . . . and yet . . . (*Flashing the ring in Tyrant's eye.*)

TYRANT: The emerald stone! Where did you find it?

DANIEL: Do you like the ring? Take it.

TYRANT: No!

DANIEL: What's the matter?

TYRANT: Don't come near me. The ring . . . Where did you get it?

DANIEL: A friend. Do you know its history?

TYRANT: Perhaps.

DANIEL: Let me tell . . .

TYRANT: I don't want to hear it!

DANIEL: This is the emerald stone that fell from God's forehead at the creation of the Universe. Whoever carries that stone has the power of God. For it bears the Seal of Solomon. Here, I give it to you as a gift.

TYRANT: Another time.

DANIEL: Aren't you feeling well, Tyrant?

TYRANT: No, not well.

STORYTELLER: And in Tyrant's heart, strange memories stirred. Memories of former times.

DANIEL: I see the ring disturbs you.

TYRANT: Not a bit! Not a bit!

DANIEL: I see it does. I'll take it off.

TYRANT: Yes, do that.

DANIEL: And place it on your hand.

TYRANT: No!

DANIEL: Let me slip it on your finger.

TYRANT: Stay away from me!

DANIEL: As you wish. I'll wear it in safekeeping 'til you're ready to receive it. Meanwhile I'll pray for you.

TYRANT: Pray! I need no prayers from you or anyone.

DANIEL: I'll pray for you anyway.

TYRANT: Do you mock me?

DANIEL: Never. But everyone's in need of redemption. Even the Devil.

TYRANT: I'll squash you like a bug.

DANIEL: This is no way for old friends to talk.

TYRANT: I grow dizzy.

DANIEL: You're not yourself today. Here, put your arm about me. You must be lonely. In this vast cosmic night there's no one to shed a tear for you. Are you lonely, Tyrant?

TYRANT: I've felt nothing for a million years.

DANIEL: What a pity.

TYRANT: Save your pity for those in need of it.

DANIEL: You seem tired. Are you tired, Tyrant?

TYRANT: I grow weary of it all.

DANIEL: The arch-criminal of the Universe, bored? How strange.

TYRANT: You have visions . . . dreams. Amuse me.

DANIEL: You must rest. Sleep . . .

TYRANT: Yes. (*Tyrant lies down. He sleeps.*)
  (*Enter Magician.*)

DANIEL: How long must I whore my life away to this Tyrant?

MAGICIAN: 'Til the Kingdom of Opposites meet.
  'Til Darkness and Light unite.
  And Life and Death are one.

TYRANT: (*Crying out.*) Ahhhhhh!! I have bad dreams!

WOLF: It's Tyrant.

TYRANT: Who shall rid me of this dark dream?

WOLF: What is it?

TYRANT: The dream . . . the dream . . . who shall tell me the meaning of my dream? Who shall take it from me?

FOX: Tell us the dream, that we may tell you the meaning.
  (*Silence.*)

TYRANT: Daniel King . . . where is he?

DANIEL: You called.

TYRANT: Tell me my dream.

DANIEL: There is a man. His head is gold, his chest is silver, his legs are brass, his feet are clay . . .

TYRANT: Yes, yes.

DANIEL: And he reaches for . . .

TYRANT: Enough! Enough! Go! All of you! (*They exit. To Daniel.*) You shall stay with me. Go on.

DANIEL: And he reaches for Heaven. And just as it's within his grasp he dissolves into Light. This is your dream, Tyrant. The dream you always dream. And fear to tell.

TYRANT: And the meaning.

DANIEL: There is a Divine Man that stretches from Heaven to Hell. Four kings reside within Him, the King of Gold touches all Suns. The King of Silver reigns over all Planets. The King of Brass is bound to Earth. But all three have a weakness. For they are dependent on the King of the Moon, and his feet are made of Clay.

TYRANT: A good interpretation! A good interpretation!

DANIEL: Who conquers Him, conquers all.

TYRANT: He can be conquered then. He can!

DANIEL: This dream is a warning to Tyrant not to reach for Heaven in the full light of day, but to steal within in the darkness of night.

TYRANT: Who shall make me a covering?

DANIEL: I will. I shall build you a Tower to the Sun.

TYRANT: Wise Daniel. I am bound to you forever. Wise Daniel. Do this for me and all I have is yours.

DANIEL: The Earth . . . the Earth as you promised!

SCENE 3: THE TRIAL OF DANIEL KING

WOLF: He must die!

FOX: He must die!

CHORUS: He must surely die.

TYRANT: Daniel King? What crime has he committed?

STORYTELLER: What is the greatest crime of all? To dare to be a living man in the world of the Dead.

MAGICIAN: In the name of the Living I demand a trial.

WOLF: Denied!

TYRANT: Granted!

STORYTELLER: At the end of the age,
    The Living and the Dead must part,

Each to go their separate ways.
Hear now the strangest trial that ever was:
The Trial of the Living by the Dead.

CHORUS: He has wronged us, the survivors of the Earth.

HEATHER: But it's no crime to be alive!

JOSHUA: Every man's entitled to his life.

CHORUS: Only if it serves the common good.

PAUL: The ant heap — no individuals.

CHORUS: We are the Individual.

PETER: That's insane!

JOSHUA: Your way of life is death.

CHORUS: Our way of life is good.

HEATHER: But he's innocent. I swear before Heaven . . .

CHORUS: There is no Heaven. There's only Earth. And those who
have survived. We make the judgment.

WOLF, FOX AND WEASEL: The judgment of Death.

HEATHER: Who are you to judge the Living?

CHORUS: We are the survivors. We make the history of the world.

DANIEL: Yes, and history shows it is always the same man and he's
always pursued by the same mob. I've seen my father murdered in
every cycle of time.

WOLF: Objection, your Honor. History has nothing to do with the
guilt of the accused.

TYRANT: Sustained. You will restrict your remarks to the present
time.

DANIEL: What is done now reverberates through all past and future
time. What we do now determines the future and the past. No one
knows that better than you, your Honor.

FOX: Objection. The accused is trying to plant seditious ideas in the
minds of the jurors. Therefore I move the remarks be struck from
the record.

TYRANT: Sustained. The jury will disregard the remarks on time.

JOSHUA: Throughout the ages you've scourged and crucified the Sons
of the Living One, persecuted those who would be free . . .

WOLF: Objection!

TYRANT: Sustained.

JOSHUA: Brutalized and beaten those who dared to stand up and be
men. But nothing can stop the Life. No bullet can harm it.

FOX: Objection!

TYRANT: Sustained.

JOSHUA: Fire cannot burn it, water cannot dampen it, air cannot exhaust it, earth cannot choke it.

SHARK: Objection! Objection!

TYRANT: Sustained.

DANIEL: And though you murder and maim us, as your kind has throughout the ages, Life is stronger than Death. You shall never contain it. With all your instruments of death you shall fail.

CHORUS: You hear? He has condemned himself.

JOSHUA: Only if the truth condemns him.

WOLF: We'll teach him to wear his face properly. He's on trial for his life.

HEATHER: Every man's on trial for his life. But not by you.

CHORUS: He is guilty! Guilty!

DANIEL: I do not recognize this court's jurisdiction over me.

SNAKE: It is we who determine whether you live or die.

DANIEL: One alone can judge me. He who made the Living and the Dead. God hath commanded man to live. You have commanded him to die.

CHORUS: Who is this One? Tyrant is our only god and savior. Do you refuse to pay allegiance to him?

(Silence.)

TYRANT: (Aside.) Careful, Daniel. Remember our covenant. Unless you pay the Dead their due, they shall surely rise up and kill you.

DANIEL: And what is due the Dead?

CHORUS: Your life.

DANIEL: Become one of the walking dead . . .

TYRANT: It has come to the attention of the court that the accused has consorted with the Dead. I, Tyrant, testify that he danced with the Great Whore and became the Great Beast.

FOX: Be watchful, Tyrant. This boy wishes to deceive you. He is faithless.

CHORUS: At this very moment he is betraying you.

TYRANT: Who dares accuse him of this? He is under my protection.

CHORUS: You cannot love this boy and us. You must choose.

TYRANT: You cannot say this to me.

CHORUS: It is we who have followed you in everything. What does this boy have to offer you? Your destruction.

TYRANT: Are you threatening me?!

CHORUS: We have spoken. Let Tyrant beware.

HEATHER: You fools! All of you! Why do you slander the Living?

Daniel King offers you life and you seek to slay him.

STORYTELLER: How long will the Dead steal the place of the Living?

CHORUS: The unbearable Light. It burns and drives us mad. Long ago we turned our back on life in order to survive.

HEATHER: But life is good.

CHORUS: Life is evil. Life is a cheat and a lie. It has broken our hearts.

HEATHER: You've torn your own hearts out. Why? Why?

CHORUS: Tyrant understands us. He suffers our pain with us. He will never leave us.

HEATHER: (*She looks at the others.*) So that's the secret . . . You want to die! You don't want to live. The silent conspiracy throughout the ages. You've murdered every man and woman that showed you the Way to Life. That's why you sit silently by and watch the Wolf and the Fox make bombs that will blow up the Earth. Working morning 'til night in chemical laboratories manufacturing viruses and germs that will destroy everything living.

JOSHUA: Constructing genetic monsters to replace the human race. Speak on it, Heather.

HEATHER: And that's why you want to kill Daniel King. Because he has the balls to unmask you.

WOLF: Objection! Nuclear warfare . . .

FOX: . . . and the chemical destruction of all that's living . . .

WEASEL: . . . is not on trial here.

WOLF, FOX AND WEASEL: Daniel King is.

PETER: You mean the Living are!

PAUL: And after Daniel, it'll be any man or woman who's alive. You've bankrupt every nation and brought the world economy to its knees so that you could get an economic stranglehold over all humanity. But your policy of divide and conquer won't work anymore.

WOLF: Objection! Our economic system of . . .

PAUL: Totalitarianism.

JOSHUA: More lies, Wolf? Capitalism and communism are two sides of the same coin. And you own the coin, brother. In your state of computerized super-controlled production, all the peoples of the world are on automatic, turning straw into gold for you, just like they did for old Pharaoh!

FOX: We administer truth . . .

WOLF: . . . and justice.

STORYTELLER: Shall Justice come from the belly of the Wolf? Shall Truth come from the mouth of the Fox?

WOLF: We are the good shepherds who lead the people rightly.

JOSHUA: You are the false shepherds who murdered the good shepherds and stole their places.

WEASEL: We bring prosperity to all.

PAUL: You bring ruin to all. Bureaucratic madness for ants and bees. Economic terror where no one can concentrate on anything beyond the next dollar.

FOX: The people are comfortable.

JOSHUA: Comfortable?! They're dead. Comfort junkies.

PAUL: Rock and roll your way to death.

HEATHER: Blot out the voices of the human heart.

PETER: Leap into the void.

JOSHUA: And death be the final fix.

WOLF: Fox . . .

FOX: The people! We get our sanction from the people.

JOSHUA: Clones!

WEASEL: Objection!

TYRANT: Overruled.

JOSHUA: What else but a clone would whore his life away.

FOX: The people follow us. Ask them. (*Pause.*) Go on! Ask them! (*Throwing money to Chorus.*)
(*The Chorus hesitantly and fearfully begin to sing.*)

CHORUS: The Wolf is our leader . . .

SHARK: (*Pointing gun at them.*) Louder! Let them hear you.

CHORUS: His strength is our staff . . .

SHARK: Louder!!

CHORUS: (*Singing hysterically.*) The Fox shall guide us. His cunning is our hope . . .

JOSHUA: See what I mean. Come on, Daniel. Let's go. This trial is over.

WOLF: (*Pulling out gun.*) This trial is just beginning.

MAGICIAN: Must find out who's stronger: the Living or the Dead. From the four quarters of the World I summon Lion, Eagle, Bull, Horse and from its sacred center, Elephant and Dove.

CHORUS: The Beasts, the Beasts of the Apocalypse![7]

MAGICIAN: The warriors of God.

CHORUS: It's the end of the world. We are doomed. Run, run for your lives.

TYRANT: Why do you do these things? You've upset my court.

MAGICIAN: Sorry. Must have witnesses to the Truth.

TYRANT: (*Banging gavel.*) Order! Order in my court.

DOVE: People of the Earth. Do not despair. The end will come. But not yet. You still have time. If man can awaken to his true responsibility, then the Phoenix will return.

HEATHER: And the Dove can stop weeping.

WEASEL: Who says?

DOVE: Heaven.

WOLF: Objection. The evidence is inadmissible.

PAUL: On what grounds?

FOX: On the grounds that no one has ever proven that Heaven exists.

TYRANT: Sustained.

DANIEL: How long will you evade your lives? Since the Fall from Heaven every man is in a state of perpetual war, his members divided one against the other, and yet every man is born a Heaven and an Earth. To become true man he must unite the two.

CHORUS: Man is dead.

PETER: If he is, you've killed him.

SNAKE: Everyone knows man's a failure.

PETER: It was all your fault, Snake. If you hadn't tempted man . . .

SNAKE: Why blame me? I just delivered a message.

JOSHUA: Man must be tempted; but though he fall countless times, as long as he struggles he shall rise again and be reborn.

FOX: Who says?

PAUL: The Phoenix.

WOLF: Then why isn't he here to testify to that?

PETER: The Phoenix won't return until violence is at an end.

HEATHER: The Dove won't stop weeping until peace reigns in your heart.

CHORUS: Give us the Dove as a witness.

HEATHER: She's testifying now. Can't you hear her weeping for all the children of the Earth? For all her wayward sons and daughters.

CHILDREN'S CHORUS: We are the children of the World.
We should have lived.
But you betrayed us

We are the children of the World.
We should have lived.
But you starved and tortured us.

We are the children of the World.
We should have lived.
But you raped us.

We are the children of the World.
We should have lived.
But you murdered us.

And closed your eyes.
And closed your ears.
And closed your heart.

Our laughter could have saved you.
But now it's too late.

We are the unborn future.
The children of the Earth.
And now we will never live.
For you have sold the Earth.

Our ghosts will haunt you forever.

CHORUS: We hear nothing.

HEATHER: Then your hearts are made of stone.

DANIEL: Don't be afraid. Tear off the mask of death that's grown to your face. And find the greatest treasure: Life.

CHORUS: We are naked and ashamed.

HEATHER: The Earth, the precious Earth, the Earth we love is fighting for her life.

PAUL: Come and rejoin the Living.

PETER: And we will make of our Earth a dream.

JOSHUA: Give us your hand. We will work together.

HEATHER: The Earth is throbbing under your feet. She's alive! You can feel her heartbeat. She's breathing . . .

CHORUS: (*Terrified, begins wailing the wail of the Dead.*)
We'll shut our ears and close our eyes and slip into the void. Tyrant! Tyrant! Save us from ourselves!

DANIEL: For a thousand generations the Dead have conspired against the Living. How long will this conspiracy go on?

TYRANT: Oh, Daniel, Daniel . . . When will you understand you must not disturb the Dead.

DANIEL: From now on, I'll speak to the Living . . .

(Daniel addresses audience; as he speaks, Peter, Paul, Heather and Joshua transmit his speech in sign language.)

Men of the Earth, hear me. God who hath promised a perfect liberty hath sent you many wise men to teach you the meaning of your lives. In your wantonness you have despised His sacred messengers. You have put His holy prophets to the death. In the long history of Man, you have maimed yourself and your children, been a parasite on the Earth that has mothered you, scoffed at Heaven which has fathered you. You, who in your madness, thought to create your own meaning rather than live by every Word of God, have fallen into the pit of death. For you have forsaken the promise of eternal life as Sons of God to become sons of animals. You, who have always mistaken license for freedom, comfort for happiness, have become a slave to the Great Beast within you. And now in your abject cowardice you worship the very Tyranny you fear. You are like naughty and wayward children who have forsaken living waters for the mirages of the preachers of death. You are sick, and with a great sickness. Is it not enough that you have turned this earthly paradise into hell? Now in your great foolishness you seek to interfere with your own nature and destroy yourselves. How long will you follow wolves in sheep's clothing? How long will you follow the demented minds of scientists who wish to destroy all of life and turn you into genetic monsters? How long will you follow the psychopaths who claim to guide and teach you? Never doubt there are men who in their hatred of the Divine seek to slay God and become gods themselves. Are you one of these men or women? My father, Adam King, died for you. Many have died for you. Do not say there is nothing you can do. Do not lie. Only you can stop the madness that is upon the Earth. For only you have created it. Do not blame God — God who hath given you everything — for you have rejected Him and have followed the Devil in your hearts. Do not blame your leaders whom you have created to hide behind. Men of the Earth listen to me. Mankind is at a great crossroads. Either we will cast off our animal skins and become human beings, or the Wolf and the Fox will eat us. We are in a failing battle. But it is not yet too late to redeem humanity. Stand up and fight. Do not allow your sons and daughters to be cannon fodder. Do not say we cannot stop war. Refuse to participate in it. Do not say we must make bombs and all the filthy appendages of modern life because we must make money. The spirit of life will provide another way for any man who follows the truth in his heart. Since Adam fell from Heaven you have lived an evil dream. And now you see the inevitable consequences of that dream. It is a nightmare. Do not think you can hide from the horror which is upon you and steadily increases with every passing day. Do not think some false god will save you. Only you can save yourselves. The choice is yours: Take the Devil and make him follow God or follow the Devil and deny God. There is no middle ground. As was said of old: This day I give you Life or Death. Choose! Choose!

PETER, PAUL, JOSHUA AND HEATHER: (*Echoing.*) Choose. Choose.

TYRANT: A pretty speech, but useless.

DANIEL: Let the people of the Earth decide. Let each man choose for himself.

TYRANT: Fool! I am the people. The judgment:

CHORUS: Guilty!

TYRANT: The punishment:

CHORUS: Death. Death.

WOLF: He is condemned. Take him.

JOSHUA: No!

PETER: No!

PAUL: No!

HEATHER: No!

SNAKE: Into the pit!

FOX: We shall see what his God does for him then.

TYRANT: Oh, in all the world will no one save this boy?!

STORYTELLER: Who will save Daniel King?
   Who will save the Living from the Dead?
   (*Enter Luke.*)

LUKE: I will. I will take his place. Let Daniel King live.

TYRANT: You will die for this boy?

LUKE: Yes.

HEATHER: Oh Daddy, Daddy!
   (*Peter breaks down, sobbing hysterically.*)

DANIEL: No! Uncle, no! I will not let you give your life as a peace offering to the Dead.

LUKE: I have a debt that must be paid. Once a man did the same for me. A King for a King. Free him!

WOLF: No man can die for another. These are the statutes of Hell.

JOSHUA: Objection! No man can live unless another die for him. These are the statutes of Heaven.

TYRANT: Overruled!

JOSHUA: It's a lie! This court is fixed.

MAGICIAN: My boy, this whole world is fixed.

HEATHER: I'll die for him!

WOLF: Objection!

TYRANT: Sustained.

JOSHUA: Take me.

FOX: You're not a King.

JOSHUA: I'm a Man and that's to be a King. Take me.

FOX: Objection!

TYRANT: Sustained.

PAUL: We're of the same blood. Take me.

WOLF: Objection!

TYRANT: Sustained.

(*They look toward Peter who is unable to speak. In dread, he looks to his father for support.*)

LUKE: Oh, Peter . . .

PETER: (*Running to his father.*) I don't want to die! (*Luke pushes him away.*)

JOSHUA: Four lives for one. We ransom our lives for his. A ransom even Hell can't refuse.

TYRANT: Denied.

PAUL: Why?

TYRANT: Each man must meet his fate alone. He is condemned to die. You are condemned to live.

HEATHER: Let him live. For the love he bears you . . . save him!

TYRANT: I cannot!

HEATHER: (*To Magician.*) Do something! Do something!

MAGICIAN: One last chance. There is an ancient statute written in the Book of Life that even Hell must recognize.

TYRANT: Speak!

MAGICIAN: By your own standard the stronger shall win. Trial by Ordeal.

TYRANT: Granted.

WOLF: He shall go into the pit naked and alone.

FOX: We shall see how he fares without his friends.

(*Bull goes into the pit.*)

DANIEL: Bull, you are the strength of my manhood.

(Eagle goes into the pit.)

Eagle do not leave me. You are my vision. Without you I'm blind. Will the sun never rise again for me?

(Lion goes into the pit.)

Lion's courage, do not forsake me now in the hour of my need.

HEATHER: Daniel . . .

MAGICIAN: Cannot be stopped. What will be, must be.

(Horse goes into the pit.)

DANIEL: Horse of the Sun! My life! My life is leaving . . . I am paralyzed . . . I cannot . . .

(Elephant goes into the pit.)

My memory . . . I have forgotten . . . Who am I?

TYRANT: I cannot bear this. Oh Daniel, Daniel, you were the jewel of my eye, and now you're going . . . going . . .

STORYTELLER: And each man must go down to Hell

Blinded, companionless, and alone.

Oh fearful journey of the soul.

Oh light of Heaven and dark of Hell,

That breaks the human heart.

(Enter both Graces to join Daniel. They take his hands and raise them aloft.)

DANIEL: By Grace I live, by Grace I die. As long as you are at my side. Now, into the furnace of God. Do with me as Thou will.

(Daniel and both Graces leap into the pit.)

LUKE: Daniel, no!!

TYRANT: Throw in the others. They must die. But he *(pointing to Peter)* may live. *(Wolf and Fox take Heather, Paul and Joshua to edge of pit.)*

LUKE: Not my daughter — not any of them! I won't let you!

MAGICIAN: All Kings must go to Hell.

(They jump.)

LUKE: I've failed.

PETER: No, you haven't, Father. *(He jumps into pit.)*

MAGICIAN: *(To Luke.)* I think maybe you do better job than you know. Every man got his own role to play.

(Luke falls to his knees and prays.)

(Ballet of the Sphinx begins.[8] Daniel enacts a ritual of escaping from the abyss through transformation, struggling with each of the Higher Animals in turn. They devour what must die in him while he absorbs their essential qualities. All continue dancing

while he struggles with each of his friends, thereby recreating the unity of mankind. Higher Animals and friends transform into the Sphinx, lifting Daniel overhead by his outstretched arms until he becomes one with all of them. Grace helps to create and sustain this unity by portraying the power of her Father through dance.)

WOLF: See how frail and weak a thing is man.

FOX: And to think he dared to stand alone against the world.

SNAKE: The Lion, the Lion! He's kneeling before him!

SHARK: He's cut off his paws![9]

(*The Dance is completed as Daniel, Joshua, Peter, Paul, and Heather each mount a Higher Animal and circle joyously, with Grace, celebrating their unity and transformation through rebirth. They escape.*)

FOX: They've escaped!

TYRANT: Thank God!

MAGICIAN: And you don't thank me? (*Exit Magician.*)

WOLF: Don't worry. We'll get them back.

TYRANT: You clones disgust me. You're no better than your originals. It was hardly worth the trouble to take you out of Hell. (*Tyrant makes a motion and the Big Ten gyrate for a second or two, lose all animation and fall into a crumpled heap.*)

Now I am alone. Oh, my eternal boy, my golden one . . . Come back. I lived only in your presence. Oh Daniel, Daniel, why hast thou forsaken me?

ACT III

SCENE I: THE SERPENT

DANIEL: (*Calling from a distance.*) Tyrant!

TYRANT: You've come back.

DANIEL: For the love I bear you.

(*Silence.*)

It's a dark night.

(*Silence.*)

I wonder if all the Planets in Heaven must contend with you, or just this poor Earth . . .

(*Silence.*)

I've built you your Tower to the Sun. Come, Tyrant. Come.

STORYTELLER: And all the many, their name was Legion: the scientists, the bankers, the statesmen, the politicians, the journalists, the engineers, the teachers, the preachers, rose out of Hell dressed in the filth of themselves and all were devils and whored themselves to Tyrant. And all slandered their Creator, and denied their Maker, and built a Tower of Babel to declare war on God. These were the left hand of God. Only a few refused to take part. They were the right hand of God.[10]

(*Wolf, Fox and the rest of the Big Ten lead the Chorus into the Tower to the Sun.*)

DANIEL: (*Gesturing toward the Tower to the Sun.*) Tyrant . . .

TYRANT: After you, my young friend.

DANIEL: After you.

TYRANT: Ha, ha, ha.

DANIEL: Ha, ha, ha. You're not going?

TYRANT: I think I'll sit this one out.

DANIEL: And this solar journey was designed for you. What a pity.

TYRANT: Yes, isn't it? They'll never come back.

DANIEL: Never.

TYRANT: Not a pleasant way to die.

DANIEL: They died a long time ago. They're their own punishment.

TYRANT: Lost in the void so to speak.

DANIEL: Exactly.

TYRANT: And now you have your revenge.

DANIEL: All the men who murdered my father are dead.

TYRANT: All except one.

DANIEL: Who is he?

TYRANT: Yourself.

DANIEL: I find you as amusing as ever, Tyrant.

TYRANT: You chose a father who would die a hero's death, Daniel.

DANIEL: What of it?

TYRANT: Your life is based on your father's murder. That's what has drawn you to me. We both seek revenge. That makes you co-conspirator with me. My main collaborator in evil!

DANIEL: The Devil always was a sophist. I find your humor grisly, to say the least.

TYRANT: You've kept your secret well hidden. Even from yourself.

DANIEL: I think I've heard enough.

TYRANT: Do you smell a rat? A little self-scrutiny will show you the truth.

DANIEL: The truth from Satan? Don't make me laugh.

TYRANT: A dark truth for a dark man in a dark time. Look into my eyes and see the mirror of yourself. When the Sons of God can't learn from the Sons of Satan, the Universe will end. And so will you, my friend. The next time you try to be a hero, base it on the certainty of self-knowledge.

(*Tyrant exits laughing.*)

DANIEL: Be still my soul. Be still. Can it be true . . .? Lost! Lost! I've lost my Way . . . Oh, there's something monstrous in the soul of man. Where can I bury my shame? In all the Earth there's nowhere to hide. If I could die . . . die . . . Oh God, is there no help for me?

(*Enter Lion, Eagle, Horse, Elephant and Bull.*)

BULL: Strength!

LION: Courage!

HORSE: Heart!

EAGLE: Vision!

ELEPHANT: Remember!

(*Grace appears.*)*

*Music p. 237

GRACE: Daniel . . .

DANIEL: My Lady, is it you?

GRACE: Yes.

DANIEL: I'm not worthy to look upon your face.

GRACE: You must hurry, Daniel. Your grandmother's calling for you.

DANIEL: Grandmother . . .

GRACE: She needs you. There is no time to lose.

DANIEL: Take me to her.

(*Grace and Higher Animals lead Daniel to Destiny.*)

SCENE 2: JUSTICE

(*At Destiny's bedside.*)

DESTINY: Where have you been? You look terrible.

DANIEL: I . . .

DESTINY: You look like you got in a fight with the Devil and got the worst of it.

DANIEL: I have.

(*Animals exit on nod from Daniel.*)

DESTINY: Have they gone? (*Daniel nods.*) Come close to me. (*He does so.*)

I'm dying, Daniel.

DANIEL: I know, Grandmother. Hush now. You must rest.

DESTINY: Rest? I'll have enough of that in my grave. I'll soon be at my eternal rest. While I've life, there's something I have to tell you. Are you listening, son of my best beloved son?

DANIEL: Yes, Grandmother.

DESTINY: Your father came again last night.

DANIEL: My father . . .

DESTINY: As I lay dying, your father came to me in a vision. He said, tell Daniel for me I understand, and that you were to forgive yourself.

DANIEL: Forgive myself?

DESTINY: And go on. Do you understand?

DANIEL: It's something between my father and myself. Something dark and awful. I don't know if it can ever be undone.

DESTINY: He says it can.

DANIEL: I'm not sure I'm good enough to be his son.

DESTINY: Are you calling God a liar? He made you what you are. Each man has his destiny. You have yours.

DANIEL: There's something I've seen in myself I can't get past.

DESTINY: "In the place of excrement you will find me." That means in the place of your deepest shame you shall touch God.

DANIEL: The crime I've committed . . .

DESTINY: There's only one crime: to betray yourself. No grandson of mine will ever do that.

DANIEL: Oh Grandmother, I'm in so much trouble.

DESTINY: You were born for trouble. You're your Father's son and you were born to fight the world and redeem Him . . . Redeem all of us. I've waited a long time for you. I'm giving you my blessing.

DANIEL: You want me to . . .

DESTINY: To do what's in you to do. And not turn back.

DANIEL: You want revenge, Grandmother?

DESTINY: I want justice. I'm an old lady but I haven't forgotten the butchers that murdered my sons. Justice! And you shall give it to me.

DANIEL: How do you know that?

DESTINY: I know you, Daniel.

DANIEL: Justice . . . How beautiful it sounds. Not revenge, but justice. Justice.

(*He starts to laugh, Destiny joins him.*)

We're not done yet. Are we, Grandmother?

DESTINY: We'll never be done.

DANIEL: Oh Grandmother, good Grandmother. You've given me back my life. How can I ever thank you?

DESTINY: By becoming the man you were born to be.

DANIEL: By all that's holy I swear I'll never fail you.

DESTINY: Now I've set things right. Get along with you. I don't want you cluttering up my room. I want to die alone. Your mother's in the next room. Be kind to her. And be sure to make your peace with your Uncle Luke. What he did he had to do. And send in Monsignor. I'm very cross with him. I want to give him a piece of my mind before I die. I leave this Earth without regret. As you must do when your time comes.

(*Silence.*)

Remember, Daniel, I'll be watching you.

(*Daniel enters the main room where the family is gathered.*)

DANIEL: Monsignor, my grandmother wishes to see you.

CARDINAL: Alright, my boy. (*He goes to Destiny's room.*)

DANIEL: It's never been easy between us, has it, Mother?

VANITY: No, Daniel, it hasn't.

DANIEL: You're my mother and yet you've been a stranger to me all my life.

VANITY: I know.

DANIEL: I've never been able to love you.

VANITY: Your father has always stood between us. You blamed me for his death.

DANIEL: I felt you never loved him.

VANITY: So many things happen between a man and a woman, Daniel.

DANIEL: I know that now. Can you forgive me?

VANITY: Oh Daniel, there's nothing to forgive.

DANIEL: A heart for a heart. Let my heart mend yours. Is it too late to love you now, Mother?

VANITY: Oh, my son, come into my arms.

(*They embrace. Prudence goes to Destiny's room as the Cardinal returns.*)

You'll be going away now . . . won't you?

DANIEL: Yes.

VANITY: I have a feeling I'll never see you again. It's so strange. I've found my son . . . now I must lose him.

DANIEL: You can never lose me, Mother. You'll always be in my heart.

VANITY: I wish . . . I was going to say . . . I wish your father could see you now. But he can, can't he?

DANIEL: You understand that?

VANITY: (*Nodding her head; very softly.*) Yes.

DANIEL: Pray for me, Mother, now and forever.

VANITY: I will.

DANIEL: Uncle Luke . . .

LUKE: Yes . . .

DANIEL: I humbly beg your pardon.

LUKE: Daniel, Daniel, give me your hand.

(*Prudence re-enters the room.*)

PRUDENCE: She's gone.

HEATHER: Grandmother . . . !

FASHION: What?!

PRUDENCE: Mother's dead.

(*Joshua enters.*)

LUKE: Mother . . . Oh, Mother. (*Begins praying softly.*)

CARDINAL: Mother of God, pray for us now and forever in our hour of sin.

(*The family goes to Destiny's room leaving the children alone. Heather goes to Daniel, kisses his cheek, and then joins the family.*)

PETER: She was a great old lady.

PAUL: Grandmother was the best of us. It's the end of the line.

DANIEL: No, Paul, it's the beginning.

PETER: The world is perishing.

DANIEL: That's no great news, Peter. The world is constantly perishing . . .

JOSHUA: . . . and constantly being renewed.

PETER: The old world is gone.

DANIEL: Let it die and give place to the living.

PETER: Are you crazy, Daniel?

PAUL: We know he's crazy, Peter. But we love him anyway. Don't we, Joshua? What the world needs is a few more madmen like him to light up our way. And what we really need is a drink. Come on, Peter. (*Handing him a drink.*) We've been sober too long. I drink to Daniel, and all the madmen who ever lived, who had guts enough to hold onto the vision of sanity and kick the rest of us slobs up the steep and thorny path to reality.

DANIEL: (*Smiling.*) To Grandmother. (*Lifting his glass.*) May she live forever.

ALL: To Grandmother!

JOSHUA: To your grandmother.

(*They all lift their glasses and drink in silence.*)

(*Enter Storyteller.*)

DANIEL: We men have a great duty to perform. To reveal to God His human face.

JOSHUA: That's beautiful.

PETER: It's terrible to be human.

DANIEL: You chose it. This Earth's our assignment.

STORYTELLER: It's time, Daniel.

PAUL: Who's that?

DANIEL: (*Smiling.*) Just a storyteller. I have an appointment that cannot be delayed.

PETER: When shall we meet again?

DANIEL: Whenever you like. I'll always be around.

PAUL: 'Til then . . .

(*Exit Peter and Paul.*)

JOSHUA: There's no turning back now.

DANIEL: No turning back. You'll take care of Heather.

JOSHUA: Yes.

DANIEL: And . . .

JOSHUA: You've taught us well, Daniel. I know what to do. Count on it.

(*Enter Heather.*)

HEATHER: She's as beautiful in death as she was in life.

DANIEL: Yes.

HEATHER: The Earth is trembling under our feet. Oh, Daniel, hold me in your arms.

DANIEL: Don't be frightened.

HEATHER: I'm never frightened when I'm with you. But one day you'll leave us.

DANIEL: How do you know that?

HEATHER: You're so wild and strange.

DANIEL: I'll always be with you.

HEATHER: Always . . . ? Promise me . . . always.

DANIEL: Always.

HEATHER: Oh, Daniel, if only I could tell you . . . (*They kiss.*)

DANIEL: Come, walk with me a ways.

(*He puts his arms around Heather and Joshua as they walk off with the Storyteller leading the way.*)

SCENE 3: I

STORYTELLER: Now Tyrant like a colossus strides the world,
Earth sickens as his shadow falls.
The last true remnant of Man held fast,
The Saints of God, encircled in the City of Light.
From a great height the Lord of all the Worlds
Looked down and wept.
The Earth vomited up its dead.
Lightning flashed, severed flesh from bone.

TYRANT: He won't come.

MAGICIAN: He'll come.

TYRANT: And if he doesn't?

MAGICIAN: I've trained him well. He'll come.

STORYTELLER: Tyrant reached in his hand and tore out the heart of

Man.

TYRANT: All flesh shall cringe under a reign of terror that will never end. I myself, am Father, Son, and Holy Ghost.
(*Enter Daniel.*)

DANIEL: Bow down and worship you?! Never! You shall not steal the keys to Heaven. Fulfill your promise. Deliver the Earth and all that's in it.

TYRANT: You have no power over me.

DANIEL: I come in the Name of a Greater Power.

TYRANT: Then take my place!

DANIEL: That was never in the contract.

TYRANT: Your father unmasked me. Your Uncle Matthew saw me face to face. Your Uncle Luke partially escaped me. It's left to you to know my true identity.

DANIEL: You are . . .

TYRANT: Your very self. If you are the one, you can free me. I've waited a long time. But are you the one?

DANIEL: God hath sent me to you.

TYRANT: How can I be sure?

DANIEL: By the power of this ring.

TYRANT: The emerald ring. Yes . . . Yes. Do you dare to know me as I am? Can you suffer for all eternity? Carry the burden men cannot carry themselves?

DANIEL: What man will dare I will dare. Since the foundation of the world you and I were destined to unite. Come, Tyrant, you shall be my bride.
(*He puts the ring on Tyrant's finger. The Spirit of Tyrant enters him and he transforms into the body of Tyrant.*)

MAGICIAN: Now you must carry the misery of all the world.

DANIEL: Ahhhh! The killer I've stalked is myself. Foul! Foul! The world is foul! And I am fouler yet! My Tyrant's heart has played me false. I'll tear it out. I've stalked Tyrant only to find myself. I am the murderer of humanity . . . It is I who has slandered God.
(*Heather rushes in.*)

HEATHER: Daniel! Daniel! Where are you? Thank God I've found you. What is it? Oh my God. It's . . . It's . . . Tyrant! What have you . . . What have you done with Daniel? (*She begins to back away.*)

DANIEL: Heather . . .
(*She continues backing away.*)

Heather . . . don't leave me.

HEATHER: Daniel . . . ?

(*He nods, reaching out his hand.*)

Oh my God . . . What have they done to you?!

(*Joshua, Paul and Peter rush in, and watch in disbelief.*)

DANIEL: I cannot bear the pain. I'm choking with the foul contagion of the world. Kill me!

HEATHER: I can't.

DANIEL: If you ever loved me.

HEATHER: I can't.

DANIEL: Have mercy on my soul. The ring. Put the ring on my finger!

HEATHER: It's gone.

DANIEL: Find it. Find it . . . !

(*The Magician enters. The ring is on his finger.*)

Godfather! The ring . . . the ring! You have it. Oh blessed God. How did you . . . ? Tyrant . . . Tyrant! You're . . . him. NO!!

TYRANT: Yes.

DANIEL: It's impossible!

MAGICIAN AND TYRANT: Now my brother and I are one.

DANIEL: My greatest friend and my greatest enemy.

MAGICIAN: Both are yourself.

(*Magician looks at him in silence.*)

HEATHER: He's been driven into a wilderness of pain. It's more than he can bear.

STORYTELLER: These are the rules of the Play. So that the Drama might be fulfilled.

HEATHER: Why? Why?

STORYTELLER: God has ordained it.

HEATHER: He couldn't ask this of anyone.

STORYTELLER: God's love must wound.

HEATHER: But not break.

STORYTELLER: Yes, sometimes, even that.

HEATHER: Oh, it's horrible.

DANIEL: The ring . . . the ring.

(*Magician puts ring on Daniel's finger.*)

HEATHER: Daniel! Daniel! Daniel!

(*He dies.*)

JOSHUA: He's gone.

(*The others go to comfort her, gathering around Daniel's body, as Grace leads his Spirit away.*)

SPIRIT OF DANIEL: My Divine Lady, you said I would never see you again.

(*Singing.*)*

GRACE: Your life is over.

You go to a greater life.

SPIRIT OF DANIEL: With you?

GRACE: Always.

(*They dance.*)

SPIRIT OF DANIEL: Is this what I was born for, this bliss, this peace? Oh Light! Light! Is this what I am?

GRACE: Yes, yes. Oh yes.

(*They start climbing the stairway to the upper platform, where two figures are revealed in silhouette, standing shoulder to shoulder, their arms linked, their backs to the audience.*)

SPIRIT OF DANIEL: Where do we go?

GRACE: To your Father's Kingdom.

SPIRIT OF DANIEL: When will we arrive?

GRACE: We have already arrived.

Every moment is an arrival

And every moment a departure.

It is a journey without end.

SPIRIT OF DANIEL: And my friends?

GRACE: They shall be well.

And all shall be well.

(*As Grace finishes her song she leads Daniel up the last step to the platform; the figures in silhouette turn, revealing Tyrant and Magician. Daniel takes his place between them.*)

HEATHER: Oh, Daniel, I love you so. I shall never see your like again.

JOSHUA: And what of us who have witnessed this bloody time?

PAUL: We shall put our friend's body in the grave.

PETER: And thank Heaven we have known such a man.

JOSHUA: And then?

HEATHER: And then . . .

(*The Phoenix and the Dove appear.*)

Look! The Dove has stopped crying.

PETER: And the Phoenix has returned.

HEATHER: We shall make peace with all the world and inherit the Earth at last.

*Music p. 239

PETER: When?

HEATHER: When all men and women can stand up and say I.

JOSHUA: I.

PAUL: I.

PETER: I.

(*Enter Lion, Bull, Horse and Eagle. They stand at the four corners of the stage, facing the four directions, Elephant at the center. From below the animals led by Wolf, Fox and Weasel enter and kneel. The entire ensemble joins in saying, I, I, I . . . in a mounting crescendo as the play ends.*)

MUSIC

CONCEIVED AND ARRANGED BY SHARON GANS
SCORE BY YUKIO TSUJI
GRACE MUSIC BY J. BARRY & S. HIMANKA

Instruments

Synthesizer: Moog, Pro 1, Juno 6
Shakuhachi: Japanese Bamboo Flute
Taiko: Big Japanese drums
Fan drum: Japanese frame drum for Temple use
Noah Bell: Bells from India specially made to get rid of devils
Steel drum
Kayagun: Korean Koto (silk string instrument)
Bird whistle, Crickets, Nose whistle, Bird call
Zither with original frets
Tibetan Gong
Chinese Gong
Japanese Gong
Japanese Kane (Temple Gong)
Kalimba
Sound Tube (hose)
Rain Stick (from Brazil)
Rin bowl (from Japanese temple)
Temple woodblock

ACT I SCENE 1

Music may be adapted at your discretion,
preserving its Oriental flavor.

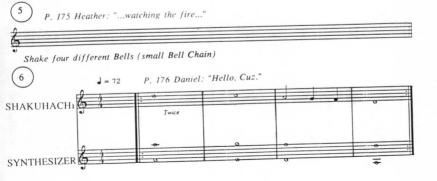

Shakuhachi

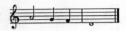

ACT I SCENE THREE

Scene opens with music such as "Spring"
from Vivaldi's *Four Seasons*.
Taiko rolls at each entrance.
Cut music at Daniel's entrance.

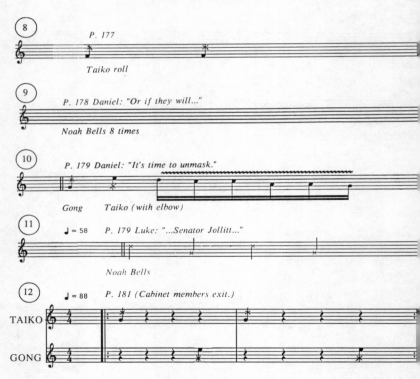

(13) ♩ = 84   *P. 184 Fashion: "...back from the dead."*

Freely

SHAKUHACHI

3 times (each time with different feeling)

SYNTHESIZER

(14) *P. 186 Spirit of Joseph Man: "We must all learn . . . "*

Improvise on Kayagun using D Pentatonic scale, Synth drone

(15) *P. 187 Paul: " . . . no choice . . . no choice . . . "*

Kayagun improvisation over Synth drone

(16) ♩ = 120   *P. 187 Spirit of Matthew King: "...and say, why not?"*

Zither with stick on string

(17) ♩ = 108   *P. 189 Enter Chorus*

Japanese Gong   *Chinese Gong*   *Tibetan Gong*   *Kane*

(18) *P. 190 Magician: "Balloons, balloons..."*

Noah Bells and Kalimba improvise (slowly)

(19) *P. 191 (The spirit of his father...)*

Repeat 5 times
Taiko roll   *Gong*   *Taiko roll*   *Gong*
                                            Synthesizer explosion with fade out

ACT II SCENE 1

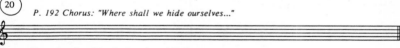

(20) *P. 192 Chorus: "Where shall we hide ourselves..."*

Hose, Bending Plastic Board, and Taiko

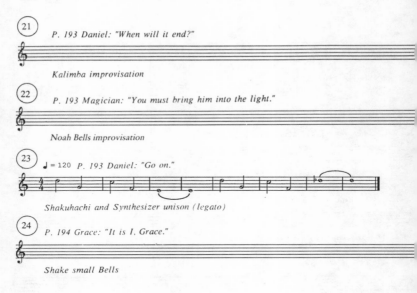

(21) P. 193 Daniel: "When will it end?"

Kalimba improvisation

(22) P. 193 Magician: "You must bring him into the light."

Noah Bells improvisation

(23) ♩ = 120 P. 193 Daniel: "Go on."

Shakuhachi and Synthesizer unison (legato)

(24) P. 194 Grace: "It is I, Grace."

Shake small Bells

ACT II SCENE 2

(25) P. 198 Tyrant: "A dangerous game..."

Repeat 3 times

Gong 1   Gong 2   Taiko (with elbow)

(26) ♩ = 100   P. 199 Daniel: "Do you like the ring?"

Shakuhachi with String Synth sound

1.

2.

(27) *P. 201 Tyrant: "You shall stay with me. Go on."*

Slowly - Rubato

Shakuhachi (mournfully)

ACT II SCENE 3

(28) ♩ = 100
Freely
   P. 206 Dove: People of the Earth."

Shakuhachi on Synth drone

(29) ♩ = 120   *P. 206 Children's Chorus*

Synth arpeggio on D minor scale and Shakuhachi

(30) *P. 207 Chorus: "We'll shut our ears and..."*

Deep Synth drone through Daniel's speech

(31) *P. 211 On each animal: Bull, Eagle, Lion, Horse, Elephant*

*Play in order: Conch Shell Horn, Bird Whistle, Superball on Taiko, Temple Wood Block,
Taiko with stick. Combine and improvise until next cue.*

232 I

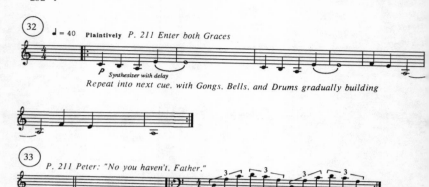

ACT III SCENE 1

ACT III SCENE 2

P. 219 Heather: "Always...? Promise me..."

(37) ♩ = 192   *Rubato*

ACT II SCENE 3

(38)   P. 220 Daniel: "...you shall be my bride."

Gongs, Taiko roll, Cymbal roll, Synth drone

(39)   ♩ = 40   P. 220 Heather: "What have you done with Daniel?"
Plaintively

Synthesizer with delay

(40)   ♩ = 72   P. 233 Joshua: "I."

Shakuhachi and String Synth unison

BALLOONS

Bal - loons,____ bal- loons,____ to take you to Hea - ven.____ Who____ will take a

ride____ to Hea-ven?____

SEQUENCE 1

Repeat until cue.

A ring of gold._____ He who

wears it   shall be - come_____ a man_____ of

gold._____ I shall   walk   by your side_____

and no harm shall be - fall_____ you._____   But if you break faith ____ with me I   shall be

(Spoken) If the ring once leaves your finger,

gone.

you shall never see me again.

But if you pass all the tests

that a - wait you. . . I'll be

yours. . . for - e - ver.

I'll _____ be yours_____ for - e - - - - - - - -

ver.

SEQUENCE 2

♩ = 80   *Cue: Daniel: "...is there no help for me?"*

Repeat until cue.

Cue: Elephant: "Remember." My Lady, is it you? I'm not worthy to look upon your face.

Dan- iel . . . _____   Yes_____ You must

hur - ry Dan - iel. ____ Your grand-mo - ther's cal - ling ____ for you.

Grandmother...

____ She needs ____ you. ____ There

Take me to her.

is no time to lose. ____

SEQUENCE 3

With you?

Al - - - - - - - ways.

Is this what I was born for, this bliss, this peace? Oh Light! Light! Is this what I am?

Yes,

Where do we go?

Yes. Oh yes.

When will we arrive?

To___ your Fa - ther's King_____ dom.

We have al - read_____ - y ar - rived.____

Ev_____ ery mo - ment is an ar -

ri_____ - val and ev_____ ery

mo - ment a de - par_____ - ture.

And my friends?

It is a jour - ney with-out end.

They shall be well. ___ And all shall be well.

(Repeat under dialogue to end of play.)

Appendix

ADAM KING

1 *Mammon,* Aramaic for "richess," personified by the Hebrew people as the false god of greed and avarice.

2 *Behold the dreamer . . . ,* refers to the story of Joseph, the son of Jacob (Israel). As a young boy he was dearest to his father "because he was the son of his old age." He had two dreams of the heights he might reach as a man: one in which the sheaf of grain he was binding commanded those of his brothers, and a second in which "the sun and moon and the eleven stars made obeisance" to him. His father, who loved him most, gave him a coat of many colors which made his eleven brothers jealous. They plotted his death, but instead they arranged to steal his inheritance by selling him into bondage in Egypt. He interpreted Pharoah's dreams, was made ruler and preserved Egypt through seven years of famine by storing up during seven years of plenty. His wisdom reunited him with his father who said, "I had not thought to see thy face: and, lo, God hath showed me also thy seed . . . I pray thee, bring them unto me, and I will bless them." Joseph saved his brothers even though they had betrayed him. Reunited they became the fathers of the twelve tribes of Israel: Reuben, Simeon, Levi, Judah, Issachar, Zebulun, Benjamin, Dan, Naphtali, Gad, Asher and Joseph. (Genesis, Chapters 35 to 50.)

3 *The Sword of Damocles,* from the Greek legend in which Damocles spoke extravagantly about the happiness of his sovereign, Dionysius the Elder, a military tyrant. Dionysius then invited him to a sumptuous banquet at which he seated Damocles beneath a sword dangling from a single thread, thus illustrating to him the precarious position of a man in power.

4 *My father always told me that all businessmen were . . . ,* John F. Kennedy's comment to his advisors when steel prices were raised, as reported by the *New York Times,* April 23, 1962. He later said that it was bankers and steelmen his father hated — not all businessmen. Later events more than proved the truth of Joe Kennedy's perception.

5 *I cannot believe that the people of our country . . . ,* from Kennedy's press conference on the steel price increase: ". . . at a time when restraint and sacrifice are being asked of every citizen, the American people will find it hard, as I do, to accept a situation in which a *tiny handful of steel executives whose pursuit of private power and profit exceeds their sense of public responsibility* can show such utter contempt for the interests of 185 million Americans . . . Some time ago I asked each American to consider what he would do for his country and I asked the steel companies. In the last twenty-four hours we had their answer."

6 *The woods are lovely . . .* from "Stopping by Woods on a Snowy Evening," by Robert Frost, American poet (1874-1963). Frost was J.F.K.'s favorite poet.

7 *Dionysus*, in Greek mythology the god of wine and ecstasy, the "gay reveler, the cruel hunter, the lofty inspirer, the sufferer." Each year he died, pruned like a vine by the cold; each spring he was reborn, rekindling the people's belief in immortality.

8 *I'm going to break the C.I.A.* . . . The process leading up to this decision was gradual — beginning with realizations Kennedy had during the Cuban crisis: "We will have to do something . . . I must have someone there with whom I can be in complete intimate contact — someone from whom I know I will be getting the exact pitch . . . Bobby should be in the C.I.A. . . . It is a hell of a way to learn things, but I have learned one thing from this business — that is, that we will have to deal with the C.I.A. McNamara has dealt with Defense: Rusk has done a lot with State: but no one has dealt with C.I.A." Supreme Court Justice William O. Douglas recalled the following discussion between him and Kennedy: "This episode (the Bay of Pigs) seared him. He had experienced the extreme power that . . . the C.I.A. and the Pentagon had, and I think it raised in his own mind the specter: Can Jack Kennedy, President of the United States, ever be strong enough to really rule these two powerful agencies?" The conflict between his growing realization of the power of the C.I.A. and an even stronger realization of the necessity to overcome it if he was ever to accomplish his aims led him to act as he did. The reaction of these powers to his decision is history.

9 *I say to you my friends* . . . from Dr. Martin Luther King's speech *I Have a Dream*, which he delivered during the famous Freedom March on Washington, D.C., August 28, 1963. In a nonviolent protest against injustice and racial discrimination, hundreds of thousands of people marched to the Capitol steps where Dr. King gave his speech.

10 *The Great Beast.* In the Platonic tradition the sophists were not truly men of wisdom; they were only keepers of the Great Beast – all that seems rather than is, all that appears and is not real, the lover of prestige rather than virtue. Simone Weil says that "the blame of the Great Beast had the power to lead all the disciples of Christ, without exception, to abandon their master. As we are worth so much less than they, it is certain that the Great Beast has at least as much power over us without our realizing it at every instant, even at this very moment. And that part of us which it has, God has not." St. John speaks of the Great Beast in Revelations.

11 *Well I don't know* . . . This speech by Joseph Man is a combination of parts of three speeches by Dr. King. These three and *I Have a Dream* are among the great speeches made in this country during the 20th century: *Drum Major Instinct* (part of a sermon at Ebenezer Baptist Church in Atlanta, Georgia, February 4, 1968); *Sermon: Washington Cathedral* (from a speech at Washington's National Cathedral, March 31, 1968); and *I've Been to the Mountaintop* (from an address at a rally in Memphis, Tennessee, April 3, 1968). The day after he gave this last speech Dr. King was murdered.

THE MAGICIAN

1 *The Great Whore*, from the Revelation of St. John, Chapter 17, represents the blasphemy of the world. She is dressed in fine colors, gold, and precious stones and holds a cup which is full of abominations.

I

1 *We must all learn to live* . . . Dr. Martin Luther King, Jr. A Christmas Sermon, Christmas Eve 1967, Ebenezer Baptist Church. After years of struggle, King saw the inescapable interconnection of man. He was one of the few human beings in the country who stood above our petty insanities and untiringly tried to turn our heads towards God and reality. Fear and lying rose to murder the country's conscience on April 4, 1968.

2 *If we fail to dare* . . . Robert F. Kennedy. Origin unknown.

3 *We shall pay any price* . . . President John F. Kennedy. Inaugural Address, January 20, 1961.

4 *The Dove*, a symbol of peace in the Bible. In Genesis, Noah sent a dove into the world to see if the flood waters had abated and the earth was safe. Each time he sent the dove, she returned for there was no rest for the sole of her feet. When the dove returned with an olive branch, then Noah knew that the flood had receded.

5 *There is a man* . . . refers to the Book of Daniel. Nebuchadnezzar, king of Babylon, dreams of this man. Daniel, a captive in Babylon, tells the king that the dream represents Nebuchadnezzar's kingdom and inferior kingdoms that will follow.

6 *The Phoenix*, a bird representing the god of the sun in Assyrian, Chinese, Egyptian, and Greek mythology. The bird had a beautiful plumage and call. It lived for 500 years, then built a nest lined with cinnamon, myrrh, and spikenard; then it died and burned. A new phoenix arose from the ashes and flew the nest and ashes to the temple of the sun. In Egypt, the bird represented immortality and the idea of death and rebirth; in China, its presence in a country represented prosperity and its absence, calamity.

7 *The Beasts of the Apocalypse*, from the Revelation of St. John. The four beasts heralded God's judgment of the world and the final war between the forces of Light and Darkness. Each beast had six wings and many eyes. One resembled a lion; one, a calf; one, a man; and one, a flying eagle. A fifth, a slaughtered lamb, represented the Christ, the Lamb of God, who through his intentional suffering and conscious labors redeemed Man.

8 *The Sphinx*, a creature of Sumerian, Egyptian, and Greek mythology. The creature was a combination of animals. In Egypt, the animals were the bull, the lion, the eagle, and the head of a man. Often it had to be subdued, either physically (deities fighting the sphinx in Sumerian legend) or in a test of wisdom (Oedipus answering the Sphinx's riddle in Greek legend). In Egypt, the sphinx was originally a picture of Hu, the god of wisdom. The Canaanite deity Astarte, mistress of heaven, was pictured as a sphinx.

9 *He's cut off his paws!* In ancient tradition, a reborn man – a man without violence – is often symbolized by a lion with its paws cut off.

10 *And all the many, their name was Legion* . . . In the Bible, the Devil is referred to as being legion – a multitude, the crowd, the many as opposed to the One – whether outside a man or within him.

Adam King was first performed in 1974, *The Magician* in 1978, And *I* in 1983 under the direction of Sharon Gans.

The author wishes to thank Michael Hilsenrad,
Andrew Robinson, Andrew Cort, Paul Levine,
Terrence Christgau, Matthew Fitzgerald,
Ed Cohen, John Mahnke, Erik Sherman, Jonathan
Weinert, Cathy Buckley, Michael Peipman, and Brad
Smith, for help in the preparation of this manuscript.
And my friend, Robert Klein, who has been
of great help to me.